CHAPTER 1

The State of Software Testing Today

T he director asked the tester, "So you tested it? It's ready to go to production?

The tester responded, "Yes, I tested it. It's ready to go."

The director asked, "Well, what did you test?"

The tester responded, "I tested *it*."

In this conversation, I was the tester. It was 1987 and I had just completed my first test assignment on a commercial software system.[1] I had spent six months working with and learning from some very good testers. They were very good at finding bugs, nailing them down, and getting development to fix them. But once you got beyond the bug statistics, the testers didn't seem to have much to go on except *it*. Happily, the director never asked what exactly *it* was.

The experience made me resolve to never again be caught with such a poor answer. I could not always be so lucky as to have management

---

[1] Commercial software is software that is commercially available and can be purchased by the public. This distinguishes it from safety-critical, proprietary, or military software.

that would accept *it* for an answer. All my training as a structural engineer had prepared me to give my management a much better answer than *it*.

Suppose the supervisor on a building project asked if I tested the steel superstructure on Floor 34 and needed to know if it was safe to build Floor 35. If I said "yes" and if the supervisor then asked, "What did you test?" I would have a whole checklist of answers on the clipboard in my hand. I would have a list with every bolt connection, the patterns of those connections, the specified torque wrench loading used to test the bolts, and the results from every bolt I had touched. I would know exactly which bolts I had touched because each would be marked with fluorescent paint, both on my chart and on the steel.

Why should software testing be any different? I could certainly give my management a better answer than *it*. Many of these better answers were around when the pyramids were being built. When I am asked those questions today, my answer sounds something like this:

> *As per our agreement, we have tested 67 percent of the test inventory. The tests we ran represent the most important tests in the inventory as determined by our joint risk analysis. The bug find rates and the severity composition of the bugs we found were within the expected range. Our bug fix rate is 85 percent.*
>
> *It has been three weeks since we found a Severity 1 issue. There are currently no known Severity 1 issues open. Fixes for the last Severity 2 issues were regression-tested and approved a week ago. The testers have conducted some additional testing in a couple of the newer modules. Overall, the system seems to be stable.*
>
> *The load testing has been concluded. The system failed at 90 percent of the design load. The system engineers believe they understand the problem, but they say they will need three months to implement the fix. Projections say the peak load should only be at 75 percent by then. If the actual loading goes above 90 percent, the system will fail.*
>
> *Our recommendation is to ship on schedule, with the understanding that we have an exposure if the system utilization exceeds the projections before we have a chance to install the previously noted fix.*

The thing that I find most amazing is that answers like these are not widely used in the industry today. I regularly hear testers and developers using *it* metrics.

Throughout the 1990s I gave out a survey every time I taught a testing course. Probably 60 percent of the students taking these courses were new to testing, with less than one year as a tester. About 20 percent had from one to five years' experience, and the remainder were expert testers. The survey asked the student to define common testing terms like *test*, and it asked them to identify the methods and metrics that they regularly used as testers. The complete results of these surveys are presented in the appendix of this book. I will mention some of the highlights here.

- The only type of metrics used regularly have to do with counting bugs and ranking them by severity. Only a small percentage of respondents measure the bug find rate or the bug fix rate. No other metrics are widely used in development or testing, even among the best-educated and seemingly most competent testers. It can also be inferred from these results that the companies for which these testers work do not have a tradition of measuring their software development or test processes.

- Few respondents reported using formal methods such as *inspection* or *structured analysis*, meaning some documented structured or systematic method of analyzing the test needs of a system. The most commonly cited reason for attending the seminar was to learn some software testing methods.

- The majority of testers taking the survey (76 percent) had had some experience with automated test tools. Today an even greater percent of testers report that they have used automated test tools, but test automation is also voted as the most difficult test technique to implement and maintain in the test effort.

- The respondents who are not actively testing provided the most accurate definitions of the testing terms. The people performing the testing supplied the poorest definitions of the testing tasks that they are performing most frequently.

Overall, I believe that the quality of the tester's level of awareness is improving, and, certainly, software testing practices have improved in the commercial software development sector. Today there are more publications, tools, and discussion groups available than there were 10 years ago. There are certainly more shops attempting to use formal methods and testing tools. But the survey results haven't changed much over the years.

How did we get to this mind-set? How did these limitations in perceptions—and, unfortunately, all too often in practice—come about? To understand that, we need to examine the evolution of software development and testing during the last two decades.

A Quick Look at How We Got Where We Are

Most of the formal methods and metrics around today had their start back in the 1970s and 1980s when industry began to use computers. Computer professionals of that time were scientists, usually mathematicians and electrical engineers. Their ideas about how to conduct business were based on older, established industries like manufacturing; civil projects like power plants; and military interests like avionics and ballistics.

The 1980s: The Big Blue and Big Iron Ruled

By the 1980s, computers were widely used in industries that required lots of computation and data processing. Software compilers were empowering a new generation of programmers to write machine-specific programs.

In the 1980s computers were mainframes: big iron. Large corporations like IBM and Honeywell ruled the day. These computers were expensive and long-lived. We expected software to last for five years, and we expected hardware to last even longer—that is, how long it takes to depreciate the investment. As a result, buying decisions were not made lightly. The investments involved were large ones, and commitments were for the long term, so decisions were made only after careful consideration and multiyear projections.

Fact: Computers in the 1980s: expensive, long-term commitment, lots of technical knowledge required

Normally a vendor during the 1980s would sell hardware, software, support, education, and consulting. A partnership-style relationship existed between the customer and the vendor. Once a vendor was selected, the company was pretty much stuck with that company until the hardware and software were depreciated; a process that could take 10 or more years.

These consumers demanded reliability and quality from their investment. Testing was an integral part of this arrangement and contributed greatly to the quality of the product. Only a few vendors existed, and each had its own proprietary way of doing things. Compared to today's numbers, only a few people were developing and testing software, and most of them were engineers with degrees in engineering.

For the most part, during this period any given application or operating system only ran in one environment. There were few situations where machines from more than one vendor were expected to exchange information or interact in any way. This fact is very significant, since today's software is expected to run in many different environments and every vendor's hardware is expected to integrate with all sorts of devices in its environment.

The 1990s: PCs Begin to Bring Computing to "Every Desktop"

In the 1990s, the PC became ubiquitous, and with it came cheap software for the public consumer. All through the 1990s, computers kept getting more powerful, faster, and cheaper. The chip makers successfully upheld Moore's law, which states that the number of circuits on a single silicon chip doubles every 18 to 24 months. To put that in perspective, in 1965 the most complex chip had 64 transistors. Intel's Pentium III, launched in October 2000, has 28 *million* transistors.

Fact: Computers in the 1990s: keep getting cheaper, no commitment involved, almost anybody can play

The price of a PC continued to fall during the 1990s, even though their capabilities expanded geometrically. The software developers were driven to exploit the bigger, better, and faster computers. And the consumers were driven to upgrade, just to remain competitive in their business; or at least that was the perception.

Software makers adopted rapid application development (RAD) techniques so that they could keep up with the hardware and the consumers' demands in this new industry, where being first to market was often the key to success. Development tools make it easier and easier for people to write programs. So, a degree becomes less important.

Unlike the 1980s, when the "next" release would be a stronger version of the existing software, in the 1990s, a new version of a product was often significantly different from the previous version and often contained more serious bugs than its predecessor.

Fact: What we got from rapid application development in the 1990s was a new product, complete with new bugs, every 18 to 24 months.

The demanding delivery schedule left little time for testing the base functionality, let alone testing the multiple environments where the product might be expected to run, such as computers made by different vendors, and different versions of the operating system. So, it was mostly tested by the users, with product support groups plugging the holes.

Who would have dreamt then how developments in software and the Internet would eventually affect the state of software testing? The outcome proves that truth is stranger than fiction. Consider the following note I wrote about software testing methods and metrics in 1995:

> *In the last couple of years, there has been a marked increase in interest in improved product reliability by several successful shrink-wrap manufacturers. I had wondered for some time what factors would cause a successful shrink-wrap marketing concern to become interested in improving reliability. I used to think that it would be litigation brought on by product failures that would force software makers to pay more attention to reliability. However, the standard arguments for accountability and performance do not seem to have any significant effect on the commercial software industry. It seems that the force driving reliability improvements is simple economics and market maturity.*

> *First, there is economics of scale. The cost of shipping the fix for a bug to several million registered users is prohibitive at the moment. Second, there are the decreasing profit margins brought on by competition. When profit margins become so slim that the profit from selling a copy of the software is eaten up by the first call that a user makes to customer support, the balance point between delivery, features, and reliability must change in order for the company to stay profitable. The entrepreneurial company becomes suddenly interested in efficiency and reliability in order to survive.*

At the time, I honestly expected a renaissance in software testing. Unfortunately, this was the year that the Internet began to get serious notice. It was also the year that I spent months speaking at several large corporations telling everyone who would listen that they could radically reduce the cost of customer support if they developed support Web sites that let the customers get the information and fixes they needed for free, anytime, from anywhere, without a long wait to talk to someone. Somebody was listening. I was probably not the only one broadcasting this message.

Enter: The Web

Within months, every major hardware and software vendor had a support presence on the Web. The bug fix process became far more efficient because it was no longer necessary to ship fixes to everyone who purchased the product—only those who noticed the problem came looking for a solution. Thanks to the Internet, the cost of distributing a bug fix fell to almost nothing as more and more users downloaded the fixes from the Web. The customer support Web site provided a single source of information and updates for customers and customer service, and the time required to make a fix available to the users shrank to insignificance.

The cost of implementing these support Web sites was very small and the savings were huge; customer satisfaction and profit margins went up. I got a new job and a great job title: Manager of Internet Technology. Management considered the result a major product quality improvement, but it was not achieved through better test methods. In fact, this process improvement successfully minimized any incentive for shipping cleaner products in the first place. Who knew? But don't despair, because it was only a temporary reprieve.

The most important thing was getting important fixes to the users to keep them happy until the next release. The Internet made it possible to do this. What we got from the Internet was quick relief from the new bugs and a bad case of Pandora's box, spouting would-be entrepreneurs, developers, and experts in unbelievable profusion.

Consumers base their product-buying decisions largely on availability and advertising. Consumers are most likely to buy the first product on the market that offers features they want, not necessarily the most reliable product. Generally, they have little or no information on software reliability because there is no certification body for software. There is no true equivalent in the software industry to institutions like Underwriters Laboratory (UL) in the United States, which certifies electronics products. Software consumers can only read the reviews, choose the manufacturer, and hope for the best. Consequently, software reliability has been squeezed as priorities have shifted toward delivery dates and appealing functionality, and the cost of shipping fixes has plummeted—thanks to the Web.

Given this market profile, the PC software market is a fertile environment for entrepreneurs. Competitive pressures are huge, and it is critically important to be the first to capture the market. The decision to ship is generally based on market-driven dates, not the current reliability of the product. It has become common practice to distribute bug-fix releases (put the patches and fixes on the Web site) within a few weeks of the initial release—after the market has been captured. Consequently, reliability metrics are not currently considered to be crucial to commercial success of the product. This trend in commercial software exists to one degree or another throughout the industry. We also see this trend in hardware development.

The next major contribution of the Web was to make it possible to download this "shrink-wrap" software directly. This type of software typically has a low purchase price, offers a rich appealing set of functionality, and is fairly volatile, with a new release being offered every 12 to 18 months. The reliability of this software is low compared to the traditional commercial software of the 1970s and 1980s. But it has been a huge commercial success nonetheless. And the Web has helped keep this status quo in effect by reducing the cost of shipping a bug fix by letting users with a problem download the fix for themselves. And so we coasted through the 1990s.

The Current Financial Climate

In the aftermath of the dot-com failures and the market slump in 2001 and 2002, investors are demanding profitability. I always expected consumers to rebel against buggy software. What happened was that investors rebelled against management gambling with their money. This change is inflicting fiscal responsibility and accountability on management. It is not uncommon today to have the chief financial officer (CFO) in charge of most undertakings of any size.

Fact: Nobody seems to feel lucky right now.

The first task is usually to cut costs, adjust the margins, and calm investors. Along with the CFO come the auditors. It is their job to find out what the information technologies (IT) department is, what it does, and if it is profitable or not. If it is not profitable, it will either become profitable, or it will be cut. The financial managers are quick to target waste in all its forms.

Slowing Down

The 1990s were a time of rapid growth, experimentation, and great optimism. We were always eager to buy the "next" version every time it became available, without considering if we really needed it or not. It was sort of the I-feel-lucky approach to software procurement. We kept expecting "better" products, even though what we got were "different" products. But we kept buying these products, so we perpetuated the cycle. There always seemed to be a justification for buying the next upgrade. A new term was coined—*shelfware*—to describe software that was purchased but never installed.

Further, even software that did get installed was rarely fully utilized. Studies showed that users rarely used over 10 percent of the functionality of most common business software. There was obviously a feature bloat.

Fat client/server applications were quickly replaced by lightweight, limited-function, browser-based clients. Most users never missed the 90 percent of the functions that were gone, but they appreciated the fast response, anytime, anywhere.

Getting More from What We Have

It seems that there is a limit to how small transistor etchings on a silicone wafer can get. To make microchips, Intel and AMD etch a pattern of transistors onto a silicon wafer. But the more you cram onto a chip, the smaller everything gets. Electrons carry the 0 and 1 information through the transistors that power our current computers' computing capabilities. When the transistors get down to the atomic level, electrons are too large to flow.

Fact: Many prognosticators believe that the dominance of Moore's law is coming to an end.

In addition, the cost of producing "Moore" complex chips is rising. As chips become more complex, the cost to manufacture them increases. Intel and AMD now spend billions to create fabrication plants.

With silicon chips nearing the end of their feasibility, scientists and engineers are looking to the future of the microprocessor. Chip makers are now focusing on the next generation of computing. But it is going to be expensive to ramp up new technologies like DNA computers and molecular computers.

DNA computing is a field that will create ultra-dense systems that pack megabytes of information into devices the size of a silicon transistor. A single bacterium cell is about the same size as a single silicon transistor, but it holds more than a megabyte of DNA memory and it has all the computational structures to sense and respond to its environment. DNA computers and molecular computers do not use electrons and 0/1 bits. They can solve more complex problems faster than transistor-based microchips because of the way in which they work. So, in the meantime, we will probably have the chance to create some new uses for the technology that we have.

Fact: We are not buying.

Microsoft's corporate vision statement was "A PC on every desktop." They have come a long way toward achieving this goal. However, the indications are that hardware prices won't fall much lower, and even though the price of some software is going up, sales are falling.

When Microsoft introduced the Windows 2000 operating system, it failed to sell at the rate they had expected; the climate had begun to change. In the following year, Microsoft Office XP, with its short-sighted and inflexible licensing, also failed to gain acceptance. Most of us decided not to upgrade.

In the 1990s, developers successfully argued that investing in better tools would build a better product, rather than investing in a better test process. Since most of the quality improvements in the past 10 years have come from standardization and development process improvements, they usually got what they wanted.

However, the real product failures had to do with products that missed the mark on the functionality, and applications that simply did not run well in large systems or systems that were so costly to maintain that they lost money in production. These are things that development tools cannot fix. They are things that testing can identify, and things that can be fixed and avoided.

In today's climate, the financial people will not allow that server from last year to be tossed out until it has been fully depreciated. Neither will they approve the purchase of new operating systems nor office software without a cost-benefit justification. Customers are not in the mood to go out and spend lots of money upgrading their systems either.

Note: Testers, here is our chance!

When consumers are not willing to buy a new product just because it's "new," things are starting to change. When consumers demand reliability over features and cost, the quality balance shifts back from trendy first-to-market toward reliability. The value of using formal methods and metrics becomes the difference between the companies that survive and the ones that fail.

With so many groups competing for budget, the test group must be able to make a compelling argument, or it will become extinct. A test manager who can make a good cost-benefit statement for the financial folks has a chance. The bottom line for testers is that the test effort must add value to the product. Testers must be able to demonstrate that value.

Note: The way to develop a good cost-benefit statement, and add real credibility to software testing, is to use formal methods and good metrics.

Regardless of the cause, once a software maker has decided to use formal methods, it must address the question of which formal methods and metrics to adopt. Once methods or a course toward methods has been determined, everyone must be educated in the new methods. Moving an established culture from an informal method of doing something to a formal method of doing the same thing takes time, determination, and a good cost-benefit ratio. It amounts to a cultural change, and introducing culture changes is risky business. Once the new methods are established, it still takes a continuing commitment from management to keep them alive and in use.

In ancient times this was accomplished by fiat, an order from the king. If there were any kings in the 1990s, they must have lived in development. Today, however, it is being accomplished by the CFO and the auditors.

Guess What? The Best Methods Haven't Changed

The auditors are paid to ask hard questions. They want to know what *it* is. The auditors are paying attention to the answers. And, since the financial folks use a very stringent set of formal methods in their work, they expect others to do the same.

What the Auditors Want to Know from the Testers

When testing a product the auditors want to know:

- What does the software or system do?
- What are you going to do to prove that it works?
- What are your test results? Did it work under the required environment? Or, did you have to tweak it?

Clearly, the test methods used need to answer these questions. Before we try to determine the best methods and metrics to use to ensure that proper, thorough testing takes place, we need to examine the challenges faced by testers today.

The Challenges a Tester Faces Today

The position and contribution of a tester has been severely eroded since I joined testing in 1987. The average tester today is facing quite a few challenges. Many are new to testing, many are experienced testers facing poor budgets, and many are facing a "testers don't get no respect" climate that is dominated by ship date pressures, where testers can easily be seen as a problem rather than a part of the solution. Sadly, this is true both for testers in commercial software development and for testers in the more traditionally formal areas such as business and safety-critical and high-reliability software.

No Specification Means No Testing

The first problem in making a convincing case for software testing today is that no one can *test* without a specification. In software development, the word *test* is even more misunderstood than the word *quality*.

 Note: To test means to compare an actual result to a standard.

If there is no standard to compare against, there can be no *test*. In the survey discussed earlier, only one person in 50 provided the correct definition for the word *test*. In shops where some form of RAD is in use, people think they are testing. However, since specifications are produced after the software is finished, testing is an impossibility. This is also true for most of the RAD descendants: the Agile methodologies; eXtreme Programming (XP), Lean Development (LD), Adaptive Software Development (ASD), and so on. The one possible exception to this situation is the Dynamic Systems Development Method (DSDM). We will discuss the RAD/Agile methodologies and how to accomplish testing them in more detail in the next chapters.[2]

The Institute of Electrical and Electronics Engineers (IEEE) defines *test* as "a set of one or more test cases." The IEEE defines *testing* as "the process of analyzing a software item to detect the differences between existing and required conditions [that is, bugs] and to evaluate the features of the software item." This definition invites the tester to go beyond comparing the actualities to a standard (verification) and *evaluate* the software (validation). Effectively, the definition invites testers to express opinions without giving them guidelines for the formulation of those opinions or tools (metrics) to defend those opinions. The IEEE definition makes testers responsible for both verification and validation without distinction. This practice, when pursued energetically, is more likely to incite riot among developers than it is to lead to quality improvements. To understand what I am getting at, consider the definitions of the words *verification* and *validation*.

According to *Webster's New World Dictionary*, *verify* means "(1) to prove to be true by demonstration, evidence, or testimony; confirm or substantiate; (2) to test or check the accuracy or correctness of, as by investigation, comparison with a standard or reference to the facts." *Verification* is basically the same process as testing with a bias toward correctness, as in, "to verify that a thing performs according to specification." Verification answers the question "Does the system do what it's supposed to do?"

Webster's New World Dictionary defines *validity* as "the state, quality, or fact of being valid (strong, powerful, properly executed) in law *or in argument*, proof or citation of authority." *Validation* is the process by which we confirm that a thing is properly executed. Validation requires a

---

[2] I will refer to all the RAD descendants as RAD/Agile efforts for simplicity.

subjective judgment on the part of the tester. Such a judgment must be defended by *argument*, for example, "I think it's a bug because . . . ." Validation answers the question "Is what the system doing correct?" Just because a system was designed to do things a certain way and is doing those things in that way does not mean that the way things are being done is the right way or the *best* way.

Comparing the system's response to the standard is straightforward when there is a specification that states what the correct system response will be. The fundamental problem with testing in a RAD/Agile environment is that, since there are generally no standards, it is impossible to *test*. RAD/Agile testers are *exploring* the software and performing bug finding and validation on the fly. To convince development that something is invalid when there are no standards to quote, one must have a *convincing argument* and high professional credibility. How much chance does a tester have of convincing development that something is invalid or seriously wrong if they are using *it* metrics and the best argument they can give is "I think *it* is a bug because I think *it* is a bug."?

Also, it is virtually impossible to automate testing if there is no standard for the expected response. An automated test program cannot make on-the-fly subjective judgments about the correctness of the outcome. It must have a standard expected response to compare with the actual response in order to make a pass/fail determination.

Being First to Market: Market/Entrepreneurial Pressures Not to Test

In our entrepreneur-driven first-to-market development environment, managers are eager to cut any costs or activities that don't add to the bottom line. They are also eager to remove any barriers that might negatively impact a ship date. Testing has not demonstrated that it is a requirement for success in the shipped product.

The fact is, it has not been necessary to use formal software test methods or metrics in many parts of commercial software development in order to succeed commercially. This type of software that I call commercial software is intended for business and home consumption, generally on the PC platform; hopefully, it is not used in safety-critical systems. This is software that anyone can buy at a store or over the Internet, like word processors, graphics programs, and spreadsheets.

Common reasons given for not using formal test methods are usually of the form, "We don't need formal methods. We are just a small shop." The general conception seems to be that formal methods have to be written by somebody else and that they must be specialized and complicated. *Formal* simply means following a set of prescribed or fixed procedures. The real problem here is the lack of really productive testing. It is a cultural problem.

Testing is perceived to be a cost center—not a contributor to the bottom line. So in some shops the perception is that testing doesn't add much value to the product. If it doesn't add much value, it won't get much funding.

Since most commercial test efforts are typically underfunded and staffed with warm bodies rather than trained testers, mediocre test results are the norm, and so over the past years, I have seen more and more companies disbanding the software test group altogether.

The Lack of Trained Testers

One of my first mentors when I started testing software systems had been a tester in a boom-able[3] industry for many years. He explained to me early on how a very good analyst could get promoted to programmer after about five years of reviewing code and writing design specifications; then after about five years in development, the very best programmers could hope for a promotion into the system test group. The first two years in the system test group were spent learning how to test the system.

This situation still exists in some safety-critical shops, but it is not the norm in commercial software shops at all. The simple fact is that few testers or developers have received any training in formal methods, especially test techniques. Dorothy Graham, a noted author in the field of test inspection and tester certification, estimated in the late 1990s that only 10 percent of testers and developers had ever had any training in test techniques. The results of the survey I mentioned earlier support this assertion.

Where do software testers get their training? In the United States, software testers are homegrown, for the most part. The bulk of test training available in North America comes through public and private seminars.

[3] So-called "boom-able" because if something goes wrong, something goes "boom."

In Europe, a larger percentage of students attending the test seminars have science or engineering degrees than attendees from the United States, but, again, the bulk of software test training is done in public and private seminars. Few metrics are in use even among the better-educated testers.

Few universities offer software testing classes. Even fewer require software testing classes as part of the software engineering curriculum. Unfortunately, this sends the message to business and the development community that software testing is not worthwhile.

Academia is largely uninvolved with the actual business of producing commercial software. Software testing is not the only topic that is missing from the curriculum. Cellular communications, digital video editing, and multimedia development represent other omissions. University instructors are busy teaching well-established subjects and exploring future technologies. Few institutions cover the ground that serves the current needs of industry, such as training the next generation of professional testers.

Traditionally, in the United States, test groups were staffed with computer science graduates looking for entry-level programming positions. But since 1990, we have seen the number of testers with any type of science degree dwindle. People currently being hired to perform testing do not come from a tradition of experimental practice or science or engineering because the entrepreneurs see no need to pay for such people to fill testing positions. This trend is reinforced by the focus on market demands rather than product reliability. Even if the need for these skills were recognized, few formally trained testers would be available.

In the 1990s, finding information on many testing topics was difficult to do. Few college courses were available on software testing, and only a few conferences were devoted to the subject. Since the advent of the Internet, this situation has changed dramatically. The Internet has made it possible for testers to find a great deal of information on software testing easily. If you enter "Software+Testing" on your favorite Internet search engine today, you are likely to get hundreds of thousands of matches. But these improvements have not improved the overall status of the software tester or the test effort.

I don't think that there is one simple answer for this situation. The situation is a result of several factors. One contributor to the current situation is that in most companies, testing is not a respected career; it is a phase. Most testers are transients—they are moving though testing to get to something else. For example, it's common for nontechnical personnel or just-out-of-school computer scientists to use a stint in the test group to bridge themselves into a job in operations or development. So, they don't stay in testing.

The poor funding that test groups routinely get today also contributes to it being a phase rather than a career. There aren't enough resources for education (especially the time necessary to go and take a class). Management must consider the questions "Why educate testers if they are just going to move on to other careers?" and "Why spend money on a test effort that probably won't be very good?"

Testing lacks the credibility that it once had. So, as the knowledge level of testers is reduced to *it* metrics and ad hoc methods, the quality of the test effort is reduced. The fact is, the real quality improvements in commercial software are coming about because of the Internet and the international acceptance of standards. Let me explain.

Standards Reduce the Amount of Testing Required

Fact: **Quality improvements in the 1990s have been driven by standardization, not testing or quality assurance.**

I already mentioned how the Web allowed software makers to cut support costs and get bug fixes to users quickly and efficiently, instead of spending more to remove bugs in the first place. Another kind of improvement that has caused testing to be less important is the rapid adoption of standards in our large systems.

When I wrote my first paper on system integration in 1989, I described integrating the system as building a rock wall with my bare hands out of a mismatched combination of oddly shaped stones, wires, and mud. The finished product required operators standing by in the data center, 24/7, ready to stick a thumb or a monkey wrench into any holes that appeared.

Each vendor had its own proprietary thing: link library, transport protocol, data structure, database language, whatever. There were no standards for how various systems would interoperate. In fact, I'm not sure that the term *interoperate* existed in the early 1990s. For example, when we created online banking at Prodigy, we wanted our IBM system to "talk" to the Tandem at the bank. We had to invent our own headers and write our own black boxes to translate IBM messages to Tandem and vice versa. All the code was new and rightfully untrustworthy. It had to be tested mercilessly.

System modules were written in machine-specific languages; each machine had its own operating system. The modems and routers had their own manufacturer-specific ways of doing things. A message could be broken down and reconstructed a dozen times between the application that built it and the client on the other side of the modem receiving it. Testing a system required that each component be tested with the full knowledge that something as simple as a text string might be handled differently by each successive element in the network.

Integrating applications into the networks of that day required major-league testing. During my first two years as a systems integrator, my best friend and only tool was my line monitor. I actually got to the point where I could read binary message headers as they came across the modem.

We have come a long way in the intervening years. I am not saying that all manufacturers have suddenly agreed to give up their internal proprietary protocols, structures, and ways of doing things—they have not. But eventually, it all runs down to the sea, or in our case, the Internet, and the Internet is based on standards: IP, HTML, XML, and so on. This means that, sooner or later, everyone has to convert their proprietary "thing" to a standards-based "thing" so that they can do business on the Web. (See the sidebar on standards that have improved software and systems.)

Because of standardization, a lot of the more technical testing chores are no longer necessary, like me and my line monitor. This has also contributed to management hiring fewer senior technical testers and more entry-level nontechnical testers. The rise of fast-paced RAD/Agile development methods that don't produce a specification that the tester can test against has also eliminated many testing chores.

Obviously, there is great room for improvement in the software testing environment. Testing is often insufficient and frequently nonexistent. But valuable software testing can take place, even in the constraints (and seeming chaos) of the present market, and the test effort can and should add value and quality to the product. Our next chapter examines that very topic.

Some of the Standards That Have Improved Software and Systems

Several standards are in use today that support e-business interoperability. They are used to enable interoperability to put information flows into a form that can be processed by another component in the system, between various business services, applications, and legacy systems. Open Buying on the Internet (OBI), cXML, and XML/EDI are a few of the most popular business-to-business (B2B) standards in use today. BizTalk, another standardized offering, is a framework of interoperability specifications. BizTalk applications support information flows and workflows between companies, allowing rules to be created that govern how flows from one process are translated, stored, and otherwise manipulated before being sent on to the next component in the flow.

With the adoption of XML, it is now possible to host a Web service on an intranet or the Internet. A Web service is simply an application that lives on the Web and is available to any client that can contract with it. It represents a "standardized" version of an application that can be located, contracted, and utilized (Microsoft calls this "consuming" the Web service) dynamically via the Web.

In the near future we will find that we don't know where our information is coming from as our applications automatically and transparently reach out and query universal description discovery and integration (UDDI) servers anywhere on the planet to locate and contract with Internet-hosted Web services to do X, Y, and Z as part of the application.

Today, bringing up an e-commerce application does not require a line monitor. Nor does it require the exhaustive testing that was required before the Web. Applications have a higher reliability from the beginning because they are based on standards. Typically, availability of a Web-based system is measured in 9s, with 99.999 percent availability being the norm for a commercial system. That translates to less than 8 hours downtime each year.

What we can do, how we can interoperate, and how reliable our systems are has improved enormously as a result of our adoption of the Internet and its standards.

DEVELOPMENT TOOLS ALSO SUPPORT STANDARDS

Our development tools have gotten a lot better as well. For example, the .NET development API, Visual Studio .NET, can be set up to enforce design and coding standard and policies on developers through the use of templates. These templates can be customized at the enterprise level. They can impose significant structure on the development process, limit what programmers can do, and require that they do certain things, such as the following:

◆ Always use the company-approved name for a specific feature.

◆ Always use a certain data structure to hold a certain kind of information.

(continues)

Some of the Standards That Have Improved Software and Systems (*continued*)

♦ Always use a certain form to gather a certain kind of information.

♦ Submit a program module only after every required action has been completed on it, such as providing all the tool tips and help messages.

When this template approach is applied to an enterprise, it eliminates entire classes of bugs from the finished product.

Installation is a matter of copying compiled files to a directory and invoking the executable. Programs do need to be registered with the system where they are running. The .NET framework contains a standardized application execution manager that controls just-in-time (JIT) compilation and application loading into managed memory. A memory manager ensures that programs run in their own space, and only in their space.

The .NET framework is based on a set of unified libraries that are used by all languages. The result of these features is that all programs are using the same set of link libraries, regardless of what language they were written in. Consequently, if a library routine is tested in one module, it can be assumed that it will behave the same way when used by any other module. A string, for example, will always be treated in the same way instead of each different language compiler bringing with it its own set of link libraries to the system, complete with their own different bugs.

Programmers can write in the language that fits the job at hand and their skill set. The end product will perform the same no matter which language it was written in, because all languages are compiled into a standardized binary file that uses the unified library routines and runs in its own protected memory space.

This architecture is *very* similar to the one run at Prodigy in 1987 using IBM's Transaction Processing Facility (TPF) operating system and Prodigy's own object-oriented language and common code libraries. It worked very reliably then, and it will probably work very reliably now as well.

Summary

Software testing today seems to have four main problems.

First, changes in the way that software is developed have eroded the value of software testing. New development methodologies are developed iteratively through trial and error. These methods typically don't produce specifications for the tester to test against, so testers are left to hunt for bugs.

Second, in recent years, software development has been driven by entrepreneurial pressures, schedule, and constantly evolving product definition. For these and other reasons, management is not always convinced that testing is necessary or worthwhile. In many types of development effort, testing by an independent test group is not believed to be worthwhile or to add value.

Third, there are few trained testers using formal methods and metrics, and most of the software testers out there are just passing through testing on their way to some other (more promising and rewarding) career. As a result, the test effort is not producing the kind of high-quality results that help demonstrate how the test effort improves the quality of the product and the bottom line.

Finally, the most important, and visible, software quality improvements in the past several years have not come as a result of testing, but of standardization driven by the Internet. This increased use of standards has had a profound effect on the quality of the final product and on the ability of multiple software systems to interact and interoperate. It has also removed the need for extensive low-level testing in these areas, so the demand for senior technical testers is decreasing.

In the end it comes down to the question "Does your test effort add enough value to make it worthwhile?" It used to be assumed that the answer to this question was yes. Today, however, this is not true. A test effort that just finds bugs is not enough. Testers must be able to demonstrate that their effort is adding value to the bottom line. There are many ways to measure that value, but you have to be measuring all along in order to demonstrate the value added. Managers and auditors, and just about anyone looking at the bottom line, expect to see a real, measurable demonstration that every part of the development of a product is contributing. This book shows you many ways to show this value. In the next chapter, we discuss some of the problems with traditional quality assurance in today's software development environment.

CHAPTER 2

Maintaining Quality Assurance in Today's Software Testing Environment

The quality assurance person said, "You are not following the process in the quality manual. We worked hard to write these procedures and you are changing it in the middle of the project. You can't do that."

The developer answered, "I am not changing the process; I am *automating* the process you published in the quality manual."

"But you *are* changing it," the quality assurance person insisted.

The developer took a deep breath and tried again, "I'm not changing it; I'm putting it *online*. See, this electronic form is exactly like your paper checklist form except it's online. This way we can all see it and it is really easy to fill out. No more wondering what happened to it, whose desk it's stuck on. Most of the information is already filled in by the system." The developer beamed. Certainly the quality assurance person would finally understand.

"No, you are changing it," repeated the quality assurance person. "The way you are doing it is not what's described in the quality manual. You just can't do it now."

"But why? We already know this automation will save about 40 person hours and 3,000 pages of paper each week. It will pay for itself in about eight weeks." The developer was becoming exasperated.

"Yes, that may be, but we would have to get together and rework the whole process. Then we'd have to change the quality manual, get it approved, redistribute it, call in all the old copies. You have no idea how much is involved. We are in the middle of the delivery schedule.

"No, you will have to wait until the next release. We just do not have time right now," concluded the quality assurance person.

What's Wrong with This Picture?

Before anyone gets offended, I want to say that I have found myself on both sides of this debate. What people perceive to be wrong with this picture will depend largely on the type of development process they are following. In a carefully planned and controlled development effort, quality assurance would win and the innovation would be held up until it could be fit into the schedule. In a RAD/Agile shop, a dynamic creative process will not be stifled simply because it is difficult and inconvenient to update *paper* documentation. In a RAD/Agile shop, the innovation would most likely be put in place as quickly as it is available, and the quality assurance procedure that cannot keep up with technology and innovation is likely to be discarded.

For the past several years, I have hosted special collaborative Web sites that provide features such as single-source documentation, proactive notification to subscribers of changes, interactive discussions and live chats, task lists, and schedules with automatic reminders and notifications. I have trained several teams on how to use these Web sites to minimize the problems described here and to mediate disagreements. However, even after training, these same problems persist, even when updates are instant and notification is automatic. These problems are caused by our culture, and culture is difficult to change. Even though the technology exists to solve the problem, or at least improve the situation, it will not succeed unless the culture can be changed.

To determine how to achieve and maintain proper quality assurance, now and in the future, we need to evaluate what's lacking in the current quality assurance environment. The following section looks at some common, faulty perceptions of what quality assurance is and then examines six faulty assumptions of what quality is and how it should be measured with respect to software systems.

Problems with Traditional Quality Assurance

Let's consider the traditional definition of quality assurance. The following definition is taken from the British Standard, BS 4778:

> **Quality Assurance:** *All those planned and systematic actions necessary to provide adequate confidence that a product or service will satisfy given requirements for quality.*

Testers and managers need to be sure that all activities of the test effort are *adequate* and properly executed. The body of knowledge, or set of methods and practices used to accomplish these goals, is *quality assurance*. Quality assurance is responsible for ensuring the quality of the product. Software testing is one of the tools used to ascertain the quality of software. In many organizations, the testers are also responsible for quality assurance—that is, ensuring the quality of the software. In the United States, few software development companies have full-time staff devoted to quality assurance. The reason for this lack of dedicated staff is simple. In most cases, traditional formal quality assurance is not a cost-effective way to add value to the product.

A 1995 report by Capers Jones, "Software Quality for 1995: What Works and What Doesn't," for *Software Productivity Research*, gives the performance of the four most common defect removal practices in the industry today: formal design and code inspections, formal quality assurance, and formal testing. The efficiency of bug removal for these methods used individually is as follows:

Formal design inspections   45%–68%

Formal software testing   37%–60%

Formal quality assurance   32%–55%

No formal methods at all   30%–50%

When taken in combination:

Formal design inspections and formal code inspections   70%–90%

The best combination:

Formal design inspections, formal quality assurance, formal testing 77%–95%

When used alone, formal quality assurance does only 5 percent better than no formal methods at all. It is not possible to determine its relative worth when used in combination with other methods. However, it can be argued that considering the following problems, the contribution of formal quality assurance is minimal.

Traditional Definitions of Quality That Are Not Applicable

Quality assurance defines quality as "the totality of features or characteristics of a product or service that bear on its ability to satisfy stated or implied needs." The British Standards 4778, and ISO 8402, from the International Standards Organization (ISO), definitions cite "fitness for purpose" and "conformance with requirements."

Quality is not a thing; it is the measure of a thing. *Quality is a metric.* The *thing* that quality measures is *excellence.* How much excellence does a thing possess? Excellence is the fact or condition of excelling; of superiority; surpassing goodness or merit.

The problem is that the methods put forward by the experts of the 1980s for achieving quality didn't work in the real market-driven world of the 1990s and probably won't be particularly useful for most commercial software makers in the coming decade. For example, Philip B. Crosby is probably best remembered for his book, *Quality Is Free* (Mentor Books, 1992). In it he describes in nontechnical terms his methods for installing, maintaining, and measuring a comprehensive quality improvement program in your business. The major emphasis is on doing things right the first time. Crosby maintains that this quality is free and that what costs dearly is the rework that you must do when you don't do it right at the get-go.

According to Mr. Crosby's teachings:

- The definition of quality is **"conformance with requirements."**
- The system for achieving quality is "prevention, not cure."
- The measure of success is **"the cost of quality."**
- The target goal of the quality process is "Zero defects—get it right the first time."

These concepts are most certainly laudable, but they require a very high level of discipline and maturity to carry out. The fact is that this set of concepts doesn't fit the commercial software development process. The reason for this is that the assumptions that they are based on are inaccurate in today's software development process. This situation is especially true in an environment where no one has ever gone before, and so no one knows what "right the first time" means.

Metaphorically speaking, the folks writing the definitions of quality and the procedures for achieving it were all from some major department store, but the market demand was going toward volume discount pricing. At the time of this writing, Wal-Mart is the dominant player in this field. Wal-Mart developed its own definitions for quality and invented its own methods for achieving it. It did its own market research and tailored its services to meet the actual (real) needs of that market. It didn't just leave it to the designers to guess. The other major point of distinction is Wal-Mart's overwhelming commitment to customer satisfaction. This sets it apart from most commercial software makers. Notice that there is nothing about customer satisfaction in Mr. Crosby's points. By the way, Wal-Mart is bigger than Microsoft.

Fact: If all you have is a hammer, then everything looks like a nail.

Get the right tool for the job. Overplanning and underplanning the product are two of the main failings in software development efforts today. While a safety-critical or high-reliability effort will fail if it is underplanned, in today's market, it will also fail if it falls into the trap of overplanning—trying to build too good a product for the technology environment and the market. The entrepreneurs are more concerned with planning to make money. They are not going to be bogged down by cumbersome quality assurance procedures that might give them only a marginal improvement.

So, on one end of the spectrum, we have the PC-based commercial software developers who have successfully marketed all manner of semifunctional and sometimes reliable products, and on the other end, we have the high-reliability and safety-critical software developers who must always provide reliable, functioning products. Over the years, consumers have come to expect the price and rapid release schedule of the entrepreneurial commercial software systems. The real problem started when they began to demand the same pricing and release/update schedule from the high-reliability folks. Mature companies like Boeing and Honeywell have faced a terrible challenge to their existence because they must maintain best-practice quality assurance and compete with the shrink-wrappers at the same time.

Some sobering thoughts . . . I found it a truly terrifying experience when I realized that the software monitoring system I was testing on the Microsoft Windows platform would be monitoring critical systems in a nuclear power plant. This was the same operating system that would let my fellow testers lock up the entire air defense system network of a small but strategic country by moving the mouse back and forth too fast on an operator console. These are only a couple of examples of the types of compromises software developers and the market are making these days.

Some Faulty Assumptions

Formal quality assurance principles are based on a number of precepts that are not a good fit for the realities of commercial software development today. The following six precepts are among the most prevalent—and erroneous—in the field today.

✔ ### Fallacy 1: Quality Requirements Dictate the Schedule

The Facts:

- For most software systems, market forces and competition dictate the schedule.

Traditional development models cannot keep up with the demand for consumer software products or the rapidly changing technology that supports them. Today's rich development environment and ready consumer market has sparked the imagination of an enormous number of entrepreneurs. Consequently, this market is incredibly competitive and volatile. Product delivery schedules are often based on a first-to-market strategy. This strategy is well expressed in this 1997 quote from Roger Sherman, director of testing at Microsoft Corporation:

> *Schedule is often thought to be the enemy of quality, but at Microsoft it is considered to be part of the quality of the product.*

(Microsoft studied their market and made their own definitions of quality based on the needs of that market.) Most software developed in RAD/Agile shops has a life expectancy of 3 to 12 months. The technology it services—PCs, digitizers, fax/modems, video systems, and so on—generally turns over every 12 months. The maximum desirable life expectancy of a current hardware/software system in the commercial domain is between 18 and 24 months. In contrast, traditional quality assurance principles are geared for products with a design life expectancy measured in *decades*.

✔ ### Fallacy 2: Quality = Reliability

This equation is interpreted as "zero defects is a requirement for a high-quality product."

The Facts:

■ Reliability is only one component of the quality of a product.

The commercial software market (with a few exceptions) is not willing to pay for a zero-defect product or a 100 percent reliable product.

Users don't care about faults that don't ever become bugs, and users will forgive most bugs if they can work around them, especially if the features are great and if the price is right. For example, in many business network environments in 1994 and 1995, users religiously saved their work before trying to print it. The reason: About one in four print jobs submitted to a certain type of printer using a particular software printer driver would lock up the user's workstation and result in the loss of any unsaved work. Even though many thousands of users were affected, the bug was tolerated for many months because the effects could be limited to simply rebooting the user's workstation occasionally.

Safety-critical and mission-critical applications are the notable exceptions to this fact. Consumers are willing to pay for reliability when the consequences of a failure are potentially lethal. However, the makers of these critical software systems are faced with the same market pressures from competition and constantly changing technology as the consumer software makers.

✔ ### Fallacy 3: Users Know What They Want

The Facts:

■ User expectations are vague and general, not detailed and feature-specific. This situation is especially true for business software products. This phenomenon has led to something that we call *feature bloat*.

For example, if you asked several banking customers if they would like to be able to pay their bills online, many would say yes. But that response does not help the designer determine what type of bills customers will want to pay or how much they will use any particular type of payment feature. Consequently, in a well-funded development project, it is common to see every conceivable feature being implemented.

I once ported a client server application to the Web that produced 250 different reports on demand. When I researched the actual customer usage statistics to determine which reports were the most requested and therefore the most important to implement first, I discovered that only 30 of these 250 reports had *ever* been requested. But each one had been implemented to satisfy a customer request.

✔ Fallacy 4: The Requirements Will Be Correct

This fallacy assumes that designers can produce what the users want the first time, without actually building product or going through trial-and-error cycles.

The Facts:

- Designers are commonly asked to design products using technology that is brand new and poorly understood. They are routinely asked to guess how the users will use the product, and they design the logic flow and interface based on those guesses.

- Designers are people, and people evolve good designs through trial-and-error experimentation. Good requirements also evolve during development through trial-and-error experimentation. They are not written whole at the outset. A development process that does not allow sufficient time for design, test, and fix cycles will fail to produce the right product.

✔ Fallacy 5: Users Will Accept a Boring Product If the Features and Reliability Are Good

The Facts:

- To make an excellent product, we must consistently meet or exceed user expectations. For example, text-based Web browsers in cell phones have failed to captivate the consumer (up till now), even though they provide fast and efficient use of the slow data transmission rates inherent in the current cellular networks.

- Software must be innovative in order to compete. The software leads the users to new accomplishments. Some examples of competitive innovations in the home consumer market include digital video editing, 3D animation, imaging, and video conferencing.

- As corollaries of the preceding facts, the software must provide a competitive advantage to the business user and it must educate users.

For example, let's consider color and graphics. DOS, with its simple black-and-green appearance on screen, was very reliable compared to the first several Windows operating systems, yet it passed away and became extinct.

Color printers have come to dominate the printer world in only a few short years. The cost to purchase one may be low, but the life expectancy is short. The cost of ownership is high (color ink is very expensive), yet they have become the status quo, successfully supplanting the tried-and-true, fast, reliable, and economical black-and-white laser printer.

Third Generation (3G) cell phones don't have 3G networks to support them yet in the United States, yet because of their brilliant color displays, their ability to use picture screen savers, and their ability to play tunes, they are outselling excellent 2G cell phones that offer superior feature sets that work reliably in today's cellular networks.

✔ *Fallacy 6: Product Maturity Is Required*

The Facts:

- Product maturity has little to do with the consumer's buying decision. Price and availability are far more important considerations in most business scenarios.

The very mature premier high-end digital video creation software system has been supplanted by two new software editing systems that provide about 10 percent of the features it does, at 10 percent of the price. In addition, the new systems can be purchased and downloaded over the Internet, whereas the premier system cannot. We are also seeing this trend in large system software. The typical scenario involves dropping a massive, entrenched, expensive client/server system and replacing it with a lightweight, Web-based, database-driven application.

This relates also to *Fallacy 3: Users know what they want.* When analysis is performed on the current system, a frequent discovery is that the customers are paying for lots of features they are not using. Once the correct feature set has been determined, it can often be implemented quickly in a new Web-based application—where it can run very inexpensively.

Feature maturity is a far more important consideration than product maturity. As I have already pointed out, most consumers have realized that the "latest release" of software is not necessarily more reliable than the previous release. So product maturity is most often a myth. A mature product or system is typically overburdened by feature bloat.

What's Not Working: The Traditional Tools for Controlling Quality

So, now I have pointed out some of the problems associated with the ideas underlying what quality assurance is. But how do we control quality and bring about effective testing to ensure effective products and services? To determine that answer, we need to examine some of the tools used by traditional quality assurance people and see where there is room for improvement.

What, then, is quality control? The British Standard 4778 defines quality control as "the operational techniques and activities that are used to fulfill requirements for quality."

We try to *control* quality and defects in software by instituting processes to control design, coding, testing, delivery, and so forth. The idea is that if we standardize the process by which something is done, we can establish *repeatability* in the process and reliable *uniformity* in the product of the process. Further, we can automate a standardized process, eliminating the need to have people participate in it at all. People are nonuniform by nature. Process is a good tool for minimizing the impact of (nonuniform) people on a project. But, when all is said and done, software is written by people to be used by people. It is this fact that may ultimately be our salvation even though it is proving to be a challenge during this time of transition.

Software development is a creative, innovative process. Quality assurance principles were developed for manufacturing, which is based on repeatability and is rarely innovative. Traditional quality assurance principles are a poor fit for the needs of today's fast-paced software development environment.

Traditional quality assurance principles equate quality primarily with reliability. This definition is too simplistic for today's market, which means that the priorities of traditional quality assurance are out of synch with the needs of the software development community.

Manufacturing has not been excessively concerned with human factors. Manufacturing was founded in an environment where the largest asset was machinery, where repetitive mechanical processes could be institutionalized by managerial decree, and where the role of people was to service the process.

In entrepreneurial software shops, the largest asset is the people and the intellectual property that they generate. Only a process that is accepted by the people doing the work will succeed. And only a process that treats people as assets will be accepted.

Traditional QA and Testing Tools Can't Keep Up

The following are traditional tools used by quality assurance and software testers:

Records.   Documentation that keeps track of events, answering the questions when, where, who, how, and why.

Documents.   Standards, quality plan, test plan, process statements, policy.

Activities.   Reviews, change management, version control, testing.

These are primarily paper-dependent tools. Most traditional quality assurance tools rely on *paper*. It is virtually impossible to perform work that is more precise than the tools used to create the work. How can quality assurance and test groups be expected to be more effective than their best tools?

The Paper Problem

Paper is the biggest single impediment to software quality today. It is no coincidence that document inspection and reviews are the most effective ways to take bugs out of our software. Inspections and reviews test the *paper* documentation. *Paper documentation is the single biggest bug repository in software development.* In addition to the number of design errors, miscommunications, ambiguities, and fallacies we introduce and entrench in our products, the number of errors introduced by outdated or discrepant paper documentation is a major quality problem. Furthermore, the creation and compilation of paper documents is expensive and slow.

The main problem with traditional quality control in RAD is that the productivity-enhancing tools used by software developers have far outdistanced the paper-producing tools used by quality assurance groups, testers, and documentation groups. The development of software proceeds at a pace that is faster by several orders of magnitude than the knowledge transfer, composition, layout, and review of paper documentation. The result is paper-producing groups not keeping up with the pace of development.

The distribution of information through paper documents is expensive and slow. Paper documentation is typically at least somewhat out-of-date by the time it is printed. When we need to distribute information to more people, we make more paper copies. When we need to update information, we must make enough copies to replace all existing earlier versions and try to distribute these new paper copies to everyone who had a copy of the earlier version. This is a manual version control process. It cannot hope to keep all distributed information fresh.

In the time it takes to explain the paper problem, I can make major changes in the functionality of a software application, recompile it, and have it ready for testing. The paper documentation is now out-of-date.

In general, development takes hours to build a release, but change management needs days to approve the release and the testers need weeks to test it. Meanwhile, the design changes daily, and documentation simply cannot keep up.

Solution: Improving the Quality Process

To improve a quality process, you need to examine your technology environment (hardware, networks, protocols, standards) and your market, and develop definitions for quality that suit them. First of all, quality is only achieved when you have balance—that is, the right proportions of the correct ingredients.

Note: *Quality* is getting the right balance between timeliness, price, features, reliability, and support to achieve customer satisfaction.

Picking the Correct Components for Quality in Your Environment

The following are my definitions of the fundamental components that should be the goals of quality assurance.

- The definition of quality is *customer satisfaction.*
- The system for achieving quality is *constant refinement.*
- The measure of quality is *the profit.*
- The target goal of the quality process is *a hit every time.*

Note: Quality can be quantified most effectively by measuring customer satisfaction.

My formula for achieving these goals is:

- Be first to market with the product.
- Ask the right price.
- Get the right features in it—the required stuff and some flashy stuff that will really please the users.
- Keep the unacceptable bugs to an absolute minimum. *Corollary*: Make sure your bugs are less expensive and less irritating than your competitor's bugs.

As far as I am concerned, this is a formula for creating an *excellent* product.

A Change in the Balance

Historically, as a market matures, the importance of being the first to market will diminish and reliability will become more important. Indications show that this already happening in some cutting-edge industries. For example, I just completed a study of 3G communications devices in the Pacific Rim. Apparently, the first-to-market service provider captures the early adopter—in this case, young people, students, and professionals. However, the higher volume sales of hardware and services go to the provider who can capture the *second* wave of buyers. This second wave is made up of members of the general public who need time to evaluate the new offerings. The early adopters serve to educate the general public. Further, the second wave of buyers is non-technical and they are not as tolerant of bugs in the system as the early adopters.

Elimination by Market Forces of Competitors Who Fail to Provide Sufficient Quality

The developers and testers who are suffering the most from the problems of outdated and inefficient quality assurance practices are the software makers who must provide high reliability. A market-driven RAD shop is likely to use only the quality assurance practices that suit their in-house process and ignore the rest. This is true because a 5 percent increase in reliability is not worth a missed delivery date. Even though the makers of firmware, safety-critical software, and other high-reliability systems are feeling the same pressures to get their product to market, they cannot afford to abandon quality assurance practices.

A student said to me recently, "We make avionics. We test everything, every time. When we find a bug, we fix it, every time, no matter how long it takes." The only way these makers can remain competitive without compromising reliability is by improving, optimizing, and automating their development processes and their quality assurance and control processes.

Clearly, we must control quality. We must encourage and reward invention, and we must be quick to incorporate improvements. What we are looking for is a set of efficient methods, metrics, and tools that strike a balance between controlling process and creating product.

Picking the Correct Quality Control Tools for Your Environment

Earlier I mentioned the traditional tools used by quality assurance to ensure that quality is achieved in the product: records, documents, and activities (such as testing). Improving these tools is a good place to start if you are going to try and improve your quality process. We need all of these tools; it is just a matter of making them efficient and doable.

I also talked about the failings and challenges associated with using paper in our development and quality processes. And, in Chapter 1, I talked about the fact that trained testers using solid methods and metrics are in short supply. In this section, I want to talk about some of the techniques I have used to improve these three critical quality assurance tools.

Automating Record Keeping

We certainly need to keep records, and we need to write down our plans, but we can't spend time doing it. The records must be generated automatically as a part of our development and quality process. The records that tell us who, what, where, when, and how should not require special effort to create, and they should be maintained automatically every time something is changed.

The most important (read: *cost-effective*) test automation I have developed in the last four years has *not* been preparing automated test scripts. It has been automating the documentation process, via the inventory, and test management by instituting online forms and a single-source repository for all test documentation and process tracking.

I built my first test project Web site in 1996. It proved to be such a useful tool that the company kept it in service for years after the product was shipped. It was used by the support groups to manage customer issues, internal training, and upgrades to the product for several years.

This automation of online document repositories for test plans, scripts, scheduling, bug reporting, shared information, task lists, and discussions has been so successful that it has taken on a life of its own as a set of project management tools that enable instant collaboration amongst team members, no matter where they are located.

Today, collaboration is becoming a common theme as more and more development efforts begin to use the Agile methodologies.[1] I will talk more about this methodology in Chapter 3, "Approaches to Managing Software Testing." Collaborative Web sites are beginning to be used in project management and intranet sites to support this type of effort.

I have built many collaborative Web sites over the years; some were more useful than others, but they eliminated whole classes of errors, because there were a single source for all documentation, schedules, and tasks that was accessible to the entire team.

Web sites of this type can do a lot to automate our records, improve communications, and speed the processing of updates. This objective is accomplished through the use of team user profiles, role-based security,

[1] The Agile Software Development Manifesto, by the AgileAlliance, February 2001, at www.agilemanifesto.org.

dynamic forms and proactive notification, and messaging features. Task lists, online discussions, announcements, and subscription-based messaging can automatically send emails to subscribers when events occur.

Several vendors are offering Web sites and application software that perform these functions. I use Microsoft SharePoint Team Services to perform these tasks today. It comes free with Microsoft Office XP, so it is available to most corporate testing projects. There are many names for a Web site that performs these types of tasks; I prefer to call such a Web site a collaborative site.

Improving Documentation Techniques

Documentation techniques can be improved in two ways. First, you can improve the way documents are created and maintained by automating the handling of changes in a single-source environment. Second, you can improve the way the design is created and maintained by using visualization and graphics instead of verbiage to describe systems and features. A graphical visualization of a product or system can be much easier to understand, review, update, and maintain than a written description of the system.

Improving the Way Documents Are Created, Reviewed, and Maintained

We can greatly improve the creation, review, and approval process for documents if they are (1) kept in a single-source repository and (2) reviewed by the entire team with all comments being collected and merged automatically into a single document. Thousands of hours of quality assurance process time can be saved by using a collaborative environment with these capabilities.

For example, in one project that I managed in 2001, the first phase of the project used a traditional process of distributing the design documents via email and paper, collecting comments and then rolling all the comments back into a single new version. Thirty people reviewed the documents. Then, it took a team of five documentation specialists 1,000 hours to roll all the comments into the new version of the documentation.

At this point I instituted a Microsoft SharePoint Team Services collaborative Web site, which took 2 hours to create and 16 hours to write the instructions to the reviewers and train the team to use the site. One document specialist was assigned as the permanent support role on the site to answer questions and reset passwords. The next revision of the documents included twice as many reviewers, and only 200 hours were spent rolling the comments into the next version of the documentation. Total time savings for processing the reviewers' comments was about 700 hours.

The whole concept of having to call in old documents and redistribute new copies in a project of any size is so wasteful that an automated Web-based system can usually pay for itself in the first revision cycle.

Improving the Way Systems Are Described: Replacing Words with Pictures

Modeling tools are being used to replace descriptive commentary documentation in several industries. For example, BizTalk is an international standard that defines an environment for interorganizational workflows that support electronic commerce and supply-chain integration. As an example of document simplification, consider the illustration in Figure 2.1. It shows the interaction of a business-to-business automated procurement system implemented by the two companies. Arrows denote the flow of data among roles and entities.

Microsoft's BizTalk server allows business analysts and programmers to design the flow of B2B data using the graphical user interface of Visio (a drawing program). They actually draw the process flow for the data and workflows. This drawing represents a business process. In BizTalk Orchestration Designer, once a drawing is complete, it can be compiled and run as an XLANG schedule. XLANG is part of the BizTalk standard. This process of drawing the system is called *orchestration*. Once the annalist has created this visual design document, the programmer simply wires up the application logic by attaching programs to the various nodes in the graphical design image.

Figure 2.2 shows the movement of the documents through the buyer and seller systems as created in the orchestration process. It also shows the interaction between the XLANG schedule, BizTalk Messaging Services, and the auxiliary components.

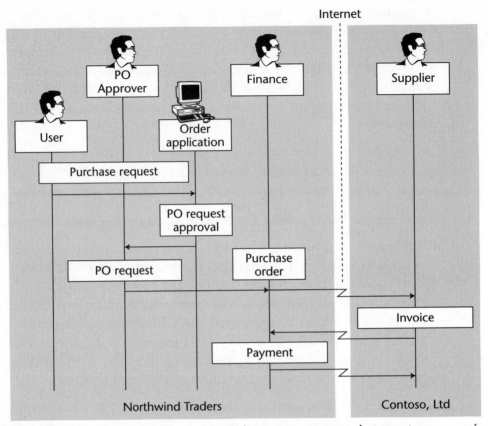

Figure 2.1   Business-to-business automated procurement system between two companies.

Fact: **One picture (like Figure 2.2) is better than thousands of words of commentary-style documentation and costs far less to create and maintain.**

It can take anywhere from 15 to 30 pages of commentary to adequately describe this process. Yet this graphic does it in one page. This type of flow mapping is far more efficient than describing the process in a commentary. It is also far more maintainable. And, as you will see when we discuss logic flow maps in Chapters 11 and 12, this type of flow can be used to generate the tests required to validate the system during the test effort.

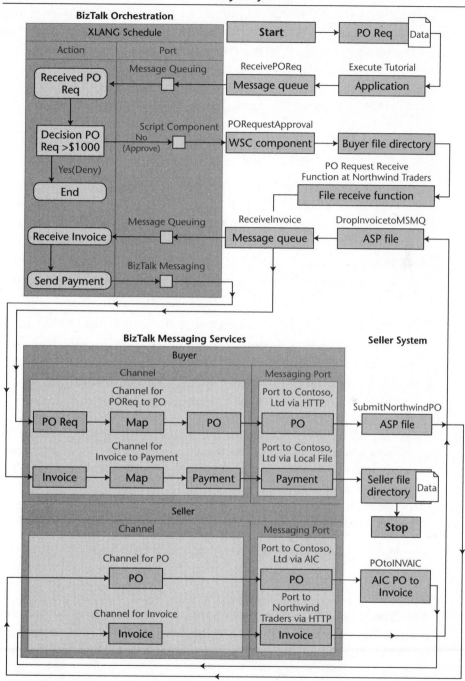

Figure 2.2 The movement of documents through the system.

Visualization techniques create systems that are self-documenting. I advocate using this type of visual approach to describing systems at every opportunity. As I said in Chapter 1, the most significant improvements in software quality have not been made through testing or quality assurance, but through the application of standards.

Trained Testers Using Methods and Metrics That Work

Finally, we have the quality assurance tool for measuring the quality of the software product: testing.

In many organizations, the testers are limited to providing information based on the results of verification and validation. This is a sad under-use of a valuable resource. This thinking is partly a holdover from the traditional manufacturing-based quality assurance problems. This traditional thinking assumes that the designers can produce what the users want the first time, all by themselves. The other part of the problem is the perception that testers don't produce anything—except possibly bugs.

It has been said that "you can't test the bugs out." This is true. *Test* means to verify—to compare an actuality to a standard. It doesn't say anything about taking any fixative action. However, enough of the right bugs must be removed during, or as a result of, the test effort, or the test effort will be judged a failure.

Note: In reality, the tester's product is the delivered system, the code written by the developers minus the bugs (that the testers persuaded development to remove) plus the innovations and enhancements suggested through actual use (that testers persuaded developers to add).

The test effort is the process by which testers produce their product.

The quality of the tools that they use in the test effort has a direct effect on the outcome of the quality of the process. A good method isn't going to help the bottom line if the tools needed to support it are not available.

The methods and metrics that the testers use during the test effort should be ones that add value to the final product. The testers should be allowed to choose the tools they need to support the methods and metrics that they are using.

Once the system is turned over to test, the testers should own it. After all, the act of turning the code over for testing states implicitly that the developers have put everything into it that they currently believe should be there, for that moment at least, and that it is ready to be reviewed.

As I observed in Chapter 1, there is a shortage of trained testers, and practicing software testers are not noted for using formal methods and metrics. Improving the tools used by untrained testers will not have as big a benefit as training the testers and giving them the tools that they need to succeed.

Summary

Traditional quality assurance principles are not a good fit for today's software projects. Further, the traditional processes by which we ensure quality in software systems is cumbersome and inflexible. Even more important, the traditional tools used by quality assurance are not able to keep up with the pace of software development today. Testers constrained to follow these outmoded practices using these cumbersome tools are doomed to failure.

The quality process must be reinvented to fit the real needs of the development process. The process by which we ensure quality in a product must be improved. A company needs to write its own quality goals and create a process for ensuring that they are met. The process needs to be flexible, and it needs to take advantage of the tools that exist today.

Several new technologies exist that can be used to support quality assurance principles, such as collaboration, which allows all involved parties to contribute and communicate as the design and implementation evolve. These technologies can also help make quality assurance faster and more efficient by replacing traditional paper documentation, distribution, and review processes with instantly available single-source electronic documents, and by supplementing written descriptions with drawings.

Replacing tradition requires a culture change. And, people must change their way of working to include new tools. Changing a culture is difficult. Historically, successful cultures simply absorb new invading cultures, adopt the new ideas that work, and get on with life. Cultures that resist the invasion must spend resources to do so, and so become distracted from the main business at hand.

Software quality is a combination of reliability, timeliness to market, price/cost, and the feature richness. The test effort must exist in balance with these other factors. Testers need *tools*—that is, methods and metrics that can keep up with development—and testers need the knowledge to use those tools.

Traditionally, testing has been a tool to measure the quality of the product. Today, testing needs to be able to do more than just measure; it needs to be able to add to the value of the product. In the next chapters, we discuss various approaches to testing and some fundamental methods and metrics that are used throughout the rest of the book.

CHAPTER 3

Approaches to Managing Software Testing

M any major hotels in Las Vegas, Nevada, offer gaming schools as a free service to their patrons. The first lesson that they teach in gaming school goes something like this: The instructor takes great pains to point out the red velvet wall coverings, the crystal chandeliers, and all the rich appointments that surround you in the casino. Then they tell you, "Look around. See all the money that built Las Vegas? Always remember, *the losers built Las Vegas*. They played their hunches. They are the ones that felt lucky."

The I-Feel-Lucky Approach to Software Development

The gaming school teaches students to resist the "I feel lucky" impulse and use methods instead. They show you how to figure out if your hand of cards is more likely to win than someone else's and how to calculate odds of certain combinations of numbers showing up on a pair of dice. The methods taught in gaming school are based on simple counting techniques and probability. They are very similar to the methods taught in this book.

If you have any doubts about the results of using methods versus the I-feel-lucky approach, consider that today most casinos are populated exclusively by computer-driven games—not cards or dice. This system is in place because there are no counting techniques that can be used to successfully calculate or predict the odds of winning in computer gaming. Only a very knowledgeable hacker or someone with inside information has a chance of winning more than they invest with electronic gaming. Clearly, the financial thinkers at the casinos saw the power of good methods and moved to circumvent them.

If management does not have a method that has demonstrated value, they will take their best guess instead. If the product succeeds, management will believe in their winning streak and continue to play their hunches. Generally, no one is much interested in trying a formal method—until this luck runs out and the winning streak breaks. If you want to prove that in the long run a method works better than luck, you have to measure how well each actually performs.

Note: Methods and metrics must provide demonstrable value to have credibility and worth.

As I said in Chapter 1, currently few people feel lucky, and we (testers) once again have a good chance to prove our worth. But what should that look like? How does a tester make a case for methods with a manager who does not believe that he or she needs to test? The best way I know is to provide that manager with high-quality information that he or she can use to make decisions that have a positive affect on the bottom line.

To do that you will have to develop an approach to testing that complements (and can succeed with) the development methodology being used. You will have to measure and keep track of what you measure, and finally, you will have to convert your measurement data into that information that management finds truly valuable. And that's what this book is about.

Another way that you can demonstrate the value of methods and metrics is to measure the cost benefit of *not* using the methods and metrics and compare that to the cost benefit of using them.

For example, in a case study of an early-1990s shrink-wrap RAD project that I reported in 1994, a group of trained testers, using the methods and metrics in this book, found bugs at the rate of two to three per hour, while untrained testers, who were not using formal methods and metrics, found three bugs per day in the same applications. Further, over 90 percent of the bugs reported by the trained testers were fixed, while half of the bugs reported by the untrained testers were returned by developers as *unreproducible*.

In this study the trained testers were paid a wage that was almost double that of the untrained testers. Even at double the pay it cost an average of $13 for the trained testers to find a bug, while it cost an average of $50 for the untrained testers to find the same bug. Even when the cost of test education is taken into account, the testers using methods and metrics are far more efficient. These are facts that will motivate management to consider trying the methods and metrics used by the trained testers.

The best reason for using methods and metrics is that companies using them have a competitive advantage. They get a much better job done for less.

I firmly believe that a competent journeyman tester (the ones using methods and metrics) can successfully test any development project regardless of the development methodology being employed as long as they have sufficient resources and management support to do so. Developing or tailoring the test approach to suit the needs of the project is a critical piece of acquiring those resources and that support.

Before we examine the current approaches to testing in the field and the approaches you should take, let's examine some myths about testing and the approaches to testing. What are some of the widespread, usually erroneous assumptions about the approaches we should take to testing?

Some Myths about Art, Science, and Software

One of the most destructive myths in the industry is that somehow science and art are mutually exclusive, that scientists and engineers cannot think creatively and that artists cannot or should not be educated to be competent in measurement or science because it would hurt their creativity.

As previously noted, *feature richness* is a major component of the perceived quality of a software product. A rich set of features requires a creative and innovative approach to design. This requirement has led to an infusion of artistic talent into the software development process. Typically, this artistic talent lacks foundation training in science or engineering. Even worse, the Internet opened the door for absolutely anyone to put up a Web site and claim to be a professional-anything.

Myths about Art

Art means to join or fit together. It is commonly defined as follows:

1. The human ability to make things; creativity of human beings as distinguished from the world of nature.
2. Skill; craftsmanship.
3. Any specific skill or its application, for example, the art of making friends.
4. Any craft, trade, or profession or its principles.
5. Creative work or its principles; such as making things in a manner that displays form, beauty, and unusual perception: art includes painting, sculpture, architecture, music, literature, drama, dance, etc.
6. The quality of being artful or cunning.
7. The quality of being sly or cunning; tricky; wily.

The infusion of artistic talent into software development has undoubtedly improved features. It has also caused serious quality degradation in the software development process. One of the most popular myths in the software development community is that *only* artists are creative and that artists cannot be creative if they are constrained to follow *rules*.

I spent 25 years in the performing arts, and I am an artist as well as an engineer. No one drills harder on fundamentals than an artist. Musicians, dancers, painters, singers, and writers all practice for hours each day for many years to build something called *technique*. The depth and quality of an artist's technique is the measure of that individual's mastery of his or her discipline. An artist cannot be competitive without great technique. Because of my own experience with art and science, I am very wary of the person who claims to be an *artist* but whines about following a disciplined approach. This person is not likely to be a competent artist.

Myths about Science

Scientific methods grow out of a body of factual knowledge, not out of myth and supposition. The term *science* refers to a body of knowledge that is a body of models and generalizations that organizes and correlates observed facts. *The purpose of gathering these facts is to make predictions.* These predictions are then tested by comparing them to actual observations or experiments.

An accepted scientific conceptual scheme is usually called a *theory*. A theory is never *proved.* A theory is considered to be a valid model of reality if it correlates well with a considerable body of facts and if no one *disproves* it by finding a fact that contradicts its predictions. There is always the chance that the best-established theory will be disproved by someone who can show its predictions to be in error. At this point the theory will have to be revised, corrected, refined, or abandoned.

Science starts by systematically recording facts. These facts should be accurate, well defined, and quantitative. The scientist tries to order and correlate these facts. The product of this process is usually a *working hypothesis* that is capable of prediction. A working hypothesis is provisional. It is meant to guide further investigation and is subject to constant change and refinement. A hypothesis is incorporated into scientific theory only when it has been empirically verified in many ways. Any hypothesis is abandoned or revised if its predictions are contradicted by observation.

When a scientist publishes a new idea, it is called an invention or innovation. *Invent* means to come upon, meet, or discover. This definition includes (1) to think up; devise or fabricate in the mind such as to invent excuses; and (2) to think out or produce, such as a new device, process, etc.; or to originate, as by experiment; or devise for the first time. According to *Webster's New World Dictionary*, *innovate* means to renew, or to alter, to introduce new methods or devices to bring in as an innovation. These definitions certainly sound like creativity.

Myths about Software

The popular myth is that the artist just throws a bunch of stuff together and comes up with a miracle of creation. This is not to say that the scientist cannot be creative, ingenious, or inventive, nor that the artist is undisciplined and cannot keep good records. But that is the myth. If you are inventing something new, you use a process called *experimentation*. In commercial software, we call this process *developing a new product*. How the experiment is conducted or the development process works is what separates the scientists from the artists.

While the artist is likely to rush right in and begin following her or his creative intuition, the scientist begins by performing background research and formulating an approach to conducting the experiment. The scientist keeps careful records of the steps in the process, the assumptions, the ingredients used, and their quantities and the outcome.

Pure *art* is good at one-of-a-kind things and limited editions. Creation is about taking risks to try new and different things. Success is capricious. Uniformity and reproducibility are *not* the hallmark of art. Most of an artist's career goes into trying to find the spotlight—fabulous painting, hit song, best-selling book, or whatever. In the commercial world we need reproducible miracles. The next release of the software should be even better than the current release; art makes no guarantees.

For example, let's consider cookies. Great software and great cookies have a lot in common. They both evolve through a process. A business needs not only to develop a good cookie but it also needs to be able to make as many of these cookies as the market demands. In addition, everyone who buys a cookie wants a good cookie, so the cookies must be consistently good, batch after batch. The maker needs to be able to make lots of good cookies time after time without unpleasant surprises. It is generally not worthwhile for a business to create one batch of fabulous cookies if it cannot ever reproduce them for sale in the future.

The artist may invent a truly marvelous cookie, but there is no guarantee that it can be reproduced with the same quality. The cookie invented by the scientist may not be so marvelous, but it will most probably be reproducible with consistent quality.

Additionally, artists tend to ignore requirements that do not agree with their artistic sensibilities. So, it is not unusual for the marvelous cookie that the artist created to be a poor fit for the cookie-buying market. While it is true that a scientist's creativity may be inhibited by his or her knowledge of the facts, the artist's creation can be crippled by ignorance of the facts.

Fact: What is required is a *balance* between creativity and method. This is where engineers come into the picture.

The Engineering Approach

It seems that people's perception of software engineers is based on programmers, who are regularly called software engineers. However, programmers might not be engineers, they might not act like engineers, and they might not conduct business as engineers do. The traditional branches of engineering—civil, mechanical, electrical, chemical—have a licensing process that engineers must go through to become *professional engineers*. This process helps ensure that an acceptable level of knowledge and competence exists in the profession. There is no such certification in software engineering.

According to *Webster's New World Dictionary*, engineering is "(a) the science concerned with putting scientific knowledge to practical uses. . . (b) the planning, designing, construction, or management of machinery, roads, bridges, buildings, etc. (c) the act of maneuvering or managing. . . ."

Engineers are scientists who apply science to solve problems. We are the practical folks in the sweaty hats. There is *art* in the definition of engineering also.

Notice the reference in the dictionary definition to *management*. Management is, according to *Webster's New World Dictionary*, "the act, *art*, or manner of managing, or handling, controlling, directing . . . ."

The *practice of engineering* is applied science (application of the bodies of knowledge of the various natural sciences), supplemented as necessary by art (*know-how* built up and handed down from past experience).

The know-how built up and handed down from past experience is also called *engineering practice*. In civil engineering, engineering practice refers to a body of knowledge, methods, and rules of thumb that consist of accepted techniques for solving problems and conducting business.

Accountability and Performance

The reason for the existence of this body of knowledge, engineering practice, is that engineers are *accountable*. If a structure fails, the engineer is the one who is probably going to be held responsible.

Nobody knows everything, and mistakes will happen despite the best preparation possible. Engineers must show that they performed their duties according to the best of their abilities in accordance with accepted standards. This is called *performance*. The engineer's defense will be based on demonstrating that he or she followed acceptable engineering practice.

Engineering practice has some fundamental rules that are of particular interest and value to software engineers and testers:

- State the methods followed and why.
- State your assumptions.
- Apply adequate factors of safety.
- Always get a second opinion.

Each of these rules is described in the paragraphs that follow.

Stating the Methods Followed and Why

The International Standards Organization's ISO 9001/EN quality management and quality assurance standards are famous for demanding that software developers "say what they do, and do what they say." But this is only one of the rules that engineers must follow in order to justify and defend what they did or what they intend to do. Most of the content of this book is the "say what I do" part of this requirement. In civil engineering, it is more a case of "say what you do and prove you did it."

Scientific method uses measurements to establish fact, so a discussion of engineering methods would not be complete without a discussion of the metrics used to support the methods. I will formally introduce the metrics used to support the test methods in this book in the next two chapters.

Stating Your Assumptions

No one knows everything or has all the answers. To solve problems in the absence of a complete set of facts, we make *assumptions*. Assumptions are frequently wrong. The way to mitigate the effects of incorrect assumptions is to publish all assumptions for as wide a review as possible. This increases the chances that someone will spot an incorrect assumption and refute or correct it. If an engineer makes an incorrect assumption but publishes it along with all the other assumptions about the project, if no one challenges or refutes this assumption, the engineer will have a defensible position in the event of a failure. The engineer performed in an acceptable and professional manner.

Our software systems have become so complex that no one can accurately predict all the ramifications of making a change to one. What we do not know for sure, we assume to be this way or that. Assumptions need to be made to fill in the gaps between the known facts. And those assumptions need to be published so that others have the opportunity to refute them and to plan for them. For example, a common assumption is that the test system will be available 100 percent of the time during the test effort. If the system goes down, or if there are resource problems because other groups need access, the loss of system availability can cause a significant impact on the test schedule.

How to Recognize Assumptions

Learning to recognize assumptions takes time and practice. We make assumptions constantly. It takes a conscious effort to try to identify them. The technique I use to recognize an assumption is to first try and identify all the things that I am depending on, and then to put the words "it is assumed that" in front of all those dependencies. If the dependency statement sounds more reasonable with the assumption clause, it goes in the test agreement as an assumption. For example, the statement "The test system will behave as it has in the past" becomes "It is assumed that the test system will behave as it has in the past." System support personnel can then confirm or modify this statement during review of the test agreement. When considered in this way, it becomes clear very quickly just how much we take for granted—like the existence of gravity.

One of the most frightening mistakes I ever made in estimating a test effort was to assume that "bugs found during testing would be fixed within published [previously agreed upon] turnaround times so that testing could continue." For example, a showstopper would be fixed as fast as possible, meaning within hours, and a serious bug would be fixed in a day.

Unbeknownst to the test group, the development manager dictated that "developers would finish writing all the code before they fixed any bugs." The bug fixes necessary for testing to continue never materialized. The developers never really finish writing code, so they never fixed any bugs. All my test agreements now state this assumption explicitly.

Types of Assumptions

The following are some examples of typical assumptions for a software test effort.

Assumption: Scope and Type of Testing

- The test effort will conduct system, integration, and function testing.

- All unit testing will be conducted by development.

Assumption: Environments That Will Be Tested

- The environments defined in the requirements are the only environments that the test effort will be responsible for verifying and validating.

Environment State(s)

- All operating system software will be installed before testing is begun.

System Behavior

- The system is stable.

- The system will behave in the same way it has in the past.

System Requirements and Specifications

- The system requirements and specifications are complete and up-to-date.

Test Environment Availability

- The test environment will accurately model the real-world environment.

- The test environment will be available at all times for the duration of the test effort.

Bug Fixes

- Bugs found during testing will be fixed within published turn-around times according to priority.

Apply Adequate Factors of Safety

We have already discussed that we use methods and take measurements in order to make *predictions.* A factor of safety is a metric. It is the measure of how far wrong a past prediction was, applied to a current prediction to make it more accurate or safe. Engineers adjust their predictions to cope with this reality by applying factors of safety. We will discuss this metric now because it is part of engineering practice in general, rather than software testing in particular.

Demands placed on a design can extend far beyond the original purpose. The engineer is accountable for the integrity of the product. Even if the product is put to uses that were never imagined, there is still a performance requirement. When an engineer designs a bridge, every component and every design specification has a factor of safety applied to it. Say, for example, that the design specification states, "the bridge will be able to carry the load of tractor trailers, all loaded to capacity, parked end-to-end on the bridge deck, during a flood." The engineer would calculate all the loads produced by all those trucks and the flood, and she or he would then multiply that load by a factor of safety, generally 2, and design the bridge to hold double the original required load. This is why bridges very seldom collapse even though they must survive all manner of loads that were never anticipated by the engineer who designed them. I have seen people drive across bridges when the floodwaters were so high that the bridge was completely under water, even though common sense dictates that such a situation is very risky.

Factors of safety are not widely used in commercial software development. If a network architect has a requirement for a switch that can handle 49 simultaneous transactions, the network architect will likely buy the switch that is advertised as capable of handling 50 simultaneous transactions. That same architect will be surprised when the switch fails in real-time operation as the load approaches 40 simultaneous transactions. The reason the system failed is important. But from a reliability standpoint, the failure could have been avoided if a factor of safety had been included in the system design.

In safety-critical software, factors of safety are more commonly implemented using redundant and fault-tolerant systems rather than by expanding design capacity.

How to Determine a Factor of Safety

In this book we use factors of safety primarily in the test estimation process to help get an accurate time line for the test effort. In most branches of engineering, there are established values for factors of safety for many applications. I am not aware of any established factors of safety in software engineering test estimation. The only project management approach commonly used in software development is to allow a few "slack days" in the schedule to absorb overruns and unforeseen events. I disagree with this practice because it is often arbitrary; the time is not budgeted where it will be needed in the schedule, and the amount of time allotted has nothing to do with the real risks in the project.

Factors of safety should be determined based on the error in the previous estimation and then adjusted as needed. Even if a process does not use measurements to arrive at an estimate, a factor of safety can be established for future similar estimates. For example, a test effort was estimated to require 14 weeks. In reality, 21 weeks were required to complete the test effort. The estimate was low by a factor of:

$$21/_{14} = 1.5$$

When the *next* test estimation effort takes place, if the same or similar methods are used to make the estimate, even if it is based on an I-feel-lucky guess, multiply the new estimate by a factor of 1.5, and you will get an estimate that has been adjusted to be in keeping with reality.

Not all factors of safety are determined analytically. One of my favorite managers was a software development manager whom I worked with for three years at Prodigy. He took every project estimate I gave him and multiplied my estimate by his own factor of safety. While it was normally between 1.5 and 2, it was sometimes as high as 3.5. His estimates were always right, and our projects were always completed on time and on or under budget. Eventually I asked Gary how he knew the correct factor of safety and if he used the same factor on everyone's estimates. He told me that each person needed her or his own individual factor of safety. Gary noted that the adjustments he applied to estimates were not based on calculation but on his experience. In my case, he was correcting for the fact that I tended to push myself harder than he liked in order to meet deadlines and that as a manager he had information about project dependencies that I did not.

Note: It does not matter how a factor of safety is determined; using them improves estimates.

No one knows everything, and no method is perfect. There is no shame in producing an estimate that is initially inaccurate, only in knowingly leaving it unadjusted. Recognizing deficiencies and correcting for them before they can become problems is the goal. Factors of safety adjust estimates to accommodate unknowns.

It has been my experience that management in software houses resists factors of safety. They want to hear a shorter time estimate, not a longer time estimate. I have had good success persuading management to use factors of safety by consistently calculating the adjusted time and making it visible. It is my job to supply the information that management uses to make decisions. If management chooses to ignore my recommendations, that is their prerogative. If management selects the shorter time and if we fail to meet it, I only need to point out the adjusted time estimate to make my point. Over time, I have convinced many managers that a more accurate estimate is preferable even if it is less palatable.

Always Get a Second Opinion

No good reason exists for working without a safety net. Inspection and formal reviews are the most productive way to remove defects that we know of today. Part of the reason is that inspectors bring an outside perspective to the process, so the rest is simple human factors. My first testing mentor, Lawrence, pointed out that inspection and review works because people who do not know anything about the project are likely to find a lot of mistakes missed by people in the project. In addition, these techniques owe much of their success to the fact that it is human nature that when you are expecting company, you generally clean the house before they come over.

Having someone to check your work is very important. If you cannot get anyone to check your work, publish the fact clearly in print. This disclaimer not only protects you, but it warns those reading your work.

The Adversarial Approach versus the Team Approach

When I joined my first software project in 1985, testers worked in isolated autonomous groups separate from the development groups, and the two groups communicated mostly in writing. It was normal for the relationship between developers and software testers to become adversarial from time to time. Boris Beizer and Glenford Myers (and lots of others), experts in software testing at the time, wrote about this fact.

Dr. Beizer even dedicated a chapter in one of his books to how test managers can defend and protect their testers.

Another characteristic of the time was the way the value of a test was measured. In his wonderful book, *The Art of Software Testing*, Glenford Myers writes, "A good test is one which finds bugs." While I agree there is merit in this thought, it suggests that a test that does not find bugs does not tell us anything useful, and that is not true. The goal of finding bugs is important, but when it becomes the sole focus of a test effort, it creates a negative imbalance in the perspective of the project personnel such that only the negative aspects of a software system are valued by the testers. This tight focus on the negative aspects of a software system is sure to cause resentment on the part of development, which can lead to an adversarial relationship.

This idea that the only valuable test is one that finds a bug was a product of the time. At that time, most software testing was conducted by engineers, or people with a science background. Testing in the traditional engineering disciplines is conducted by stressing a component until it breaks. The expected outcome is always failure. In materials testing, for instance, a newly designed steel beam is placed in a machine that will apply various loads to the beam. The tester uses very precise instruments to measure the reaction of the beam to each load. The load is increased until ultimately the beam fails. The actual load at which the beam failed is compared to the theoretical ultimate loading for the beam. The ideal situation is that the calculated ultimate load agrees closely with the actual ultimate load. This means that the predicted ultimate load was correct. Concurrence between actual and predicted behavior gives the engineers increased confidence that the other predicted behaviors of the beam will correlate closely with its actual behavior in the real world.

The traditional engineering approach to testing is not always a good fit with the needs of software testing. While some parts of the software environment can be tested to an ultimate load—for instance, the maximum number of bytes per second that can be transmitted in a certain communications environment—the concept is meaningless for most software modules. A software module is *not* like a steel beam. With the level of sophistication that exists in today's software systems, the software module should never *fail*.

The best correlation for a load failure in software is data boundary testing, which is probably why it is the most productive test technique used today. But even if a data value falls outside the expected range, the software should still process it as an exception or error. As software systems become more and more robust, it becomes harder and harder to force a load failure. Where a tester used to be able to cause telephone calls to be dropped by overloading a telephone switching computer with too many simultaneous calls, now in most situations, the callers whose calls cannot be routed immediately hear an announcement to that effect.

Normally my goal as a tester is *not* to "break the product." My goal is to perform verification and validation on the product. My job isn't just to test, to verify that it does what it is supposed to do; an automation tool can be trained to do that. I must also determine if it's doing the right things in the right way.

Judging the merit of something must be accomplished by weighing its positive aspects against its negative aspects. When testers get too intent on finding bugs, they can lose track of how well the system works as a whole. They can lose sight of the goal of satisfying and delighting the customer. I have seen too many test efforts that found lots of bugs but never tested the real-life scenarios that mattered to the customers, where the testers didn't even know what those scenarios were.

I don't agree with the people who say that human testers will try to "not find bugs." Every tester I know loves to find bugs; we relish them. We show them off to each other: "Hey wanna see something really cool? I can make the display monitor turn into lots of little flashing squares!" The real issue is how we handle the communications about those bugs between testers and developers and between developers and testers.

The adversarial approach that promotes aggressive behavior does not provide satisfactory results in today's mixed male, female, and multi-cultural work place. A team approach does provide good results while maintaining good morale in the workplace. After all, we are all on the same team; our real adversaries are the bugs.

Persuasion is an art. One of the chief tools of persuasion is argument. The word *argument* has a negative connotation, being linked to confrontation and adversarial situations, but it is part of the definition of the word *validation*. The answer to the question "Does the product do the right thing?" requires subjective judgment. Persuasion will be accomplished by argument. The quality of the tester's *argument* is determined by how successful it is in convincing others of its merit. The best case or most convincing argument is made through objective measurements, but measurements alone are not always sufficient to make a successful argument.

The Eclectic Approach to Integration and Testing: Balancing Art and Engineering

When I examined the methods that I use that work well when organizing and carrying out a test effort, I found that I was relying on communications skills that I learned as a dancer and ballet mistress rather than the formal approach that I learned as an engineer. When I am planning and reporting, I use tools and methods from engineering.

Dance is not communicated through written documents but by an older form of communication; dance is communicated by an oral tradition. This contrasts sharply with engineers and musicians, who communicate via written documents, but it correlates closely with the current requirements of software development. I mention musicians because there are a significant number of musicians in software development.

An oral tradition has the advantage that there is no time lost in recording instructions on another medium, and the disadvantage that there is no permanent record of what transpired and everyone must remain in close proximity to be kept informed. Large projects cannot be controlled using oral communications alone; neither can projects with team members who are spread out in disparate locations. Recording instructions and design specifics in writing takes time, but it allows ideas to be communicated to many people in remote locations.

Dancers absorb and memorize new material through a combination of oral, aural, and visual input. Virtually every movement that the dancer makes is set by the choreographer. Dancers rarely perform ad lib. Each movement is supposed to be performed on a specific beat in some precise location and spatial orientation on the stage. This is doubly true for members of the corpse de ballet, who must perform as a single unit, with each individual dancer precisely in synch with all the others. The dancers must execute complex coordinated movements precisely, time after time, on the beat, and in the correct place on the stage, down to the tilt of the head and the angle and alignment of their fingers. It is within this very demanding and precise framework that a dancer applies his or her art to make that particular rendition of the dance exceptional and memorable. A group of testers with these characteristics is definitely in a position to do an excellent job of testing a system.

Dancers are competent professionals when they are hired. When a new production is scheduled, everyone is given a part, usually one that is well suited to her or his abilities. The main difference between the ballet and the software business is that in ballet, everyone expects to be *taught* the part that they will perform in each new production. In business, the expectation is that somehow everyone will *know* his or her part. My friend Bill says, "Everyone wants to learn, but no one wants to be taught." In business this seems to be true. But it doesn't solve the problem of how to transfer knowledge to new players in a new production and get them working together.

I have had success coping with these difficulties in business by building teams. In a team environment, every member's work is visible; if someone is not keeping up, the situation can be examined and solutions can be proposed. The biggest problems arise when individuals become isolated and their work has low visibility. Today, these precepts are considered an integral part of managing a collaborative development effort.

The ballet mistress or master is responsible for rehearsing the company, spotting and correcting any problems, and tuning the whole company to give their best performance. If some part of the production is not working, it is the ballet mistress or master who takes the issue to the choreographer. To be able to do this job, the ballet mistress or master must attend every single choreography session and rehearsal. If any written notes exist for a production, it is usually the ballet mistress or master who creates and maintains them. She or he must be able to count every phrase of the music for the production from memory, preferably while singing the main themes. She or he must know, at least in general, each dancer's part and all their entrances and exits. In a pinch she or he must be able to dance the parts of dancers who are not present so the rest of the company is not disrupted by the absence. This may mean filling in for a chorus member or a soloist.

The ballet mistress or master must be able to spot and correct mistakes and be ready to arbitrate or break the tie in any disagreements among the dancers, like, "We are supposed to be in the air on seven." "No, we are supposed to be on the ground on seven." She or he must also be able to make compelling arguments to nondancers like lighting engineers and the musicians. For instance, the ballet mistress may need to persuade the conductor that the fouetté music must be played at a slower tempo so the prima ballerina does not fall down or spin off the stage like a runaway top. By the way, this is a *validation* on the part of the ballet mistress; it is based on her judgment. Verification would require that the argument be tested to verify what actually happened to the ballerina turning at the questionable tempo.

The ballet mistress or master is primarily a technician, not a manager; however, she or he must be able to *manage* the various egos and temperaments in the company to keep everyone happy—that is, ready, willing, and able to give a splendid performance.

The company takes correction from the ballet mistress or master for two reasons. The first is that only dancers with a long and broad experience base are chosen to perform this very demanding role, and their corrections are virtually guaranteed to improve the quality of the performance. The second is that the ruling of the ballet mistress or master can only be overturned by the choreographer.

So, while the experts, like the soloists, focus on giving the best performance possible in their part of the production, the ballet mistress or master is the integrator responsible for testing and fine-tuning the production as a whole. All these players, working together, are necessary to ensure a truly excellent performance.

We are human beings. Our endeavors include these roles because they are effective in managing human undertakings, particularly ones that require cooperation—teamwork. Each discipline has a key person who performs a role similar to the ballet mistress. In the symphony it is the conductor, in singing it is the choral director, in acting it is the director, and in sports it is the coach.

In safety-critical software, the testers are generally the most experienced people on a project, and their rulings are rarely challenged or overturned. It is not hard to imagine what happens to the entire process if this integrator's role in the test process does not exist, is filled by someone who is poorly informed, or is filled by someone who doesn't have a technical background.

Many case studies show that the software testers should be involved in the software design and development phases, yet the industry continues to treat software testing as an afterthought, and testers as unskilled temporary positions that can be filled by persons with no special training.

In keeping with my role as integrator, I go to great lengths to make sure I am invited to the design meetings and brainstorming sessions whether it is part of the plan or not. If that fails, I rely on the friends that I make among the designers and programmers to keep me informed. If all of these things fail, most especially if I am forbidden access to the developers, I cannot possibly succeed. When I do contract testing, I have clauses that allow my company to withdraw from the project in this situation. Even if I cannot withdraw, I am duty bound to report to my management, in writing, that the situation is untenable and that I cannot perform my job in a satisfactory manner.

Engineers communicate in writing. Except for clarifications, the field engineer gets *all* of her or his knowledge of the project and instructions from the plans. This means that the plans must be well thought out, precise, and up-to-date. When a situation arises that is not covered in the plans, the field engineer prescribes a solution, generally after consulting with a colleague and getting a second opinion to back up her or his own. Since I have already discussed the problems associated with trying to create and maintain paper documentation in the fast-paced software development industry, it should be clear that the engineering methods applied to software development often break down at this point. Workers do what the field engineer says because the engineer is the authority in charge. The field engineer's decision can generally only be overturned by direct challenge and an inquiry by other engineers at the behest of the owner or general contractor. Even if the field engineer's decision is demonstrated to be wrong, it may not be easy to overturn it.

Since the paper documents in the software development effort are rarely able to keep up with the actual developments, the integrator who tracks the evolution of the project firsthand can be more effective in managing a software test effort than the engineer relying on the written documentation. This advantage that the integrator has via word of mouth should diminish as we focus on implementing self-documenting strategies in electronic media to replace transcribed paper documentation, but these skills are always beneficial.

Traditionally, engineers are far removed from human factors concerns. A lack of concern for or understanding of the needs and priorities of people is a serious disadvantage for anyone trying to manage people today. The company loyalty that used to allow managers and engineers to rule by decree has been severely eroded. Recent studies have shown that the employees are more likely to feel loyal to their current project than to their company.

Over- and underplanning is one of the hottest issues being debated in the software journals in 2002. The Capability Maturity Model disciples require extensive planning in the best engineering tradition; meanwhile, the Agile developers prefer to produce and test small bits in immediate response to customer requirement or evolving thinking. In the theatre this is the difference between a Shakespearean play and an evening of improvisation. Like it or not, they both have their place.

In engineering, the finished project is rarely better than the plans. In art, the project owes little allegiance to a plan; it improves and evolves continuously. It is never finished, only released.

Note: Two points for engineers in software to keep in mind:

1. You need to pick the right tool method or approach for the job at hand.

2. You need to remain flexible and plan for change.

Engineering provides methods for presenting and winning arguments through fact and measurement that are far superior to those used in the arts. The arts use the *critique* to make people aware of problems. Criticism is typically subjective and personal, as in "You made a mistake." Criticism is not easy to accept, especially for those not raised in a discipline where criticism is commonly used. The use of criticism leads to adversarial situations. Good engineering uses objective measurement and fact to make corrections. Facts and measurement are impersonal and much easier to accept, as in "There is a mistake that we must fix."

It has been said, "measure to discover," to which we should add, "not to lay blame unnecessarily." Testers who use engineering arguments, fact, and measurement are in a better position to be effective in assessing the actual importance of issues and win their points while avoiding adversarial encounters.

Sometimes neither the classical ballet mistress integrator nor the engineering approach is acceptable. Artists who are in the throes of the creative process with little or no supervision are not necessarily overjoyed to have an alternate authority introduced into their project—especially if they have succeeded in discrediting or dismantling the in-house test group.

An interesting outgrowth of this situation is the rise in popularity of the *external review*. An external review takes place when someone outside the project, or outside the company, tests the system and writes a bug report called a *review*. The review is submitted to management. Those writing the external review are disposable bad guys. Issues listed in the review are generally taken seriously by management because the source is external and uninvolved, and the arguments presented are generally unbiased. Many of the same issues may well have been logged by the in-house test group and denied by development.

Testers do not have to be *experts* in a system to test it well. *They must be trained testers, using a systematic approach, sound reasoning, and measurements to make their case.* They must also be well informed about the project and have good channels of communication to the experts. People skills are also a definite plus.

Like it or not, good testing also includes exploration. Good testers are the ones that dig in and explore the system. They want to know how it works. The ones that don't dig in aren't going to get the job done, and the ones that think they know how it works are no good either, because they are closed and biased.

The Top-Down Approach versus the Bottom-Up Approach

The approach to testing that was entrenched in the industry in 1987 when I began testing was the *bottom-up* approach. Basically the bottom-up approach to testing proceeds as follows: Each module or component is first tested alone; this is called *unit testing*. Next, the modules are combined a few at a time and tested. Simulators are used in place of components that are necessary but missing. More modules are added when the existing ones are stable until the entire system has been assembled. This very cautious approach is also from engineering; it is rigorous and thorough, but it is also very slow. It has one major drawback: Testers are testing the simulators, not the real system. I haven't seen a real system yet that behaved exactly like the simulator.

The bottom-up approach is a rigorous testing approach that comes from engineering. When applied to today's commercial development environment, bottom-up testing is like teaching each performing group their parts, then bringing them together, a few at a time, to rehearse. It is a very long and laborious process to assemble the entire cast, because the group dynamics change each time new cast members are added, creating a new set of issues at each step, none of which is relevant to the finished product. Such rehearsals are only of value if it is important to know in advance what the system behavior is likely to be if some of the members are not functioning. This type of testing may lead to a test effort that contains a huge amount of unproductive redundancy. However, sometimes it is the only way to accomplish the goal.

Top-down testing is like teaching each cast member their part individually, then getting as much of the system as possible together for a rehearsal as soon as possible. In the top-down approach to testing, each module is first unit-tested, then all the available modules are assembled,[1] and the entire group is tested as a system from the highest possible point, usually the user interface, with as few simulators as possible.

In the top-down approach, testers begin with the integration phase. This requires that the code has been unit-tested before it is delivered to the testers. If the unit testing has not been successfully completed or if the units lack integrity, top-down testing will not succeed. If the new system is too unstable to test, the best that the tester can do is subdivide it and try again. Testing the whole system will not succeed if most of the test time is spent diagnosing buggy units.

Current Testing Strategies

Let's explore the types of testing being done and the pros and cons of various strategies that place the test group in various parts of the organization.

❋ **Assumption #1. The developers have unit-tested the code.**

In both the bottom-up and the top-down approaches, the most common assumption testers state when they begin testing is this: "The developers have unit tested the code." I state this assumption in all my test agreements, and it is always a requirement in my contracts to test.

---

[1] This strategy for building a system from modules as they became available is also called *incremental delivery*.

Top-Down Broad-Focused Integration Testing

When I test, I have no particular interest in any one part of the system, but rather I am interested in the whole system. After all, my assignment is almost always to verify and validate *the system*. The system includes applications and components programmed using everything from object-oriented programming (OOP) to assembler to batch languages. Network communications protocols carry transactions between these components through various routers, switches, databases, and security layers.

The *system* is not a finite state machine; it is a society of components interacting constantly with a dynamic group of stimuli. It is practically impossible to know all the stimuli and interactions going on in even a small group of components at a given instant. The Heisenberg uncertainty principle, which states that "the more precisely the position is determined, the less precisely the momentum is known in this instant, and vice versa," certainly applies: We can only prove that these components exist, not what state they are in at a particular time.

In much the same way as no single algorithm is sufficient to map all the paths through a complex system, no single type of testing used by itself will give a satisfactory result in this case. Traditional system testing, the kind that digs deep into individual components deep in a system, can completely ignore things like the user interface. Function testing, or end-to-end testing, can completely ignore systems issues that may cause total paralysis in the production environment. And, while I am sure that they exist, I don't personally know of any companies willing to pay for different groups of experts to perform unit, integration, system, function, end-to-end, load, usability, and user acceptance testing for the same system.

As a result, I perform whatever types of tests are appropriate for the situation. The types of tests performed should be clearly illustrated in the test inventory. For examples on types of tests to perform, see Chapter 4, "The Most Important Tests (MITs) Method," where every type of test is represented on the same task list. Experts, on the other hand, each have a *specialty*, some point of fixation about which they are undoubtedly biased.

Bias is a mental leaning or inclination, a partiality or prejudice. It is natural and healthy for specialists to be biased in their view of their project. Much like a proud parent, the experts' partiality gives them a tight focus that ensures maximum quality in their project. However, all of these child projects must grow up to function as an integrated system in the real world. The contemporary software tester must make sure that they do this.

Today's test professional must be, among other things, an integrator whose focus can take in the entire system. Testers who do not have training in test techniques and a good command of test metrics will have a hard time rising to this challenge.

Organizational Strategies for Locating the Test Group

I have consulted in all types of organizations, and I am constantly amazed at the variety of places management comes up with to stick the test group. My experience indicates that no matter where the test group shows up on your org chart, it is important to pick a location in your organization that maximizes good communications and the free flow of information. Every location has its pros and cons, as I point out in the next paragraphs.

Have an Independent Test Group under Their Own Management

This approach sounds great, but unfortunately it has some major flaws. First is the fact that the test group can become squeezed between the development and operations groups. If communications fail, the testers can find themselves with adversarial situations on both sides. If the developers are late with the code, the testers will be the ones who have to either make up the time or explain the delays to operations. Testers need allies, and this organizational strategy has a tendency to put them in a situation where they are continually the bearers of bad news and often made to be the scapegoats.

Put the Test Group in Development

There is currently a trend toward moving the testing functions into the development area and away from a separate test group. There are two dominant themes behind this trend. The first is to break down barriers between the two groups to allow better communications. The other rationale is along the lines that the test group is not competent to conduct system testing; therefore, the developers are going to conduct or assist in conducting the system test.

There is a serious problem with both these rationales. The developers certainly have expertise in the system; generally, they are the ones who wrote it or maintain it. Both of these strategies achieve the same result, "having the fox guard the henhouse." Even if the developers doing the testing have training in software testing techniques, a rare thing at best, they suffer from the bias previously mentioned. Not only are they likely to miss bugs that their bias forbids them to see, they are not likely to test outside their area of expertise. A system test alone is not likely to remove bugs in the user interface or in the function sequence steps, but these bugs are the first bugs that the end user is likely to see.

Any tester who has ever had to try to convince development that an application that ties up the entire PC for a couple of minutes while it does a database query has a serious bug knows exactly what I mean. A tester arguing this point without citing some type of standard has a poor chance of being heard. Just about every user interface design guide recommends constant user feedback and response times of less than 5 seconds. Usability lab studies indicate that the user believes the application is hung after a 20-second period of inactivity. But even the tester who cites a design guide standard for response time is likely to find out either that the recommendations of the design guide have been waived or that the developers are not required to follow any of the cited design guides at all. The developer's bias may come from knowing how much trouble it was to get *it* to work as well as *it* does. They may not be anxious to take time away from current commitments to try again, especially when fixing *the bug* may mean a massive rewrite.

Another example is the situation where developers see nothing wrong with a menu option that says *Report Writer* but takes the users to a window titled *Able Baker*—especially because there are several other menu options in the same application that navigate to windows with equally mismatched titles. No matter that the design guide clearly recommends against such confusing labels. After all, if development changed one of these labels, they would probably have to change them all. Surely, the issue cannot be that important. It is very challenging to come up with an argument that will convince developers and management that the fix is worth the cost and effort.

However, having pointed out the types of problems that can arise when the test effort is moved into development, I must also say that I have seen it work very well. The environments where this approach is successful have fairly small, highly competent programming groups of three to ten programmers, producing high-reliability class software or firmware. Typically, these projects last from 6 to 12 months, and after unit testing, no developer tests her or his own software.

The other thing that these successful efforts have in common is that the systems that were being tested by developers for developers were small stand-alone systems, such as firmware for telephone operators' stations, firmware for pagers, and medical imaging software running on a single platform. When this testing strategy is used in large systems, or on components that will run in large systems, the method fails. Even if the testing is thorough, in this situation, it only amounts to a unit test, because when this product is introduced into a larger system, it must be *integrated* into the larger system. This brings me to the next interesting trend that I have observed in large networks, propping up the product with support.

Don't Have a Test Group At All

It is far too simplistic to assume that companies *must* test their products or go bankrupt. There are many companies that do little or no testing and not only survive but prosper. Their prosperity is not often the result of flawless programming. These companies often have divvied up the test group or disbanded them altogether. Whatever pre-production testing is done is done by the development group.

Note: **What happens when there is little or no testing? The users test *it*. But then what? You prop it up with support.**

These organizations typically have several layers of support personnel. The first layer of support personnel are generally junior-level people who log the issues, answer common questions, and try to identify and route the more difficult issues to the next layer of more technically competent support personnel. In times past, the testers often filled the second layer of support, since they were the experts on the system and its problems.

Problems that can't be resolved by the second level of support are escalated to the third and most expert layer. The third layer of support is usually made up of senior wizards who understand the depths of the system. These folks have the best chance of diagnosing the really tough problems. Generally, what they can't fix outright they send back to development, and they are likely to get a speedy response.

Management may not see the need to pay for highly competent and experienced testers, but that is not the case when it comes to support. The typical third-line support person is a senior-level programmer or systems engineer, whereas the programmers writing the bulk of the code rank one or two levels below that. The reason is simple: Eventually the bugs get to the users and become prioritized by the user's demands. Management doesn't have a problem justifying highly paid technicians who make the customer happy and get the *right* bugs fixed. This is a logical outgrowth of the "let the customers test it" approach started by the shrink-wrap software industry in the 1990s.

It is logical that this situation should arise given the chain of events I have described, but it is not obvious to many people that the testing is often going on after the product has been shipped. The support team may be testing the product, and the customer is almost certainly testing the product. I find it interesting that support personnel don't think of it as testing; they generally describe what they do in terms of *tuning the system* and *fixing bugs* rather than in terms like *testing*. The users are doing the testing.

Another flavor of this trend is to let the customer test the product under the guise of installing or upgrading their system, while providing one or more senior support staff to manage the process and get the bugs fixed ASAP.

This approach of propping it up with support is very appealing to the manager who shipped the product without testing. In fact, such support is required. This approach requires no test planning; no time is spent designing or tracking tests. And, only the most important bugs get fixed. The problem is that the cost of finding and fixing bugs grows geometrically the farther the bugs get from the developers. This is the most expensive way to find and remove bugs. And, again, only the most important, obnoxious bugs are removed.

Put the Test Group in Operations

I have found putting the test group in operations to be a very healthy and productive practice. This is the location I prefer. In my experience, operations is the best place to be when testing a system. The people who control the system are my best allies. Proximity to the person who can help find the problem in a complex system is invaluable.

When I am attached to operations, I am in a position to add a great deal of value to the released product, in addition to the test effort itself. Consider the following: When I am testing a system, I am really getting it ready for the customer. Often I am also writing or reviewing the user guide at the same time as I am testing. If I have to write up any special instruction to make the system or product work, like how to tweak this or that, these are passed along to customer support and thence to the customer.

Finally, a good test suite is also a diagnostics suite. So if I am a part of operations, then there is a good confidence level in the verity of my test suites, and again proximity makes it easy for operators to get expert help in maintaining and running the tests and interpreting the results. In this situation my test suites are reused, sometimes for years.

The only way to make test replay automation cost-effective is to make sure the automated tests get lots of reruns. In a single test effort, many tests are only performed once and never again, so it is not worth automating them. However, in this scenario, the automated tests can be incorporated into diagnostics suites that are run in the production environment to help make sure the system stays healthy. This type of reuse really adds value to the testers work.

The Best Approach

As the Vulcan philosopher said, "Our diversity is our strength." The more points of view represented in the testing, the more defects will be found. Ideally, use as many approaches as you need or, realistically, as many as you can afford.

I advocate putting the testers in close communications with the developers, with as few barriers as possible, but I do not advocate having them all report to the same manager. People with the same leader eventually come to have the same view. The dancers have their ballet mistress; the musicians have their conductor. Each group has its own point of view, and each needs someone to represent that point of view. All of them have the same goal: an excellent production.

An approach to management that builds a strong team working together transferring knowledge to get the job done is far preferable to one that allows testers to become isolated. Isolated testers can be overwhelmed by the size of the task they must perform.

One of the ways to cultivate good relations between developers and testers is to minimize the subjective arguments used in validation. Use fact and measurement to report problems, not opinion. Another way to cultivate good relations in any team is by being interested in what everyone is doing, like the ballet mistress who must know each person's part. The purpose is not to check up on them, but to properly appreciate the scope of their effort and the merit in their accomplishments.

Plan the best approach for the system. If the building blocks or units are good, top-down testing is the most efficient way to accomplish testing. If the quality of the units is uncertain, or if there are high-reliability, safety-critical considerations, a bottom-up approach is usually considered best practice. For example, a bottom-up approach may be necessary when a significant amount of new (untrusted) objects or processes are involved. Almost all of the examples in this book use a top-down approach.

If the development effort is some flavor of RAD/Agile, top-down testing with an integrator coordinating intergroup communications is probably the best approach. The best successes I have seen use a brief bulleted style for the design documents during the development phases. When the product nears completion, the user guide becomes the vehicle used to document the design. In high-reliability and safety-critical projects where the bottom-up approach is used, it is common to see more formal documentation carrying more of the communications between groups. The role of integrator in a bottom-up effort is traditionally filled by an engineer. Whichever approach is used, the test inventory must still be constructed for the project.

Summary

The commercial software industry is highly volatile. The current climate is one where getting the product to market first with the right features is often considered more important than product reliability. This market is very attractive to entrepreneurs who have been very successful using the I-feel-lucky approach to software development. Interest in reliability is growing, but it does not seem to be due to any increased accountability on the part of software makers. The demand for greater reliability seems to be a response to decreasing profit margins and tighter fiscal controls.

Many people in the industry call themselves engineers, but they do not conduct business in accordance with engineering principals or practice. These so-called engineers do not use metrics or calculations based on measurement, are not overly concerned with reproducible results, and are not made accountable for their actions. A demand for greater reliability inevitably will lead software makers to use scientific methods, because these methods and metrics yield predictable, reproducible results. If there are no methods and metrics being used, decisions will be based on the I-feel-lucky approach. The I-feel-lucky approach will not keep a software company profitable.

This is a good time for the tester who can demonstrate solid test methods and measure results, because management is paying attention. Testing must demonstrate its value, or it will not get budget.

The best approach to testing software will normally be a blend of several approaches:

- The precision of an engineering approach and the human factors benefits of the artistic approach.

- The depth of the test coverage achieved by testers who are specialists in specific areas and the breadth of the test coverage achieved by generalists who are competent testers across entire systems.

- The fast but minimal test coverage achieved by top-down test coverage and the slow but more thorough bottom-up test strategies.

The tester's challenge is to achieve the correct balance between creative freedom and engineering discipline, between delightful surprise and comfortable predictability. Science and engineering methods supporting a creative process provide the efficient way to establish the correct balance. The science of engineering provides methods that are a good fit for the needs of software development and testing. However, care must be taken that these methods do not become rigid and unchangeable or they will cease to be a benefit.

Many approaches to developing software are in use today, and you must select or develop an approach to testing that is effective and efficient in the development environment producing the thing that you must test. To do this, first look at the approaches that are available, and then strike the best balance for your situation. I will go into how to do this in more detail in the next chapter, when I explain the Most Important Tests method. After that, the rest of this book is about this very simple set of fundamental testing methods that bring value to any test effort individually and can have a profound effect when applied together.

CHAPTER 4

The Most Important Tests (MITs) Method

The vice president said to the tester, "This has really got to happen fast. We can't afford any slipups and the whole thing has to run perfectly."

"I understand completely. The whole team is on it," the tester told the vice president.

"It's a pretty good-sized project; how are you going to get it all done? We have to deploy in four weeks and the code has not been turned over yet. Will you have enough testers?" asked the vice president.

"Well, sir, I am glad you asked, because there are a couple of things we need, and I would really like to show you what we have in mind. Do you have a minute to take a look?" the tester smiled.

In the last chapter I talked about various approaches to managing the test effort. In this chapter I will dig down into the actual methods of accomplishing a test effort that is focused on running the most important tests.

Overview of MITs

The Most Important Tests (MITs) method was developed as an aid to sizing test efforts based on the risk of failure in the system. While it was developed to be used mainly in top-down system, integration, and function testing, the methods are viable for all levels of testing. The core of the Most Important Tests method is a form of statistical testing where testers use several techniques to identify the areas that need to be tested and to evaluate the risks associated with the various components and features and functions of the project. These risks are translated into a prioritized ranking system that identifies the most important areas for testing to focus upon. As part of this process, testers and management can focus the test effort most constructively. The thoroughness of the testing can then be agreed upon in advance and budgeted accordingly.

In the ideal situation, the tester, having completed a thorough analysis, presents a test plan to management and negotiates for the time and resources necessary to conduct a comprehensive test effort. In reality, the test effort is trapped in the space between the end of the development cycle and the project release date. The impact of this constraint can vary depending on the timeliness of the code turnover from development and the flexibility of the release date. In most cases, trade-offs will have to be made in order to fit the test effort into the necessary time frame. The MITs method provides tools to help you make these trade-off decisions.

If you are in an Agile development effort, the design changes daily. You may get new code every day as well. The tests you ran yesterday may be meaningless today. Planning tests is a waste of time, and you don't have any time to waste. The manager wants to know if the effort is on schedule, but half the functions that you had been testing (and had considered complete) are not in the latest release of the code. Your developer has decided that she can't fix the bug that is blocking your other testing until your business partner (the customer) decides on the sequence of the Q&A dialogs. How do you explain all this to your team leader? MITs can help you with this as well.

What MITs Does

In the planning phase, the MITs method provides tools for sizing that allow the test effort to be fitted into a specified time frame. The method allows testers and managers to see the impact of trade-offs in resources and test coverage associated with various time lines and test strategies. The method uses worksheets and enumeration to measure time costs/savings associated with various trade-offs. The MITs tools, such as the worksheets and the test inventory, serve as aids in negotiating resources and time frames for the actual test effort.

During the testing phase, MITs tools facilitate tracking testing progress and determining the logical end of the test effort. The method uses S-curves for estimation, test tracking, and status reporting. S-curves show the status of the testing and the system at a glance. The curves show the rate of progress and the magnitude of the open issues in the system. The graphs also show both probable end-of-the-test effort and indicate clearly when the test set has exhausted its error-finding ability.

The MITs method measures the performance of the test effort so that test methods, assumptions, and inventories can be adjusted and improved for future efforts. A performance metric based on the percentage of errors found during the test cycle is used to evaluate the effectiveness of the test coverage. Based on this metric, test assumptions and inventories can be adjusted and improved for future efforts.

How MITs Works

The process works by answering the following questions:

Q: What do we think we know about this project?

A: We find out by stating (publishing) the test inventory. The inventory contains the list of all the requirements and specifications that we know about and includes our assumptions. In a RAD effort, we often start with only our assumptions, because there may not be any formal requirement or specifications. You can start by writing down what you think it is supposed to do. In projects with formal specifications, there are still assumptions—for example, testing the system on these three operating systems will be adequate. If we do not publish our assumptions, we are deprived of a valuable opportunity to have incorrect assumptions corrected.

Q: How big is the test effort?

A: How many tests are there? We find out by enumerating everything there is to test. This is not a count of the things we plan to test; it is a count of all the tests that can be identified. This begins the expansion of the test inventory.

Q: If we can't test everything, what should we test?

A: The most important things, of course! We use ranking criteria, to prioritize the tests, then we will use MITs risk analysis to determine the most important test set from the inventory.

Q: How long will the effort take?

A: Once the test set has been identified, fill out the MITs sizing worksheet to size and estimate the effort. The completed worksheet forms the basis for the test agreement.

Q: How much will it cost? (How much can we get?)

A: Negotiate with management for the resources required to conduct the test effort. Using the worksheet, you can calculate how many tests, testers, machines, and so on will be required to fit the test effort into the desired time line. Use the worksheet to understand and explain resource and test coverage trade-offs in order to meet a scheduled delivery date.

Q: How do I identify the tests to run?

A: Use the MITs analysis and the test inventory to pick the most important areas first, and then perform path and data analysis to determine the most important tests to run in that area. Once you have determined the most important tests for each inventory item, recheck your inventory and the sizing worksheet to make sure your schedule is still viable. Renegotiate if necessary. Start running tests and develop new tests as necessary. Add your new tests to the inventory.

Q: Are we on schedule? Have we tested enough?

A: Use S-curves to track test progress and help determine the end of the test effort.

Q: How successful was the test effort? Was the test coverage adequate? Was the test effort adequate?

A: Use the performance metric to answer these questions and to improve future test efforts. The historical record of what was accomplished last time is the best starting point for improvement this time. If the effort was conducted in a methodical, reproducible way, the chances of duplicating and improving it are good.

As I said before, in the *ideal* scenario, you do all of these things because all these steps are necessary if you plan to do the very best test effort possible. The next thing to recognize is that the real scenario is rarely "ideal." The good news is this method is flexible, even agile. Any steps you perform will add to the value of the test effort. If you don't do them all, there is no penalty or detriment to your effort. Next, the steps are listed in the order that will give you the best return on your investment. This order and the relative importance of the steps is different for different types of development projects.

Different environments have different needs, and these needs mandate different priorities in the test approach. I am going to point out some of the differences and then present different ordering of the steps to complement each type of effort. Finally, I will give specific examples of three different development efforts that were all part of the same systems development effort. The MITs method was used in varying amounts in each of these development test efforts, and it was also used in the system integration test effort that successfully integrated these individual systems.

How to Succeed with MITs

A couple of factors will influence which methods and metrics are the right ones for you to start with and which ones are the most useful to you. In fact, you most probably use some of these methods already. The first factor is the ease of implementation. Some of these methods and metrics are much easier to implement and to show a good return on the investment than others. Another factor is the development method that is being used in the project you are approaching.

Plan-driven development efforts use the same MITs methods as Agile development efforts, characterized as heavyweight and lightweight, but their goals and expectations are different. So the priorities placed on the individual MITs steps are very different. I will go into this in more detail in the next section. I mention it here because, over the years, I have collected lots of feedback from students on these methods. These students come from both heavyweight and lightweight efforts. I find it interesting that testers from both types of efforts agree on the usefulness and ease of implementation of the MITs methods.

Methods That Are Most Useful and Easiest to Implement

The following lists show the methods that have been identified as most useful. They are listed according to the respondent's perceptions of their ease of implementation.

EASIEST TO IMPLEMENT

- Bug tracking and bug-tracking metrics
- The test inventory and test coverage metrics
- Planning, path analysis, and data analysis
- MITs ranking and ranking criteria (risk analysis)
- The test estimation worksheet
- Test performance metrics

MORE DIFFICULT TO IMPLEMENT

- S-curves
- Test rerun automation
- Automated test plan generation

Most companies already have well-established bug tracking tools and metrics. Some have developed very sophisticated intranet tracking systems that carry all the way through testing to system support and customer support.

Most test efforts rely heavily on their bug tracking metrics. For the most part, the bug metrics in use are fundamental metrics with a few derived metrics like mean time between failure and bugs found per hour. MITs use techniques that allow you to perform analysis based on several types of measurements taken together. Several examples of how to use these techniques to get a superior view of the state of a software system are provided in this book.

The one tool that I have seen come into its own over the last 10 years is the test inventory. Today, a test inventory is considered a requirement in most test efforts, even if it is a continually evolving one. Ten years ago, almost no one was using an inventory. Still, there is a lot more that the test inventory can do for you as a working tool, as you will see in the next two chapters.

If you are already using the test inventory, you will see some examples of how to get more value from it and how your inventory can help you make the step up to path, data, and risk analysis. Once you are performing risk analysis (even without doing any path and data analysis), you can use the test sizing worksheet—a tool that will change your life.

Test performance metrics and S-curves are closely related and can be implemented at the same time if the team has the graphing tool required to produce S-curves.[1] Ironically, the Agile groups I have worked with have been the ones to see the value in S-curves and take the time and energy to implement them. This effort is due to the Agile method's need to make quick design changes during the development in the process.

Agile managers will pay a lot for accurate information about the real status of a project from day to day. On the heavyweight front, Boeing is the only company that I know of who uses them regularly. Boeing has been using S-curves for years.

The S-curve is one of the best project-tracking imaging tools extant. These graphs provide critical progress information at a glance. Agile efforts usually have collaboration technologies in place that make it easier for them to get team members to report the test numbers that fuel S-curves. So they find it easier to institute this powerful tool than the plan-driven efforts that must go through a more complex and difficult documentation process to accomplish the same reporting.

Test rerun automation is one of the most difficult toolsets to get a positive return from, and yet just about everyone has tried it. The thing to remember about automated test rerun tools is that you only get a payback if the test is rerun—a lot.

Agile efforts are dynamic. The product is continuously evolving, and so a static test has a short life span. Capture replay is of little use to an Agile tester. In heavyweight projects, the time required to create and maintain these tests is often the issue. Even though the tests might be rerun a lot, over a long period of time, management is often hesitant to invest in the creation of tests unless they are quite certain to be replayed and the investment recaptured.

The Steps for the MITs Method

I have already introduced the spectrum of development methodologies in use today. Now I want to discuss the differences in approach and how testing in general and MITs in particular complement the differing priorities of these approaches.

---

[1] The graphing tool that comes with Microsoft Office, Microsoft Graph, is sufficient to do this.

Complimenting Your Development Methodologies

Agile and plan-driven teams use different approaches to design and implement software (see Figure 4.1). Proponents of the plan-driven methodology believe in spending up front to acquire information that will be used to formulate the design, so that they are as well informed as possible before they commit to a plan. This is called *money for information* (MFI).

Users of the Agile method choose the design early and modify it as they go. So they reserve budget to help them adjust and absorb the changes and surprises that will certainly come. This is called *money for flexibility* (MFF).

MITs contributes to both approaches by first providing the tools to gather information and predict what will be needed, and then by giving you the tools to know if you are on schedule at any time during the process so that you can take appropriate action. However, the order and priority of the steps will necessarily be different for each of the development methods—and everything in between.

The method I call structured RAD is based on my real-world experiences. It combines the flexibility of the Agile approach with the more intense up-front planning and research of the plan-driven approach. My experiences show that typically there is far less risk of failure in this structured RAD approach than in either of the other two. Notice from the figure that the structured RAD approach typically spends more on implementation than either of the others. Consider that the test budget

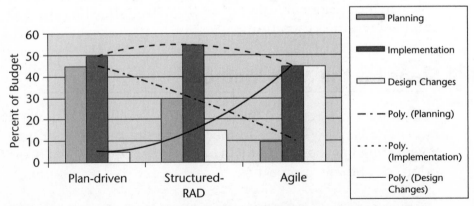

Figure 4.1 The spending priorities of different development methods.

is included in implementation and that the RAD project typically spins through many incremental evolving development iterations in the implementation phase.

Management will consider various trade-offs regardless of the method they are following. For example, managers will spend MFI when the outcome is uncertain, as with new technologies or systems. MFI is used for unpredictable but resolvable or "must-have" scenarios, like establishing system limits or actual usage patterns. Usually these are things that can be estimated early using simulation.

If the issue is unresolvable, like a complete human factors failure, for example, the customer rejects the product. Or, if a technology or component is overwhelmed and simply cannot do the job in the real environment and there must be funding to provide alternatives, this is taken care of by MFF.

Remember, whether something is resolvable is in the eye of the beholder. If the unresolvable problem is discovered late in the development cycle, the entire investment is at risk. This leads to a situation where almost no price is too high for a resolution. This can be a showstopper for the plan-driven effort, which should have discovered the unresolvable problem during the planning phase. Because of their MFF focus, the Agile effort may well have funds left to find a resolution. There is an example of this situation in the Agile project in the next section.

Fact: Maturity Is Independent of Method

The Software Capability Maturity Model (SW-CMM)[2] tells us what to do in general terms. It does not say how you should do it. The Agile methods, and any other formal methods that provide a set of best practices that specify how to implement the project, can be used with CMM practices. So, maturity can occur any time, any place; it is not dependent on the methods being used to develop or test the project.

Granted, the CMM is currently skewed in terms of inefficient paper and overburdened by policies, practices, and procedures. But that is simply the tradition and legacy of its past. There is no reason that efficient automated alternatives cannot be used to replace the legacy baggage.

---

[2] See the Glossary at the back of this book.

Consider the following sets of steps. They all use the MITs methods, but the prioritization has been tailored to the development method in use.

MITs for a Plan-Driven Test Effort

This is the original MITs process; the first four steps are devoted to planning. The fifth step sets the limits and the agreement, and the last three steps are devoted to actually testing.

1. State your assumptions.
2. Build the test inventory.
3. Perform MITs analysis.
4. Estimate the test effort.
5. Negotiate for the resources to conduct the test effort.
6. Build the test scripts.[3]
7. Conduct testing and track test progress.
8. Measure test performance.

The rest of the chapters in this book follow this outline. Chapter 5 covers most of the metrics used in the method. Chapters 6, 7, and 8 cover the foundation and implementation of the test inventory and all its parts. Chapters 9 and 10 cover the MITs risk analysis techniques used to complete the test sizing worksheet. Chapters 11 through 13 cover the path and data analysis techniques used to identify tests for the inventory. Chapter 14 completes the test estimate and discusses the in-process negotiation process. (By the way, this information is useful even to an Agile tester because management always wants to know how much testing remains to be done and how long it is going to take.)

This process offers very good tools for planning up front and fits the traditional "best practice" plan-driven approach. It works well with traditional quality assurance policies and change management practices. It offers testers a lot of protection and latitude in the testing phase as well, since they will have negotiated test priorities, test coverage, and bug fix rates in advance. The superior tracking tools also give testers the edge in predicting trouble spots and reacting to trends early. This is a good approach to testing in a business-critical environment.

[3] This book covers the first five steps of the method in detail. Steps 6 through 8 are left to a future work.

Agile Development Values

The following is the Agile Software Development Manifesto:

We are uncovering better ways of developing software by doing it and helping others do it. Through this work we have come to value:

♦ *Individuals and interactions over processes and tools.*

♦ *Working software over comprehensive documentation.*

♦ *Customer collaboration over contract negotiation.*

♦ *Responding to change over following a plan.*

That is, while there is value in the items on the right, we value the items on the left more.

Source: "The Agile Software Development Manifesto," by the AgileAlliance, February 2001, at www .agilemanifesto.org.

MITs for a Structured RAD/Agile Test Effort

This type of effort is characterized by well-trained people and a high level of professional maturity. In the CMM scale, they are CMM Level 2 and Level 3. Notice how the estimation phase is shortened and actual test inventory is created using collaboration techniques. Extra importance is placed on the measure, track, and report steps because management has a keen (you could say, life-and-death) interest in the progress of the effort.

Because a Rad/Agile effort is a "code a little, test a little" process that repeats until done, the best source of status information is the tester. Because of proximity, developer and tester are nearly in synch and the tester is actually exploring the code and measuring the response. Contrary to popular myth about testers not being required in a Agile effort and the customer being the best source of information, Rad/Agile recognized that the customer is biased and not usually trained in the use of test metrics. Also contrary to some of the popular trends, the tester is necessary in an Agile effort to prevent requirements creep, bloat, and spin.

Agile management is likely to demand the highest quality of reporting because that is their best defense against the unknowns that are most certainly lurking out there in the development time line. Remember, Agile efforts don't spent MFI up front, so they usually haven't pretested all the new technologies that they are counting on at the back. Their best defense is in early detection of an unrecoverable error so that they can devise an alternative.

In a plan-driven environment, the developers "code a lot, then the testers test a lot." Meanwhile, the developers are moving on to something else and coding something new. So, the answer to the question "Are we on schedule?" has two answers, one from developers and one from the testers. Consequently, management is likely to get two very different answers to the question. Also, in the Agile effort, bug turnaround can be nearly instant. In the plan-driven method, developers must stop what they are doing (new) and refocus on what they did (old). This refocusing causes delays and difficulties.

The following list of steps shows the type of modifications necessary to tailor MITs to fit the needs of a Rad/Agile effort.

Steps:

1. Prepare a thumbnail inventory and estimate the test effort (best-guess method, covered in Chapter 7, "How to Build a Test Inventory").

2. Negotiate for the resources to conduct the test effort; budget for head count, test environments (hardware and software), support, and time lines/schedule.

3. Build the test inventory, schedule, and plan of action including targets; include your assumptions.

4. Conduct interviews and reviews on the inventory, schedule, and plan of action; adjust each accordingly. Perform MITs risk analysis (try to renegotiate budget if necessary).

5. Generate the tests, conduct testing, and record the results.

6. Measure, track, and report the following:

   - Test progress using S-curves
   - Test coverage metrics
   - Bug metrics

7. When the product is shipped, write your summary report and your recommendations.

MITs for a Free-for-All RAD/Agile Test Effort

This type of project is a typical entrepreneurial effort in a new technology, characterized by lots of unknowns in the feasibility of the system and often plagued by floating goals. It assumes a low maturity level on the part of the sales, management, and development communities.

This situation is best addressed using good measurements and very graphic records—ones that tell the story in clear pictures. Regular reporting of status is very important so that testers keep a continual line of information and feedback going to the decision makers.

The focus of this set of steps is on tester survival. The product will probably succeed or fail based on marketing and sales, not on its own merits.

Steps:

1. Conduct interviews and construct the inventory (ramp up), schedule, and plan of action; perform MITs analysis. Estimate the test effort (best-guess method, covered in Chapter 7, "How to Build a Test Inventory").

2. Prepare a contract to test. Establish and agree to targets for coverage, acceptable bug find and fix rates, code turnover schedules, and so on. Negotiate for the resources to conduct the test effort; budget for head count, test environments (hardware and software), support, and time lines/schedule. Be conservative.

3. Start testing, and record the results.

4. Measure, track, and report:
   - Test progress using S-curves
   - Test coverage metrics
   - Bug metrics

5. When the product is shipped or the contract is up, write your summary report and your recommendations.

6. Don't work without an open PO.

Note: Crossing over, sometimes I will throw in a chart or worksheet from a different kind of effort. Don't be afraid to invent a new way of explaining the situation.

Integrating Projects with Multiple Development Methodologies

I have worked in several large projects where different systems were being developed using different methodologies. MITs give me all the tools I need to test any of these projects. But again, the order of the steps and activities will be changed to suit the needs of the project.

Each development effort can be tested using an appropriate approach that is tailored to suit its needs. The interesting part comes when you integrate all of these systems. It turns out that good integration is not related to size or development methodology; it's a matter of timing. I use the same tools to integrate a large project as I do a small one. (More about timing issues in Chapter 7, "How to Build a Test Inventory.") How rigorous the approach is will be driven by the goals of upper management and the criticality of the final integrated system. Usually if it is a *big* project, it will be critical, and so even though many parts of the project may have been developed using Agile methods, the integration of the system will likely be conducted using a plan-driven approach. In any case, timing issues require a good deal of coordination, which requires good communications and planning.

Real-World Example: Heavyweight, Middleweight, and Lightweight Development Efforts

The case we will discuss was a real project that was extremely large. It included many subcomponents that were each large systems in their own right. These systems all had their own development groups, platforms, hardware, and so on. In the real project, the main integration effort was responsible for integrating 12 major systems. For this book I have selected three of these projects that were particularly good examples of what I characterize as heavyweight, middleweight, and lightweight development efforts.

The heavyweight project was an old-style mainframe application. The middleweight project was an object-oriented multi-tier client/server application. The lightweight project, my personal favorite, was a first-generation Web application that migrated an old proprietary document management behemoth to a cutting-edge standards-based architecture. Each of these efforts used MITs methods somewhere in their process. You will see many of the examples in this book taken from these projects.

Overview of the Project

This 1998 project involved two shipping companies. One company was buying the other and integrating the assets, employees, customers, and business systems of the two. The day-to-day business conducted by the companies was highly dependent on some very large, complex scheduling systems. The object of this project was to integrate the business-critical scheduling system of the parent company with that of the acquired company.

The scheduling system was linked to several other systems for the purposes of sharing or accessing data and business logic. Most notably in this example, scheduling accessed the billing system and the automatic document generation system. It performed tasks like checking schedules against contract agreements and generating documents, which included everything from weight tables to contracts, bills of lading, and invoices. These other systems were also being modified or created and then integrated as part of the buyout. The integration of all of these systems was in the scope of the overall integration test effort.

The various development groups at the parent company were operated in what is called a *silo* structure. That is, each one was autonomous with its own budget, management, programmers, culture, and methodology. Integrating the many systems that ran the business had been accomplished one at a time over a period of years. The interaction of these many systems was only partially understood in any given silo.

To minimize the impact on the day-to-day business activities, upper management wanted all existing and new systems to come online at virtually the same time. The buyout and the subsequent integration of the acquired business was to be undertaken as a big bang effort with all the new systems scheduled to come online on the same day; this first day was called the "split" date. The integration test effort was chartered to make this big bang a success from the very first day.

The system integration effort was to be conducted by an independent group reporting to their own vice president in charge of split day integration. They were to have the full cooperation and support of the operations group and all the development groups. They were responsible for planning and designing a test effort that would integrate and test all of the new systems. The system integration team came from many different parts of the company and various contract testing organizations.

A change control board was formed, and procedures were written to control the migration of code, modules, and systems from development through the test environments and finally into production. Operations supplied the test systems and the support personnel to maintain these test systems. The membership of the change control board included the directors of each development silo and operations.

The Scheduling System

The scheduling system processed millions of transactions each day. There were several major subsystems. For example, there were hundreds of freight containers being tracked by the system at any given time, not all of them belonging to either the parent company or the acquired company. The contents in these containers could be almost anything that was not perishable. Central to the integration effort was the system that actually scheduled the freight containers to be in a certain place by a certain time so that they could be routed onward. There was a subsystem that tracked the engines that moved the containers, as well as subsystems that scheduled maintenance for both the freight containers that belonged to the company and the engines.

Failure of any part of this scheduling system was considered unacceptable. Further, the scheduling system had to be 100 percent available, and so was fully redundant. The production system and data center was "owned" by the operations group and staffed by some of the most senior technical staff in the company.

The scheduling system ran in an expanded high-reliability mainframe environment. The project did not include any architectural changes to the platform or hardware environment other than the expansion of data storage capacity and the addition of processing power to handle the predicted new loads.

The company commissioned a complete analysis of the data center under the existing and the projected new loadings. The analysis was conducted by the mainframe vendor, and the system modifications were made in accordance with their recommendations. The newly expanded system was put into service eight months before the expected big bang on the split date. Three integration test systems were also constructed and provisioned at the same time.

The scheduling system project had in excess of 160 individual Project Development Requirement documents (PDRs); each was a development effort in its own right, with its own budget and developers. The senior developers were all Subject Matter Experts, or SMEs, in one or more areas of the system. These SMEs typically participated at some level in the development of all PDRs in their area of expertise. Experienced programmers wrote most of the code, and junior programmers performed the testing and maintained the documentation.

Testing the Scheduling System

The scheduling system was implemented using a traditional plan-driven approach with a rigorous contract and requirements-based development process, overseen by outside auditors. The scheduling system was built and tested using traditional formal requirements documents, quality assurance practices, and change management. A multiphase bottom-up approach to testing was used. Code reviews, unit testing, module testing, and preliminary system testing were all conducted by developers prior to turnover to the change management board for integration testing. The methodology was about as heavyweight as it gets—except that there was no independent test group prior to the systems integration phase. No metrics were made available on these test phases.

Best practice was observed throughout, and requirements were not allowed to creep; only minor corrections were accepted by the change board. The test inventory for the integration test included thousands of test cases.

The original system integration test effort was scheduled to take nine months. The system did deploy on time but with a reduced feature set. Testing and integration continued for an additional 18 months before the parent company had actually integrated the acquired scheduling system. The end cost was 300 percent greater than the original budget. No serious failures occurred in the deployed production system. We will discuss various aspects of this test effort and of the integration test effort throughout the rest of this book.

The Billing System

The parent company's billing system was being modified to accommodate the new billing rates from the acquired company, the contractual differences between the two companies, and the predicted higher systems requirements due to the increase in volume. Each company had a proprietary system in place. Consequently, the database schema and structure of the two systems were quite different. This meant that all the data (an enormous amount of data) from the acquired company would have to be normalized, or converted into an acceptable form (or both), and then assimilated by the parent system in a short time. Failure to convert and integrate the billing data would translate into millions of dollars in lost revenue for the parent company and possible losses to the customers as well.

Because of United States antitrust laws and other legal constraints, the parent company could not start processing any data from the acquired company before the actual acquisition. The parent system was required to process and incorporate all the billing data of the acquired company within a 30-day window once the acquisition was final.

Several special data conversion programs were written and tested to prepare for the acquisition date. These were tested first by the developers and then by a special integration team that specialized in testing all types of data and message flows into the new system.

The billing system itself was an object-oriented, multi-tier client/server application system. The billing system projects were developed using Dynamic Systems Development Method (DSDM).

My Perspective on DSDM

DSDM is a descendent of RAD that was developed in the United Kingdom. It uses an iterative approach to develop each phase of the product: functional model, design and build, and implement.

I consider DSDM to be a good middleweight methodology. It is usually listed with the Agile technologies, but I would describe the DSDM projects I have worked on to be flexible, plan-driven, highly disciplined, and well-documented efforts, which also feature some of the best trained professionals of any development or test effort. Based on my experiences, I would describe DSDM as a very effective methodology for bringing middle-sized, object-oriented, business-critical projects to completion on time.

The system used a SQL-based relational database management system (RDBMS). The business logic layer ran on servers built on the UNIX platform. The clients ran on high-end PCs running the Windows Workstation operating system. The clients required standard IP LAN network connections to the server system.

Testing the Billing System

The billing system was tested using a planned incremental delivery top-down approach by the test group inside the billing silo. Major features of the new billing system were delivered to the change board and integrated one at a time by the integration test group. The code was assumed to be ready to be integrated when it was delivered. There were only a few occasions when the code was turned back for failure to pass a smoke test.

An independent contract test organization was hired to perform the system testing the project. There was one tester for every two or three developers. In addition to evolving a very comprehensive top-down test suite, these testers successfully implemented a large number of automated test suites that ran from the PC client environment. Some of these automated suites were also used by the integration test team and in production after the live date.

Bug reporting was accomplished in a private SQL-based reporting facility that lived in the billing silo and was visible only to project personnel. The business partners, who were the customers of the system, reviewed the system at milestones. If they had issues, they reported them to the testers, who then logged the issues.

Some flexibility was allowed in the systems integration testing phase, since the original plan had called for testing the billing system against the new scheduling system currently in the cleanest integration test environment. This was not possible, because the billing system was delivered on time, while the scheduling system lagged behind. So, the billing system arranged to set up their own integration test system with feeds from the real production system. There were several plan changes of this type. The eventual cost of the test effort was higher than planned, but the time frame for delivery did not slip. The test inventory included 80 PDRs and hundreds of test cases. One serious program failure did occur with the billing system, but it did not impact any scheduling system functions.

There were, however, serious deployment problems with the client application at the acquired company field sites due to the lack of a LAN network infrastructure and, more importantly, due to the older DOS-based equipment at the field offices where the client would need to run.

Various PDRs covered the hardware upgrade issues, but the human factors turned out to be the limiting factor. Newly assimilated personnel had their hands full simply getting used to all the changes in their daily routines without having to learn how to operate an entirely new mouse-driven computer system and billing application. For example, if the bill of lading for a freight container was not present when the cargo was loaded, the freight container could not be moved. The yard operator had to wade through some 50 menu choices before they could print the bill of lading to a network printer (located—they weren't sure where) for a particular container. In the first weeks after the split date, the client-side failure rate was significant.

The Document Generation System

The documentation generation facility was a new Web-based system that was being implemented using an eXtreme approach (although the method was not called by a particular name at the time).

Management had agreed to try a new RAD approach to developing this system because it was Web-based and it relied on several new database technologies that had not been proven in commercial environments. It was recognized that there were substantial risks in trusting this new technology. It was also recognized that even though the end product documents were well understood, no one really knew what the final system would look like or how it would perform the task of generating these documents. The business partners had a long list of things that they did not like about the legacy system, and that list, coupled with the required end product documents, served as the beginning requirements for the project.

Management understood that a flexible, lightweight approach to design and development with a heavy emphasis on prototyping would be most likely to succeed in this environment. The director, whose brainchild it was, was given a free hand to organize her resources any way she chose. The code developed and tested by her group joined the traditional process oriented integration effort when it was turned over to the change control board. From that point forward, all the code, modules, databases, and systems from all the projects were subject to the same rules and procedures.

Testing the Documentation Generation Facility

The documentation generation facility was developed using a methodology that was very similar to what is now called eXtreme Development Methodology (See the following sidebar). While the development community insists that individuals following the latest Agile approaches, like eXtreme Programming, are not abandoning discipline, but rather excessive formality that is often mistaken for discipline, it is not hard to imagine how a method of this type could become an "I-feel-lucky" approach. In this case, however, it did not. This project was so remarkable that I published two papers on it in 1998 and 1999: "A Team Approach to Software Development" and "The Team with the Frog in Their Pond."

---

eXtreme Programming (XP): A Thumbnail Sketch

XP is an iterative development methodology that is based on 12 basic tenets:

1. **Customer is at the center of the project.**
2. **Small releases.**
3. **Simple design.**
4. **Relentless testing.**
5. **Refactoring (adjust code to improve the internal structure, make it clean and simple, remove redundancies, etc.).**
6. **Pair programming.**
7. **Collective ownership.**
8. **Continuous integration.**
9. **40-hour work week.**
10. **On-site customer.**
11. **Coding standards.**
12. **Metaphorically, development is guided by a story view of how the system will work.**

XP is a "small project" methodology; it's not known to scale well (6 to 12 developers is considered ideal).

Source: Adapted from Kent Beck, *Extreme Programming Explained: Embrace Change* (Addison-Wesley, 1999).

The project was housed on one whole floor of a large building. The only rooms with doors were the bathrooms. All team members were given cubicles. Each developer was teamed with a tester and a business partner (the customer). This unit was called a *feature team*. The entire project had 10 to 15 feature teams. Feature teams working on related PDRs became a *cluster*. Each cluster had a dedicated leader who was responsible for administrative and reporting tasks, along with escalation activities if they were needed.

The cubicles of a feature team were always touching. If one team member wanted to talk to another member of his or her team, all he or she had to do was stand up and look over the cubicle wall. How a feature team used their three cubicles was up to them. Some teams chose to remove the dividers altogether so that they could share one large space.

Each developer submitted new code to the tester and business partner as soon as it became available. The tester was responsible for integrating the new code in the larger documentation system and for testing (finding bugs in) the code. The business partner was responsible for validating the functionality of the code. If the business partner didn't like the way the user interface worked or how the workflow process worked, they reported it as a bug. There weren't very many arguments about "is it a bug or not?" Most solutions were devised and implemented so quickly because of the proximity of the team that there was no need to log the bug.

Status meetings were held every morning. All members of the feature team were jointly responsible for meeting delivery schedule and reporting progress.

Even though the development methodology was one that could easily lack discipline, these teams successfully implemented some of the most difficult of the MITs' methods and metrics during the effort. They were able to implement and use S-curves to track their progress and estimate when the code was ready to deliver—a task that requires a high degree of maturity. They credited these methods with keeping them on track, preventing excessive feature creep, and providing an excellent communications tool for upper management. However, the methods could not have succeeded without the gifted and insightful management that governed the project.

The team added functions to the test inventory so that it would support several innovative ways to leverage the work that they put into the test inventory. They added columns to track when tests were run and categorized tasks so that sort routines could automatically generate lists of tests for the testers to perform when that code was being integrated. These "test lists" were what I would call test suites of related short form test scripts, with blank spaces for the testers to add notes and outcomes. These forms were filled out as the tester executed the various tests, and at the end of the day, they had a complete log of their testing activities. Record keeping was a matter of putting a check mark in the date column in the main online test inventory, along with the outcome and logging any open issues.

This effort also developed an excellent, highly visible, and fast method of tracking bugs, as well as a method that prioritized bugs based on their cost to fix and severity. They called this the "Z form for bug ranking." (I discuss this methodology in the paper, "The Team with the Frog in Their Pond.")

Briefly, bugs were entered into a lightweight, LAN-based, commercially available bug tracking system, but more importantly, open issues (bugs) were posted on the wall. Each feature team had its own poster on the main hall wall, showing a frog sitting on a lily pad on a pond. Bugs were posted in one of four quadrants in the pond that represented the severity of and cost to fix the bug. Everyone knew where the bugs were all the time—how many and how serious. If a group needed help, they got it, right away.

The original test inventory for the documentation facility included 100 PDRs. The final test inventory included 110 PDRs. No tests were written in advance. Test checklists were generated from the PDR-based inventory and were used by everyone testing. Once a feature or function had been tested and passed, it was checked off.

The system suffered several setbacks due to poor performance from the SQL database system that had been chosen to support the Web-based logic. This was a result of overoptimistic claims made by the database manufacturer and the newness of the entire architecture. To solve the problems, database programming consultants were hired to write and optimize SQL queries and stored procedures to bypass the poor-performing features of the database. The documentation generation facility was delivered slightly over budget, but complete and on time with some known performance issues.

The other major challenge that they faced was an integration issue that involved code collisions in the business logic of a major shared component in the scheduling system. The component was a business rule nexus used by several of the different groups. The silos rarely interacted, and so the integration team had to intervene and arbitrate a set of procedures to govern this type of component so that all changes to it were coordinated. The change management group was able to control versioning so that the collisions could be identified and minimized.

Integrating the Entire System

One internal group and two different consulting firms were invited to bid on the systems integration test effort. The internal group had experts from all the major silos on their team and boasted the most technically competent group of experts extant for the systems that would be integrated. However, they lacked formal testing experience and integration experience outside their own silos.

One of the consulting firms proposed a RAD-oriented, "test fast and furious" approach, and the other firm proposed a fairly traditional top-down, risk-based approach to the integration effort. Management inside the silos feared that the traditional approach would not be able to work quickly enough or be flexible enough to accomplish the mission and voted for the RAD-oriented approach to testing.

Upper management at both companies felt that the RAD approach could not provide as stable a system as the more conservative risk-based approach. They opted to go with the risk-based approach because, first, they felt it would provide better assurance that there would not be any major failures when the system went live and, second, they felt that the traditional risk-based approach was more defensible as a best-practice approach in the event that a failure did occur.

This integration effort was huge, and it used much of the MITs methodology. I will be giving detailed examples from this effort throughout the rest of the book. Here are some of the main points.

When the initial test inventory was submitted by the risk-based test group, it became clear that the internal group of systems experts had only estimated about 30 percent of all integration tasks in their scope. Further, they did not have the testing resources or expertise to accomplish the integration of all the systems in the given time frame. However, no one wanted to deprive these experts the opportunity to test the systems in their scope, so upper management opted to run both integration efforts in parallel. The experts tested the message flows to whatever level of detail that they deemed appropriate and necessary.

The integration test group developed a master test plan for the effort. A major component of the master test plan was the test inventory. The test inventory was prepared, and the items were priorities and cross-referenced. Sections of this inventory are discussed at length in Chapter 7, "How to Build a Test Inventory." This inventory was used by all groups for several purposes.

Initially, the inventory was used to gather information about test needs and relative priorities. The interview process was used to gather information from the various development groups. The idea was to establish the risks associated with each project directly from the developers. In reality, it didn't work quite like that. The risk analysis process for this project was a real learning experience, and we will talk about it in detail in Chapter 7 and Chapter 9, "Risk Analysis."

When the director of the integration test effort was named, he declared that the inventory was the most important single document in the effort. It became the basis for reporting and tracking throughout the integration effort. Also, and particular to this effort, the inventory became the source of delivery dependency information, contact/owner information, relative priority information, and much, much more.

Because of the size and complexity of the effort, no one had ever constructed a single Gantt that all groups could agree upon. The closest thing to it lived on the wall in the SME integration test room. But it only covered modules in their scope, which only covered 30 percent of the project. Also, when code delivery dates changed, there was no way to update a Gantt conclusively, nor could anyone guarantee that all involved parties would see it.

The inventory provided a solution to this problem that ensured that delivery-driven dependencies would be called out and noticed. We will talk about this in more detail in Chapter 7 when we discuss the interview process.

A change management board was created and tasked with overseeing and approving each movement of the code through the various integration test systems. Each new module passed a unit test phase and function test phase before being accepted into the integration test phase. Three different integration test systems were maintained throughout the effort, each one progressively cleaner and more a mirror of the actual production environment. Integration testing was conducted using captured production data and a past environment clock.

Because of the distributed nature of this integration effort, or perhaps simply because of the plan-driven nature of the effort, higher reporting functions and more complex metrics were never used. Status reporting was done using the inventory, not using the S-curves.

Summary

The methods discussed in this book provide an effective risk-based approach to software test estimation, testing, and evaluation. This approach is called the Most Important Tests method, or MITs. MITs gives testers a defensible set of test methods, metrics, and tools with which to accomplish their testing tasks.

Most software testing today is conducted without benefit of formal methods or metrics. The major distinction between a formal method and an informal method is in the measurement tools used to accomplish the goals and the quality of the product produced. The process described in the MITs' steps probably sounds familiar, but the end result of a test effort that does not use formal methods and metrics like the ones described here is likely to be described in terms like "I tested *it*." Testers using the methods in this book will have much better answers than "I tested *it*," and they will conduct a better test effort in the available time and produce a higher-quality product.

One of the best things about the MITs method is that you don't have to do all the steps as I describe them in this book, nor do you have to execute every step in the list in order to succeed. Start with the step(s) that you (1) can use, (2) need, (3) understand, and (4) think will help; add others when it makes sense. Be sure to select the methods that work in your particular situation. MITs helps the plan-driven effort predict what is coming, and it helps the Agile test group retain its flexibility. So, on the heavyweight side of development, MITs give you solid, defensible, fast ways to estimate your needs. In the middle ground, you can quickly estimate your test needs, prioritize the requirements, promise coverage, and provide accurate status reporting with a minimum of effort. On the lightweight side, you can provide quick estimates and give your management the high-quality, blow-by-blow status information that they *must* have to succeed.

Hopefully this chapter, with all its examples, will give you some ideas, or perhaps simply corroborate your own experiences.

CHAPTER 5

Fundamental Metrics for Software Testing

Would you hire a carpenter who did not have and would not use a tape measure? Probably not, because the carpenter who does not use a tape measure probably will not deliver a satisfactory job. Most people recognize readily that measuring tools are necessary to make sure that a structure is laid out according to the plan, that the floors are level and the walls plumb. Yet we buy software to do important work that has been developed and validated by people who do not use any type of measurement. In this chapter, we define the fundamental metrics that will be used in the methods described in the next chapters.

The following are some typical software testing questions that require measurement to answer:

- How big is *it*?
  - How long will it take to test *it*?
  - How much will it cost to test *it*?
- What about the bugs?
  - How bad were they? What type were they?
  - What kind of bugs were found?

- How many of the bugs that were found were fixed?
- How many new bugs did the users find?
- How much of *it* has to be tested?
- Will *it* be ready on time?
- How good were the tests?
- How much did it cost to test *it*?
- Was the test effort adequate? Was *it* worth it?
- How did *it* perform?

Good answers to these questions require measurement. If testers don't have good answers to these questions, it is not because there are no applicable metrics; it's because they are not measuring.

In this chapter, we discuss the metrics available to answer each of these questions, both fundamental and derived. The techniques used to give you good answers to questions like "How big is *it*?" are presented throughout the rest of this book; all of these techniques require measurement. In this chapter, I introduce the units and metrics used by these techniques.

Measures and Metrics

A metric is a measure. A metric system is a set of measures that can be combined to form derived measures—for example, the old English system of feet, pounds, and hours. These metrics can be combined to form derived measures as in miles per hour.

Measure has been defined as "the act or process of determining extent, dimensions, etc.; especially as determined by a standard" (*Webster's New World Dictionary*). If the standard is objective and concrete, the measurements will be reproducible and meaningful. If the standard is subjective and intangible, the measurements then will be unreproducible and meaningless. The measurement is not likely to be any more accurate than the standard. Factors of safety can correct for some deficiencies, but they are not a panacea.

Craft: The Link between Art and Engineering

My great-grandmother was a craftsperson. A craftsperson is the evolutionary link between art and engineering. My great-grandmother made excellent cookies. Her recipes were developed and continuously enhanced over her lifetime. These recipes were not written down; they lived in my great-grandmother's head and were passed on only by word of mouth. She described the steps of the recipes using large gestures and analogies: "mix it till your arm feels like it's going to fall off, and then mix it some more." She guessed the temperature of the oven by feeling the heat with her hand. She measured ingredients by description, using terms like "a lump of shortening the size of an egg," "so many handfuls of flour," "a pinch or this or that," and "as much sugar as seems prudent."

Great-Grandmother's methods and metrics were consistent; she could have been ISO certified, especially if the inspector had eaten any of her cookies. But her methods and metrics were local. Success depended on the size of her hand, the size of an egg from one of her hens, and her idea of what was prudent.

The biggest difference between an engineer and a craftsperson is measurement. The engineer does not guess except as a last resort. The engineer measures. The engineer keeps written records of the steps in the process that he is pursuing, along with the ingredients and their quantities. The engineer uses standard measuring tools and metrics like the pound and the gallon or the gram and the liter. The engineer is concerned with preserving information and communicating it on a global scale. Recipes passed on by word of mouth using metrics like a handful of flour and a pinch of salt do not scale up well to industrial production levels. A great deal of time is required to train someone to interpret and translate such recipes, and these recipes are often lost because they were never written down.

Operational Definitions: Fundamental Metrics

The definition of a physical quantity is the description of the operational procedure for measuring the quantity. For example, "the person is one and a half meters tall." We know from this definition of a person's height by what metric system the person was measured and how to reproduce the measurement. The magnitude of a physical quantity is specified by a number, "one and a half," and a unit, "meters." This is the simplest and most fundamental type of measurement.

Derived units are obtained by combining metrics. For example, miles per hour, feet per second, and dollars per pound are all derived units. These derived units are still operational definitions because the name tells how to measure the thing.

How Metrics Develop and Gain Acceptance

If no suitable recognized standard exists, we must identify a local one and use it consistently—much like my great-grandmother did when making her cookies. Over time, the standards will be improved.

Developing precise and invariant standards for measurement is a process of constant refinement. The foot and the meter did not simply appear overnight. About 4,700 years ago, engineers in Egypt used strings with knots at even intervals. They built the pyramids with these measuring strings, even though knotted ropes may have only been accurate to 1 part in 1,000. It was not until 1875 that an international standard was adopted for length. This standard was a bar of platinum-iridium with two fine lines etched on it, defining the length of a foot. It was kept in the International Bureau of Weights and Measures in Sevres, France. The precision provided by this bar was about 1 part in 10 million. By the 1950s, this was not precise enough for work being done in scientific research and industrial instrumentation. In 1960, a new standard was introduced that precisely defined the length of the meter. The meter is defined as exactly 1,650,763.73 times the wavelength of the orange light emitted by a pure isotope, of mass number 86, of krypton gas. This standard can be measured more accurately than 1 part per 100 million.

Once a standard is introduced, it must still be accepted. Changing the way we do things requires an expenditure of energy. There must be a good reason to expend that energy.

What to Measure in Software Testing

Measure the things that help you answer the questions you have to answer. The challenge with testing metrics is that the test objects that we want to measure have multiple properties; they can be described in many ways. For example, a software bug has properties much like a real insect: height, length, weight, type or class (family, genus, spider, beetle, ant, etc.), color, and so on. It also has attributes, like poisonous or nonpoisonous, flying or nonflying, vegetarian or carnivorous.[1]

I find that I can make my clearest and most convincing arguments when I stick to fundamental metrics. For example, the number of bugs found in a test effort is not meaningful as a measure until I combine it with the severity, type of bugs found, number of bugs fixed, and so on.

Several fundamental and derived metrics taken together provide the most valuable and complete set of information. By combining these individual bits of data, I create information that can be used to make decisions, and most everyone understands what I am talking about. If someone asks if the test effort was a success, just telling him or her how many bugs we found is a very weak answer. There are many better answers in this chapter.

Fundamental Testing Metrics: How Big Is *It*?

Fundamental testing metrics are the ones that can be used to answer the following questions.

- How big is *it*?
- How long will it take to test *it*?
- How much will it cost to test *it*?
- How much will it cost to fix *it*?

The question "How big is *it*?" is usually answered in terms of how long it will take and how much it will cost. These are the two most common attributes of *it*. We would normally estimate answers to these questions during the planning stages of the project. These estimates are critical in sizing the test effort and negotiating for resources and budget. A great deal of this book is dedicated to helping you make very accurate esti-

---

[1] There are well-defined quantified metrics and metrics systems available today in software testing. Unfortunately, many of these metrics are not fundamental measures; they are complex and often obscure. Function points [Jones 1995] and McCabe's Complexity [McCabe 1989] are examples. It is not immediately apparent from these names how to use these metrics, what they measure, or what benefits they offer. Special knowledge is required. Acquiring this knowledge requires an expenditure of time and resources. It is probably unreasonable to expect that practitioners can transition directly from no metrics to complex metrics.

mates quickly. You should also calculate the actual answers to these questions when testing is complete. You can use the comparisons to improve your future estimates.

I have heard the following fundamental metrics discounted because they are so simple, but in my experience, they are the most useful:

- Time
- Cost
- Tests
- Bugs found by testing

We quantify "How big *it* is" with these metrics. These are probably the most fundamental metrics specific to software testing. They are listed here in order of decreasing certainty. Only time and cost are clearly defined using standard units. Tests and bugs are complex and varied, having many properties. They can be measured using many different units.

For example, product failures are a special class of bug—one that has migrated into production and caused a serious problem, hence the word "failure." A product failure can be measured in terms of cost, cost to the user, cost to fix, or cost in lost revenues. Bugs detected and removed in test are much harder to quantify in this way.

The properties and criteria used to quantify tests and bugs are normally defined by an organization; so they are local and they vary from project to project. In Chapters 11 through 13, I introduce path and data analysis techniques that will help you standardize the test metric across any system or project.

Time

Units of time are used in several test metrics, for example, the time required to run a test and the time available for the best test effort. Let's look at each of these more closely.

The Time Required to Run a Test

This measurement is absolutely required to estimate how long a test effort will need in order to perform the tests planned. It is one of the fundamental metrics used in the test inventory and the sizing estimate for the test effort.

The time required to conduct test setup and cleanup activities must also be considered. Setup and cleanup activities can be estimated as part of the time required to run a test or as separate items. Theoretically, the sum of the time required to run all the planned tests is important in estimating the overall length of the test effort, but it must be tempered by the number of times a test will have to be attempted before it runs successfully and reliably.

Sample Units: Generally estimated in minutes or hours per test. Also important are the number of hours required to complete a suite of tests.

The Time Available for the Test Effort

This is usually the most firmly established and most published metric in the test effort. It is also usually the only measurement that is consistently decreasing.

Sample Units: Generally estimated in weeks and measured in minutes.

The Cost of Testing

The cost of testing usually includes the cost of the testers' salaries, the equipment, systems, software, and other tools. It may be quantified in terms of the cost to run a test or a test suite.

Calculating the cost of testing is straightforward if you keep good project metrics. However, it does not offer much cost justification unless you can contrast it to a converse—for example, the cost of not testing. Establishing the cost of not testing can be difficult or impossible. More on this later in the chapter.

Sample Units: Currency, such as dollars; can also be measured in units of time.

Tests

We do not have an invariant, precise, internationally accepted standard unit that measures the size of a test, but that should not stop us from benefiting from identifying and counting tests. There are many types of tests, and they all need to be counted if the test effort is going to be measured. Techniques for defining, estimating, and tracking the various types of test units are presented in the next several chapters.

Tests have attributes such as quantity, size, importance or priority, and type.

Sample Units   (listed simplest to most complex):

- A keystroke or mouse action
- An SQL query
- A single transaction
- A complete function path traversal through the system
- A function-dependent data set

Bugs

Many people claim that finding bugs is the main purpose of testing. Even though they are fairly discrete events, bugs are often debated because there is no absolute standard in place for measuring them.

Sample Units: Severity, quantity, type, duration, distribution, and cost to find and fix. *Note:* Bug distribution and the cost to find and fix are derived metrics.

Like tests, bugs also have attributes as discussed in the following sections.

Severity

Severity is a fundamental measure of a bug or a failure. Many ranking schemes exist for defining severity. Because there is no set standard for establishing bug severity, the magnitude of the severity of a bug is often open to debate. Table 5.1 shows the definition of the severity metrics and the ranking criteria used in this book.

Table 5.1 Severity Metrics and Ranking Criteria

SEVERITY RANKING	RANKING CRITERIA
Severity 1 Errors	Program ceases meaningful operation
Severity 2 Errors	Severe function error but application can continue
Severity 3 Errors	Unexpected result or inconsistent operation
Severity 4 Errors	Design or suggestion

Bug Type Classification

First of all, bugs are bugs; the name is applied to a huge variety of "things." Types of bugs can range from a nuisance misunderstanding of the interface, to coding errors, to database errors, to systemic failures, and so on.

Like severity, bug classification, or bug types, are usually defined by a local set of rules. These are further modified by factors like reproducibility and fixability.

In a connected system, some types of bugs are system "failures," as opposed to, say, a coding error. For example, the following bugs are caused by missing or broken connections:

- Network outages.
- Communications failures.
- In mobile computing, individual units that are constantly connecting and disconnecting.
- Integration errors.
- Missing or malfunctioning components.
- Timing and synchronization errors.

These bugs are actually system failures. These types of failure can, and probably will, recur in production. Therefore, the tests that found them during the test effort test are very valuable in the production environment. This type of bug is important in the test effectiveness metric, discussed later in this chapter.

The Number of Bugs Found

For this metric, there are two main genres: (1) bugs found before the product ships or goes live and (2) bugs found after—or, alternately, those bugs found by testers and those bugs found by customers. As I have already said, this is a very weak measure until you bring it into perspective using other measures, such as the severity of the bugs found.

The Number of Product Failures

This measurement is usually established by the users of the product and reported through customer support. Since the customers report the failures, it is unusual for product failures that the customers find intolerable to be ignored or discounted. If it exists, this measurement is a key indicator of past performance and probable trouble spots in new releases. Ultimately, it is measured in money, lost profit, increased cost to develop and support, and so on.

This is an important metric in establishing an answer to the question "Was the test effort worth it?" But, unfortunately, in some organizations, it can be difficult for someone in the test group to get access to this information.

Sample Units: Quantity, severity, and currency.

The Number of Bugs Testers Find per Hour: The Bug Find Rate

This is a most useful derived metric both for measuring the cost of testing and for assessing the stability of the system. The bug find rate is closely related to the mean time between failures metric. It can give a good indication of the stability of the system being tested. But it is not helpful if considered by itself.

Consider Tables 5.2 and 5.3. The following statistics are taken from a case study of a shrink-wrap RAD project. These statistics are taken from a five-week test effort conducted by consultants on new code. These statistics are a good example of a constructive way to combine bug data, like the bug fix rate and the cost of finding bugs, to create information.

Notice that the cost of reporting and tracking bugs is normally higher than the cost of finding bugs in the early part of the test effort. This situation changes as the bug find rate drops, while the cost to report a bug remains fairly static throughout the test effort.

Table 5.2   Bug Find Rates and Costs, Week 1

Bugs found/hour	5.33 bugs found/hr
Cost/bug to find	$9.38/bug to find
Bugs reported/hr	3.25 bugs/hr
Cost to report	$15.38/bug to report
Cost/bug find and report	$24.76/bug to find and report

Table 5.3   Bug Find Rates and Costs, Week 4

Bugs found/hour	0.25 bugs found/hr
Cost/bug to find	$199.79 bug to find
Bugs reported/hr	0.143 bugs/hr
Cost to report	$15.38/bug to report
Cost/bug find and report	$215.17 bug to find and report

By week 4, the number of bugs being found per hour has dropped significantly. It should drop as the end of the test effort is approached. However, the cost to find each successive bug rises, since testers must look longer to find a bug, but they are still paid by the hour.

These tables are helpful in explaining the cost of testing and in evaluating the readiness of the system for production.

Bug Density per Unit: Where Are the Bugs Being Found?

Figure 5.1 shows the bug concentrations in four modules of a system during the system test phase. A graph of this type is one of the simplest and most efficient tools for determining where to concentrate development and test resources in a project.

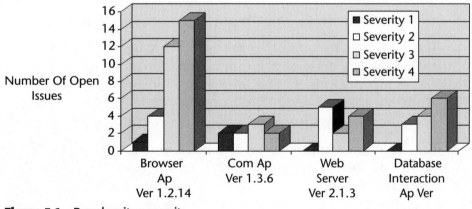

Figure 5.1   Bug density per unit.

Bug densities should be monitored throughout the test effort. The graph presented here was used successfully to allocate test and development resources toward the end of the test effort so that the product could be released on time. It shows both the number of bugs and the severity of those bugs in the four modules. Near the end of this test effort, extra programmers were assigned both to the Com Ap, because of the number of serious bugs it had open, and the Browser Ap, because of the large number of issues it had open.

Even though this type of chart is one of the most useful tools testers have for measuring code worthiness, it is one of the most seldom published. There is a common fear that these metrics will be used against someone. Care should be taken that these metrics are not misused. The highest bug density usually resides in the newest modules, or the most experimental modules. High bug densities do not necessarily mean that someone is doing a poor job. The important point is that there are bugs that need to be removed.

Bug Composition: How Many of the Bugs Are Serious?

As we have just discussed, there are various classes of bugs. Some of them can be eradicated, and some of them cannot. The most trouble-some bugs are the ones that cannot be easily reproduced and recur at random intervals. Software failures and bugs are measured by quantity and by relative severity. Severity is usually determined by a local set of criteria, similar to the one presented in the preceding text.

If a significant percentage of the bugs being found in testing are serious, then there is a definite risk that the users will also find serious bugs in the shipped product. The following statistics are taken from a case study of a shrink-wrap RAD project. Table 5.4 shows separate categories for the bugs found and bugs reported.

Management required that only bugs that could be reproduced were reported. This is a practice that I discourage because it allows management and development to ignore the really hard bugs—the unreproducible ones. These bugs are then shipped to the users. Notice that half the Severity 1 bugs found were not reported. Inevitably, it will fall on the support group to try and isolate these problems when the users begin to report them.

Table 5.4   Relative Seriousness (Composition) of Bugs Found

ERROR RANKING	RANKING DESCRIPTION:	BUGS FOUND	BUGS REPORTED
Severity 1 Errors	GPF or program ceases meaningful operation	18	9
Severity 2 Errors	Severe function error but application can continue	11	11
Severity 3 Errors	Unexpected result or inconsistent operation	19	19
Severity 4	Design or suggestion	0	0
Totals		**48**	**39**

Figure 5.2 shows the graphical representation of the bugs found shown in Table 5.4

The Severity 1 bugs reported represent 38 percent of all bugs found. That means that over a third of all the bugs in the product are serious. Simply put, the probability is that one of every three bugs the user finds in the shipped product will be serious. In this case, it is even worse than that because even if all of the serious bugs that were reported are fixed, it is probable that at least nine (unreported) hard-to-reproduce Severity 1 errors still exist in the product.

The Bug Fix Rate: How Many of the Bugs That Were Found Were Fixed?

$$\text{Bug fix rate} = \frac{\text{BugsFixedDuringTest}}{\text{BugsFoundDuringTest}} \times 100$$

There is a pervasive myth in the industry that all of the bugs found during testing are fixed before the product is shipped. Statistics gathered between 1993 and 1994 indicate that for commercial software, the actual bug fix rate is between 50 percent and 70 percent. Studies conducted in 1998 and 2000 showed bug fix rates of 80 percent to 85 percent in several commercial applications. Figure 5.3 shows the cumulative errors found and errors fixed curves in the 1998 study. The gap between the two curves at the end of the scale is the bugs that were not fixed.

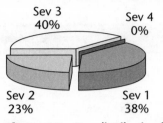

Figure 5.2 Bug distribution by severity.

Many of the shipped bugs are classified as "hard to reproduce." A study of production problems showed that two-thirds of the problems that occurred in production had been detected during the system test. However, because the test effort had not been able to reproduce these problems or isolate the underlying errors, the bugs had migrated into production with the system.

The risk of not shipping on time is better understood than the risk of shipping bugs that cannot be easily reproduced or are not well understood. If a test effort finds 98 percent of all the bugs ever found in the system but only fixes 50 percent of them, will it be a failure? If there is no estimation of the risk of shipping these bugs, management does not have enough information to make a well-informed decision. The pressure to ship on time becomes the overriding factor.

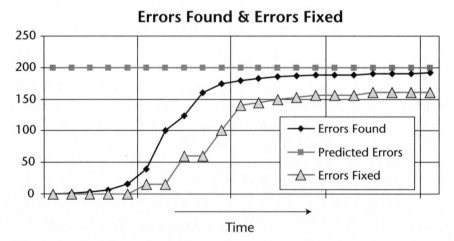

Figure 5.3 Bug fix rate from 1998 study.

Metrics to Measure the Test Effort

The next metrics help measure the test effort itself, answering questions about how much was tested, what was achieved, and how productive the effort was.

Test Coverage: How Much of It Was Tested?

Given a set of things that could be tested, test coverage is the portion that was actually tested. Test coverage is generally presented as a percentage.

$$\text{Test Coverage (Absolute)} = \frac{\text{Test Conducted}}{\text{Total Tests}} \times 100$$

For example, 100 percent statement coverage means that all of the statements in a program were tested. At the unit test level, test coverage is commonly used to measure statement and branch coverage. This is an absolute measure; it is based on known countable quantities.

It is important to note that just because every statement in a group of programs that comprise a system was tested, this does not mean that the system was tested 100 percent. Test coverage can be an absolute measure at the unit level, but it quickly becomes a relative measure at the system level. Relative because while there are a finite number of statement tests and branch tests in a program, the number of tests that exist for a system is an unbounded set—for all practical purposes, an infinite set. Just as testing can never find all the bugs in a system, neither can testers find all the tests that could be performed on a system.

For test coverage to be a useful measurement at the system level, a list of tests must be constructed that serves as the basis for counting the total number of tests identified for a system. We will call this list the *test inventory*. (The test inventory is defined and discussed in the next chapter.) System test coverage is then a measure of how many of the known tests in a system were exercised.

$$\text{System Test Coverage (Relative)} = \frac{\text{Tests Conducted}}{\text{Total Test Inventory}} \times 100$$

The value of this test coverage metric depends on the quality and completeness of the test inventory. A test coverage of 100 percent of a system is only possible if the test inventory is very limited. Tom Gilb calls this "painting the bull's-eye around the arrow."

Test Effectiveness: How Good Were the Tests?

Test effectiveness is a measure of the bug-finding ability of the test set. If a comprehensive test inventory is constructed, it will probably be too large to exercise completely. This will be demonstrated as we proceed through the next several chapters. The goal is to pick the smallest test set from the test inventory that will find the most bugs while staying within the time frame. In a test effort, adequate test coverage does not necessarily require that the test set achieve a high rate of test coverage with respect to the test inventory.

It is usually easier to devise a comprehensive test set than it is to find the time and resources to exercise it fully or to track resulting problems to their source. Therefore, the number of tests that could be performed is almost always greater than the number that actually can be performed given the time and resources available. For example, a test effort conducted with a limited test inventory may achieve 100 percent test coverage by the end of the test cycle. However, regression testing around new code and bug fixes is usually limited in its scope because of time and resource constraints.

We can answer the question, "How good were the tests?" in several ways. One of the most common is to answer the question in terms of the number of bugs found by the users, and the type of bugs they were.

The bug-finding effectiveness of the test set can be measured by taking the ratio of the number of bugs found by the test set to the total bugs found in the product.

$$\text{Effectiveness} = \frac{\text{Bugs Found in Test}}{\text{Total Bugs Found}} \times 100$$

where Total Bugs Found = bugs found during test + new bugs found by users

An effective test suite will maximize the number of bugs found during the test effort. We also want this test suite to be the smallest test set from the inventory that will accomplish this goal. This approach yields the highest test effectiveness (most bugs found) and highest test efficiency (least effort, expense, or waste). For example, if the test coverage of a system test suite covers only 50 percent of the test inventory but it finds 98 percent of all the bugs ever found in the system, then it probably provided adequate test coverage. The point is, the tests in the suite were the right 50 percent of the inventory—the most important tests. These tests found most of the bugs that were important to the user community. The benefits of increasing the test coverage for this system would be minimal.

Test effectiveness only measures the percentage of bugs that the test effort found. Some bugs will be found by both the testers and the users. These are only counted once. The test effectiveness metric differs from the performance metric, which I will introduce in a moment, in that effectiveness only counts found bugs and is not concerned with whether or not these bugs are ever fixed. Since most managers expect the test effort to result in bugs being removed from the product, the performance metric is what they want to see because it is concerned with the percentage of bugs that were found and fixed.

Test effectiveness is valuable when you are evaluating the quality of the test set. I use it as one of the selection criteria when I am distilling a test set that is a candidate for becoming a part of a production diagnostic suite. All the tests that I run during a test effort are part of the most important tests suite. The subset of these most important tests that can discover a failure are valuable indeed.

To select this subset, I use test effectiveness in conjunction with a certain class of bugs that I call *failures*. Failures are bugs that can recur even after they appear to have been fixed. (See the examples listed under the section *Bug Type Classification* earlier in the chapter.)

This failure-finding subset of the most important tests can provide years of value in the production environment as a diagnostics suite, especially if these tests are automated tests. Over the years, test suites that my team developed to test various systems and software products have been incorporated into basis suites used in real-time system monitoring, disaster recovery validation and verification, and real-time problem identification.

When the test effort can identify this test set and instantiate it in the production environment, the testers are delivering a very good return on the test investment. Some of my diagnostics suites have run for years in production environments with few changes. Often these tests are still running long after the original coding of the application or system has been retired.

Metrics to Track Testing: Will It Be Ready on Time?

The following set of derived metrics are used to track the test effort and judge the readiness of the product. By themselves, these metrics are not always helpful. They are extremely valuable in answering questions such as, "Are we on schedule?" and "Have we tested enough?" when they are used in conjunction with S-curves.

- The number of tests attempted by a given time
- The number of tests that passed by a given time
- The number of bugs that were found by a given time
- The number of bugs that were fixed by a given time
- The average time between failures

How Much Did It Cost to Test *It*?

When you use the Most Important Tests method, it is possible to show management how big it is and what a given level of test coverage will require in time and resources. From this basis, it is possible to calculate cost. These techniques are very useful in the test estimation phase. S-curves can help you stay on track during the testing phase, and performance metrics can help you determine the actual cost of testing and what you got for the effort.

Calculating the cost of the effort afterward is one of the simplest of all the metrics in this chapter, even though it may have several components. It is very useful in make a comparative case to get enough budget—next time.

Metrics to Measure Performance: Was It Worth It?

Note: Today, you have to show management that it was worth it.

Not only does the test effort have to provide proof of its performance, it also needs to show that it adds enough value to the product to justify its budget. The performance of the test effort can be most accurately measured at the end of the life of a release. This makes it difficult to justify an ongoing test effort. Constant measurement by testers is the key to demonstrating performance.

Performance is (1) the act of performing, for instance, execution, accomplishment, fulfillment, and so on; and (2) operation or functioning, usually with regard to effectiveness.

The goal of the test effort is to minimize the number of bugs that the users find in the product. We accomplish this goal by finding and removing bugs before the product is shipped to the users. The performance of the test effort is based on the ratio of the total bugs found and fixed during test to all the bugs ever found in the system.

$$\text{Test Effort Performance} = \frac{\text{Bugs Fixed}}{\text{Total Bugs Found}} \times 100$$

The performance of the last test effort, including its test coverage, bug fix rate, and the number of serious bugs that occurred or required fixes in the shipped product, are all used to evaluate the adequacy of the test effort. The cost of the test effort and the cost of the bugs found in production are also considered.

We measure to formulate theories capable of prediction. Next, we measure the results to determine the correctness of the predictions and then adjust the predictions for the next time. To evaluate the accuracy of predictions about the requirements of an adequate test effort, we need to examine several metrics.

This information can be used to adjust test coverage and bug fix requirements on the next release. For example, two test efforts conducted on similarly sized client server applications had the performance statistics shown in Table 5.5. Management determined, based on the number of calls to customer support, that the test effort for Case 1 was more than adequate, while the test effort for Case 2 was found to be inadequate.

One of the problems in Case Study 2 is that the test inventory was probably insufficient. When a poor test inventory is coupled with a low bug fix rate, the result will be a marked increase in the number of calls to customer support and a reportedly higher rate of customer dissatisfaction.

Table 5.5   Determining If the Test Effort Was Adequate

TEST COVERAGE	AVG. CALLS TO CUSTOMER SERVICE PER LICENSE IN FIRST 90 DAYS	BUG FIX RATE	PERFORMANCE RATIO (6 MO. AFTER RELEASE)	SEVERITY 1 BUGS REPORTED IN PRODUCTION	SEVERITY 2 BUGS REPORTED IN PRODUCTION
		CASE STUDY 1			
67%	5	70%	98%	0	6
		CASE STUDY 2			
100%	30	50%	75%	7	19

Severity 1 = Most serious bugs   Severity 2 = Serious bugs

It is necessary to distinguish between the adequacy of the test effort as a whole and the adequacy of the test coverage, because many of the problems that occur in production environments actually occurred during the test cycle. In other words, the bugs were triggered by the test set, but the bugs were not fixed during the test effort and consequently were shipped with the product.

The challenge here is that traditional test efforts cannot remove bugs directly. I have already talked about the management tools "argument" and "persuasion." The current trend is toward find-and-fix.

The Cost of Not Testing: How Much Did Testing Save?

As I mentioned already, this metric is very useful as a point of comparison, but very difficult to establish. The preceding case studies are good examples of how to limp around this problem. I have had the opportunity to conduct a couple of forensic studies in recent years, and I am convinced that the cost of not testing is profound, but because a product failure is such a sensitive issue, I have never been in a position to safely publish any details. It is a common managerial foil to portray a complete debacle as an overwhelming success and move right along to the next project—such are the ways of politics. If you have been involved in a failed product, you have probably experienced this phenomenon firsthand.

You can compare the cost of fixing a bug found in testing to the cost of fixing a bug in the shipped product. I have had some luck in recent years showing that my test effort had a positive cost-benefit ratio using this technique, but it requires intimate knowledge of the customer support process and the ability to track costs in the support area and the development area.

Testing never finds and removes all the bugs in a product. Testing only reduces the number of bugs and the risk of serious errors in the shipped product. If you keep good records, over time you can predict the percentage of certain classes of bugs that the test effort will find and remove. These percentages are also helpful in estimating the cost of not testing.

Other Contributions of the Test Effort

The test effort contributes other valuable things besides the finding of bugs. Testing collateral can provide several valuable resources to production, customer service, and the customers themselves.

I already mentioned the diagnostics suites for production. Installation instructions are another normal product of the test effort; they may be applicable to operations in the case of a system or to the end users in the case of a software product. Since the testers are the first expert users of the system, they are an invaluable asset to customer support in researching, explaining, and resolving customer issues.

Finally, since testers are the first expert users of a product, their questions, working notes, and instructions usually form the foundation of the user guide and seed for frequently asked questions documentation. It is a sad waste when the documentation creation process does not take advantage of this resource.

Summary

Time, cost, tests, bugs, and failures are some of the fundamental metrics specific to software testing. Derived test metrics can be made by combining these fundamental metrics. The problem is, only time and cost are clearly defined by standard units. Tests, bugs, and failures are usually defined locally—that is, much like grandmother's cookies, their definitions are local and only exist inside the organization.

In this chapter, I have introduced fundamental metrics that you can use to answer the questions:

- How big is *it*?
- How long will it take to test *it*?
- How good were our tests? (test effectiveness)
    - How many new bugs did the users find?
    - How many of the bugs that were found were fixed? (the bug fix rate)
- Was the test effort adequate? (I do this by looking at a set of test measurements.)

In addition, I have provided information on the following:

- The bug find rate
- Bug density per unit
- Bug composition
- The bug fix rate

Most of these metrics are simple sums of events. Cumulative results like these should be accumulated over time and examined carefully for trends. I use these cumulative trends to show the big picture and predict the answers to other questions that need to be answered, such as:

- Are we on schedule?
- Have we tested *it* enough?

There are many other questions that you can answer using these metrics as well. In the meantime, would you hire a tester who could not or would not measure the test effort?

CHAPTER 6

The Test Inventory

"Using a list (posted on the refrigerator) reduced my grocery bill by 23 percent. In addition, I haven't run out of anything important since I started using it, which means no emergency runs to the grocery store. Finally, everyone in the house is much happier because the things that they want are here too."
Marnie L. Hutcheson

I n this chapter I talk about methods for answering the questions "What are you going to test?", "What did you test?", and perhaps more importantly, "How big is it?"—because that is the question that gets asked the most. The auditors ask the first two questions; management asks the third. You can't get budget without a good answer to the question, "How big is it?"

The test inventory is a major component of a successful test effort. In this chapter, I introduce the test inventory and discuss how an inventory is used in preparing an estimate for a test effort and what types of items go in the test inventory. We'll also look at how the test inventory helps you conduct an adequate test effort and how it answers the question about how big it is. This process is continued through the next chapters.

Project management uses task lists to keep track of things that need doing. Test scripts are similar to tasks, but the two are not quite the same. The biggest difference is that whereas a task gets completed once, a test may be repeated many times. And this fact means that testing can be trickier to manage than a standard project.

The Goal: A Successful Test Effort

The goal of testing is a successful test effort, but what is a successful test effort? One that finds bugs? Finding bugs alone does not make a successful test effort. The successful test effort will also ensure that the bugs are removed, and it will probably introduce several improvements.

Note: **The goal of the test effort is to establish a responsive, dependable system in the shortest possible time that satisfies and delights the users while staying within budget, schedule, and resource constraints.**

The successful test effort involves several activities in addition to testing the system and finding bugs. Most of these other activities have to do with getting the bugs removed. Testers must perform diagnostics, write bug reports, and track status on the failures that occur during testing; then they must secure, integrate, and verify the fixes. The successful test effort will also complete its test activities in the allotted time. Any plan or estimate that does not take all of these factors into consideration will probably fail, because the failure of any of these activities can cause the entire test effort to fail.

During planning, the potential consequences of a failure in the product and eventually its cost must be balanced against the size and completeness (and cost) of the test effort. Testers need to select a test set that provides the best test coverage for the given time frame. In other words, testers must identify and execute the most *important* tests.

The tester must be able to communicate the size, complexity, priorities, and underlying assumptions of the test effort during planning, because that is when the schedule is established. If the testers cannot communicate these things clearly and adequately, management will not be able to make well-informed decisions about resource allocations and time frames.

Once testing begins, in addition to producing results reports, testers need to be able to calculate, at any time, how much time is required to complete the planned testing and bug-fix integration activities so they can communicate the impact of events on the schedule and adjust planned activities to control the situation. They need to get the job done in a systematic and reproducible way. This goal of a successful test effort cannot be met without a good plan and measurements.

Management must participate in planning and in building the test agreement. They must actively participate in discussions about what will be tested and what will be fixed, and they must allocate enough of the *right* resources to get the job done. This means enough time, testers, and test machines to execute the test agreement, and enough programmers to find and fix the bugs within the time allotted for the test cycle.

Management must also recognize that the test scripts are at least as valuable as the source code that they test and they must promote test reuse. This can be accomplished by setting the expectation that test resources will be reused, not only in subsequent releases but as diagnostics and basis suites. Basis and diagnostic test suites should also be shared with other groups.

Planning for Adequate Testing: How Much Is Enough?

Test coverage is the percentage of all the known tests that were actually attempted and completed. It can be used to answer the question, "How much did we test?" To calculate what percentage of the whole you have accomplished, you must have some idea how big *it* is. We use a test inventory to answer the question, "How big is *it*?"

Unfortunately, most test coverage in commercial software today seems to be estimated by gut feel. When the question is asked, "Did we test enough?", the answer is often along the lines of, "Well, we haven't found any bugs for a while; *it*'s probably okay." This is part of the I-feel-lucky approach.

To make an objective and quantitative answer to the "Did we test enough?" question, a tester must first have made an estimate of how much there is to test. In my workshops, I ask how many testers build a list of all the things there are to test in a given system. Perhaps 1 tester in 30 reports regularly building such a list. Most testers report that they just *start testing*. If no one measured how much there was to test, then no one would ever know how much of *it* was tested. This is the "ignorance-is-bliss" corollary to the I-feel-lucky approach.

These testers always know that they did not test everything; but since they do not know exactly how much they did not test, they can rationalize at least temporarily that they tested enough. Even though *enough* testing is more a function of testing the right things than testing everything, we must have some idea how big the project is. This topic is discussed in detail later in this chapter (see *Using Historical Data in Estimating Effort*).

Planning for an Adequate Test Effort

Studies of production problems that I conducted in 1993 and 1994 showed that 80 to 90 percent of the bugs found in production were encountered during testing. About 60 percent of these bugs were *difficult to reproduce*. The test effort did not have sufficient resources to track those bugs down and get them fixed. *Test coverage was sufficient, but the test effort was not.* As mentioned in an earlier chapter, one of the myths in the software industry is that we always fix every bug we find. While this is generally true in safety-critical systems, it is not the case in most commercial software. A test effort does not usually fail because bugs went undetected but because an unacceptable number of bugs were shipped with the product.

In many cases, the main reason that these bugs can be hard to reproduce is that they only exist in certain environments—that is, they are not in the software being tested but in other supporting software in the system. How can a software maker be held responsible for bugs in someone else's screen driver or printer driver program? On the other hand, how is a normal user or an average tester supposed to recognize that the reason a machine locks up sometimes when he or she selects a graphing function in the word processor is a defect in a certain screen driver?

Another reason that some bugs are hard to reproduce is that the systems where the software is running are large, multiuser systems. These are not finite state machines. Our software systems are complex, event-driven societies of interactive applications. For example, the tester is listening to her favorite CD on her PC while using her LAN-connected Internet browser to do research for the paper she is writing on her word processor, and both the word processor and the browser are open on the screen. In addition to the operating system, there are a variety of drivers, like the mouse, video, memory, fax, and the CD, running on the windowing operating system concurrently. The system locks up and the screen goes black when the fax tries to answer an incoming call. Generally duplicating or even completely documenting the actual state of such a system when the fatal event occurs is impossible, even when the system in question is a single standalone machine, let alone when it exists in a network. Consequently, re-creating the exact state(s) that existed in one of these systems at the moment a failure occurred is generally impossible.

Testers alone cannot hope to catalog and control today's complex environments; development must take a proactive approach to making the product *testable*. Studies have shown that a significant percentage of production problems have been hard to reproduce because there are insufficient diagnostics in the environment, or misleading or erroneous error messages have been displayed when the bugs occurred. Good defensive programming and rich environmental diagnostics are required in order to isolate these bugs. In some cases, the best fix possible is simply a notice that explains a bug that might happen. In any case, if the test effort fails to get *enough* bugs fixed, it will be judged a failure.

Just as the creation of the developer is the code that performs the functions in the product, the creation of the tester is tests that demonstrate the reliability of the product. The testers want to create the most bug-free product possible. The tester's frustration is that he or she cannot usually fix the bugs found. The developers must be persuaded to do it—in some cases, third-party developers. Sound test methods and good measurements are critical. They are the basis of all persuasive efforts with development and management, as well as the professional credibility of the testers. Without good measurements to give management a clear idea of the importance and possible impact of these hard-to-reproduce bugs, it will be difficult to convince them to spend money and possibly slip delivery dates to hunt for them.

The point here is that test coverage alone is not enough to ensure a successful test effort. There are two parts to the successful test effort: adequate test coverage and an adequate test effort. Both parts must be considered in the planning process.

The most effective way to determine if the test coverage is adequate is by measuring. Worksheets are an excellent tool to aid you in accumulating the measurements and applying factors of safety for various tests and related tasks. I use worksheets both for estimating the resource requirements for the test effort and for keeping track of the actual counts during the test effort. I also use them to measure the actual performance of the test effort after the product has been deployed. This performance measurement provides the basis of the factor of safety that I will be applying to correct the worksheet estimates of the *next* test effort.

The remainder of this chapter deals with building the test inventory, which is the basis of the worksheet. Each of the next three chapters deals with techniques necessary to flesh out the worksheet and the test inventory. I discuss techniques for automating the creation and maintenance of the worksheet, as well as the calculations on the worksheet, throughout.

Determining the Scope of Testing: How Big Is *It*?

Antonio Stradivari (1644-1737), better known to most of us as *Stradivarius*, made some of the finest and most prized violins and violas in the world today. Stradivari was a master craftsman; he had a special knack for understanding the properties, strengths, and weaknesses of a piece of wood. He measured the quality of his materials and craftsmanship by his senses. It is said that he could examine a piece of wood and know just by looking at it, touching it, and listening to the sound it made when he knocked on it what its best use would be. But for all the master's art and craftsmanship, when it came to doing a complete job and managing his efforts, he relied on lists.

We know that he did so because when he was through with a list, he reused the paper the list was written on, which was too valuable to be thrown away, to reinforce the inside joints of his instruments. At that time, all craftsmen were trained to keep lists. These lists might be used to satisfy a benefactor that their funds were well spent or the craft guild if the craftsman was called to make an accounting. Much of what we know of many of the masters' arts and lives comes from handwritten lists found reinforcing the insides of the fine instruments and furniture they created.

An *inventory* is a detailed list. An inventory of all the tasks associated with a project, such as all the tests identified for a test effort, is the basis for answering such questions as, "How long will it take to accomplish everything on the list?" In a test effort, *how big?* is best answered in terms of *how much?*, *how many?*, and most importantly, *how long*? The inventory then becomes the basis of an agreement between parties, or a contract for accomplishing the project. We will postpone the discussion of the test agreement or test plan until later. For now, consider the test inventory only as a means of answering the question, "How big is *it*?"

The *test inventory* is the complete enumeration of all tests, of all types, that have been defined for the system being tested. For example, the inventory for a typical end-to-end system test effort will include path tests, data tests, module tests, both old and new user scenarios (function tests), installation tests, environment tests, configuration tests, tests designed to ensure the completeness of the system, requirements verification, and so on.

The inventory can be organized in any way that is useful, but it must be as comprehensive as possible. It is normal and healthy that the inventory grow during the test effort. The inventory is dynamic, not static. It evolves with the system. When a test inventory is used, the test coverage metric can be used to measure many types of testing, such as function or specification coverage.

Test Units

The much-defamed LOC (lines of code) metric is crude, rather like that knotted string the Egyptians used that we will discuss in Chapter 11. Its biggest problem is that it is not uniform. There is no equivalence between a line of C code and a line of Ada, Pascal, or Basic. But it is better than no measure at all.

How do you measure a test? If I say, "How many tests are in this test effort?", do you think of mouse clicks, or long scripts composed of many keystrokes and mouse clicks, or huge data files that will be processed? Clearly, a test is a measure of the size of the test effort. But, like LOC, it is only useful if there is a way to normalize the way we measure a test.

Unfortunately, there is no standard definition of the word *test*. The IEEE defines *test* as a set of one or more test cases. This definition implies multiple verifications in each test. Using this definition, if we say that one test effort requires 1,000 tests and another requires 132 tests, the measure is totally ambiguous because we have no idea what a test entails. In fact, a test is performed each time a tester compares a single outcome to a standard, often called an *expected response*. In today's test lab, a test is an item or event that is verified, where the outcome is compared to a standard. A *test case* or *test script* is a set of tests, usually performed in some sequence and related to some larger action or software function. A *test suite* is a set of test scripts or test cases. Test cases in a test suite are usually related and organized to verify a more complex set of functions.

If a tester performs many steps before performing a verification, and if the comparison of the actual outcome to the expected outcome fails, the entire set of steps will have to be repeated in order to repeat the test. At Microsoft I observed that, except for simple text entry, almost every keystroke or mouse action was considered to be a test, meaning it was verified individually. When the definition of a test is this granular, the test inventory is going to be very comprehensive, at least as far as function test coverage is concerned. *This degree of granularity is necessary not only for good test coverage; it is essential if the goal is to create robust test automation.* I am not saying that we should plan to rigorously verify the result of every single keystroke in every single scenario. That level of verification may or may not be necessary or cost-effective. I am saying that we need to *count* every single keystroke or system stimuli that *can* be verified and make sure that each one is included in the test inventory.

One Test Script: Many Types of Tests

System testing is usually conducted once the entire system is integrated and can be tested from "end to end." Even though this part of a test effort is often called a *systems test* or *end-to-end test*, there are different types of test activities being performed. Statement execution is the focus of unit testing. But statement execution is the result of the user's actions, like keystrokes or mouse clicks during the higher-level tests as well. Behind every system response there are internal and possibly external module, component, and device responses. Any of these responses could be verified and validated. A single user or system input could require multiple layers of verification and validation at many levels of the system. These *tests* are all different tests even though they may all be generated by the same test script, and they may or may not all be verified and validated each time the test script is attempted.

The function tester is generally concerned with verifying that the system functions correctly from the user's perspective. The function tester cannot usually perform verification of internal system processes, only the outcomes or actual results visible to a normal user. This type of testing is called *black box testing* or *behavioral testing*. The task of verifying internal, often invisible, system processes generally falls to the system testers. System testing may use the same system stimuli as the function test—that is, the same test script, database, and so on—but what is verified as a result of the stimuli is different. System testing usually delves into the internal system response to the stimuli.

For the number of tests to have meaning as a sizing metric, there must be some way to normalize the way we measure a test. One important attribute that all tests have in common is the time required to conduct the test. The total time required to conduct all the tests in the inventory is an important measurement in estimating the test effort.

The function tester and the system tester may use the same keystrokes to stimulate the system, but the tests may take very different amounts of time to complete because the verification being performed is very different. The function tester uses the next screen he or she receives to verify the test. The system tester may have to evaluate the contents of systems log files and trapped events. Verification and validation at this low level takes a lot more time than verification from the user interface.

Low-level system verification requires a highly technical tester. Because this type of testing is difficult, time-consuming, and expensive, the trend has been to do less and less of it. After all, if the system appears to be sending the correct response to the user, why look any further? This argument has been used to justify the current top-down approach to system testing. The problem is the really tough, expensive bugs often live in these low-level areas. For example, a bug may only affect 3 percent of the users. Sounds OK, right? But what if those 3 percent happen to be those users who have over $10 million being managed by the system?

Using Historical Data in Estimating Effort

Historical data from a test effort that is similar to the one being estimated can provide a factual basis for predictions. However, even if the time required to conduct two test efforts is known, it is not possible to compare two test efforts and say which was more productive unless there is some additional basis for comparison. It is possible to establish a working basis of comparison by considering similar sets of measurements about each test effort. Consider the sample application data in Table 6.1.

A function in Release 1M is roughly *equivalent* to a function in Release 1A. They are two consecutive releases of the same application, differing only by some bug fixes. At first glance, the test set for Release 1M appears to be more comprehensive than the test set for Release 1A. This is not the case, however. The Release 1M statistics are from the original *manual* test effort. Release 1A was the *automated* version of the tests from Release 1M. When the test estimation for Release 1A was performed, all the tests from Release 1M were included in the test inventory. The test analysis showed there were many redundancies in the tests from Release 1M. These were largely removed, and new tests were added to the inventory based on the path and data analysis.[1] The values in the table marked *theoretical* were calculated values.

Efficiency is the work done (output) divided by the energy required to produce the work (input). In this example, the efficiency of Release 1A is 66 verifications per hour, while the efficiency of Release 1M was 2.6 verifications per hour. The efficiency of the tests in Release 1A in terms of verifications was roughly 25 times (66/2.6) greater than Release 1M.

Cost is the inverse of efficiency. *Cost* in this case will be measured in units of time per test, that is, the *time per verification performed* and the *time per function tested*. It took (383/236) or 1.6 hours to verify a function in Release 1M, while it took (100/236 = 0.42 hours) or about 25 minutes to verify a function in Release 1A. Verifying the 236 functions in Release 1A *cost* about one-quarter the time as Release 1M. This improvement was due to the introduction of automation tools.

---

[1] In this case, the time required to create the automated tests is factored into the total of 100 hours.

Table 6.1   Comparison of Two Releases of the Same Application

ITEM	RELEASE 1M	RELEASE 1A
1. Number of test scripts (actual)	1,000	132
2. Total user functions identified in the release (actual)	236	236
3. Number of verifications/test script (average actual)	1	50
4. Total verifications performed	1,000	6,600
5. Average number of times a test was executed during the test cycle	1.15	5
6. Number of tests attempted by the end of the test cycle (theoretical)	1,150	33,000
7. Average duration of a test (known averages)	20 min.	4 min.
Total time required to run the tests (from project logs)	383 hrs.	100 hrs.
Total verifications/hr. of testing (efficiency)	(1,000/383) = 2.6	(6,600/100) = 66
Definition of a test	Verification occurs after a user function is executed	Verification occurs after each user action required to execute a function

These types of cost and efficiency comparisons are dependent on the assumption that the program functions are similar. A program function in firmware is very different from a program function in a piece of windowing software. Program functions are similar from one release of a product to the next. Comparison of tests and test efficiency is most useful when you are planning for a subsequent release when functions will be fairly similar. Such comparisons can also be made between similar applications written in the same language.

Another measure of efficiency is the number of bugs found per test or per test-hour. If it is not possible to establish equivalence, it is still possible to measure the time required to perform the tests and use this measurement to make predictions about regression testing and other similar tests. "How long will it take?" and "How much will it cost?" are two questions for which testers need to have good answers. Using this approach, we can say:

✳ **1. The overall size of the *test inventory* is equal to the number of tests that have been identified for the project. (This is how big *it* is.)**

It does not matter that the true set of tests that exists for the project is unbounded, that is to say, virtually infinite. The techniques discussed in the next chapters are used to cut that number down to some still large but manageable number. Care must be taken that the test inventory includes at least minimum items discussed in the following chapters. If the test inventory is poor, incomplete, or simply too shallow, the resultant test effort will be unsatisfactory even if test coverage is 100 percent.

✳ **2. The size of the *test set* is the number of tests that will actually be executed to completion.**

This is the number of tests that must *pass* in order for testing to be considered complete. The test coverage that this effort achieves is the fraction of test items from the test inventory that will actually be executed until they are successful. As stated previously, we want this subset of all the tests that have been identified to be the most important tests from the inventory.

✳ **3. The size of the *test effort* will include all test activities undertaken to successfully execute the test set.**

The time required to accomplish the test effort can be estimated based on the total time required to plan, analyze, and execute tests; report, negotiate and track bugs; and retest fixes on the tests that will be run. A worksheet presented in Chapter 11, "Path Analysis," is used to total the time required for each of these tasks.

✳ **4. The cost of the test effort can be estimated based on the time and resources required to perform an adequate test effort.**

This seems too simplistic to mention, but it has been my experience that the budget for the test effort is rarely determined in this way, by adding up predicted costs. It seems that the most popular method of estimating the cost of the test effort goes something like this:

1. Pick a delivery date.
2. Estimate the date when the code should be turned over to test.
3. Subtract Step 2 from Step 1. This is the number of days available for testing.[2]
4. Multiply the days available for testing by the cost per hour and the number of testers that can be spared for the effort.

This method totally ignores the goal of an adequate test effort. Testers are somehow expected to get *it* tested in some arbitrary number of days. When the users start reporting bugs in the product, management immediately asks, "Why didn't you test *it*?"

When I became an engineer, my first manager told me, "You have to manage your management." She was absolutely correct. The way I manage management who are using this approach to figuring the budget is to show them exactly what they can get for their money—*and* what they will not get. If they eventually discover that they did not get enough, it is their problem.

In commercial software testing, this method is sufficient and I have done my job. If management chooses to ignore my professional estimate of what is required to perform an adequate test effort, so be it. I will work with whatever they leave me, being sure all the while that they understand what they are choosing *not* to test. In high-reliability and safety-critical software, the situation cannot be handled so casually. Whatever form the engineer's protestations or advisements may take, they must be documented. Such documentation is the tester's best defense against the charge that the efforts were inadequate.

Reasons for Using an Inventory

Testing without a test inventory is like going to the grocery store without a list. The shopper will probably proceed by walking down each aisle and examining each item on the shelves in order to make a determination. Do

---

[2] I will resist commenting here on what happens if this is a negative number.

I need this or not? Can I afford it? Will it fit in the basket? This continues until the shopper runs out of time, money, or energy. At that point, the shopper hurries through the rest of the store to the checkout, perhaps collecting a couple more items on the way. Let's assume that the shopper can afford to pay the bill. It's likely that when the shopper arrives at home, he will discover that he did not get certain items that he really needed, like milk or bread, which means he will have to make an unscheduled return trip to the store or do without. There is also a good chance that he made some impulse purchases, like toffee pecan ice cream, and some duplicate purchases, like another jar of green olives when he already has three in the cupboard.

An effective and efficient trip to the grocery store begins with a good list and a budget. Ideally, the shopper arrives at the store in plenty of time to get the job done. The efficient shopper will proceed on some systematic path through the store, usually aisle by aisle, finding the items on the list, checking the price, and reviewing the other offerings as well. This is how we find things we needed that were not on our list, and this is how we discover new items. "On my way down the exotic foods aisle, I saw this new fajita marinade and thought it sounded good. Let's give it a try."

If time is short, the efficient shopper will try to plot a path that will minimize the time required to acquire the items on the list and ensure that he does not have to double back to get any items on the list.

Because of the way software development works, software testers do not usually get in the store until just before it is going to close. All the experts agree that using a list is the most efficient way to do the shopping, but only 1 tester in 30 reports that he prepares a list of the tests that he thinks could be performed, or all the tests that should be performed.

Using a list helps minimize the mistakes that we can make because something was forgotten, and it reduces the waste of unnecessary purchases. How good the list is depends on how carefully the cupboards were reviewed during its preparation. The most comprehensive and therefore the best list is the public list posted on the refrigerator, where everyone can add to it.

As good as all these reasons are for using an inventory, they are not the main reason that I use test inventories.

Note: **The main reason that I use test inventories is that they protect *me*, the tester.**

If I tested everything on the list and the project failed, I have still performed my part of the agreement. This is part of project management, engineering practice, and contract law. I can show clearly what I plan to do and not do, what I have and have not done. If management or any other party sees something amiss, they are *required* to say so, or they will carry a share of the blame later. If the scheduled time has to be shortened, I can ensure that whatever time is available is spent testing the most critical items. But I am not responsible for completing an effort if agreed upon time or resources were not available.

I make management aware of every test that they are choosing to forego if they choose to downsize the test effort, or if they choose to forego the systematic approach and go with a purely ad hoc effort. Have you ever heard management say something like, "Of course you can finish it. I will give you 10 folks from editorial. They can test *it* in no time." (*It* indeed.) On the surface, this may seem like a good idea, but it is one of the poorest solutions available. There probably is not any time budgeted to train these newly designated testers on how to test or how to follow a test plan. The odds are that the test effort will quickly degenerate into an ad hoc free-for-all. The good folks from editorial will not be sure how to reproduce most of the bugs that they find. Development will probably return their bug reports as "unreproducible," and the real testers will lose a lot of time chasing chimera when they could have been performing meaningful testing.

Note: I do not write test plans anymore; I write a contract to test.

I started writing contracts to test long before I started testing as a consultant. It is too easy for a test plan to be ignored and forgotten. In a commercial software shop, the testers are usually the first ones shot when the product fails. It is not so easy to shoot testers who are holding an agreement that management signed and then chose to ignore when deadlines approached.

The Sources of the Tests on the Inventory

Tests on the inventory can and should come from a number of sources, like the complete grocery list on the refrigerator door. The tests can target any part of the system and can range from high-level user functions to low-level system tests. The following are some of the most common sources of tests in the inventory:

- Requirements
- Analytical analysis techniques
  - Inspections, reviews, and walk-throughs
  - Paths analysis
  - Data analysis
  - Environment catalog
  - Usage statistics
- Nonanalytical techniques

Tests Based on Requirements

One of the first sources of tests for the test effort should be the requirements. If you can establish the relative priorities of the requirements, then it helps greatly in establishing the rank of the tests that are designed to verify the requirements and the amount of test coverage that will be provided. Ranking provides a valuable tool for designers and developers to pass on their knowledge and assumptions of the relative importance of various features in the system. More on this when we discuss how I build a test inventory in Chapter 7, "How to Build a Test Inventory."

Analytical Methods

These are tests determined through systematic analysis of the system requirements, user requirements, design documents and code, or the system itself. There are many types of analysis techniques and methods. The following are the ones I have found most useful:

- Inspections, reviews, and walk-throughs
- Paths analysis
- Data analysis
- Environment catalog
- Usage statistics

Inspections, Reviews, and Walk-throughs

Inspection, reviews, and walk-throughs are all used to test the accuracy of *paper* documentation. Paper is also the medium currently used to store and communicate those ideas. Many of the defects discovered in paper documentation are related to paper and the limitations of paper-dependent processes, not fuzzy or incorrect human logic.

> **"The Horses for Courses Principle: Use walk-throughs for training, reviews for consensus, but use Inspections to improve the quality of the document and its process."—From *Software Inspection* by Tom Gilb and Dorothy Graham.**

Inspections

Inspection, with a capital *I*, is a formal technique used to test project documentation for defects and measure what is found. It is currently acknowledged to be the most effective method of finding and removing defects. Issues logged against the documentation through inspections are usually resolved before they can become bugs in the product. Testers do not necessarily have access to the Inspection results, unless testers hold their own Inspection (which is a very good idea). Ideally, all test documents, plans, the test inventory, and so on will be inspected by a team that includes both testers and developers.

Inspections do not generate tests that will be run against the system. Tom Gilb, noted author and management practice guru, says that "inspection is a testing process that tests ideas which model a system." Inspections are used to measure and improve the quality of the paper documentation, or the ideas expressed in it.

Reviews

Reviews, also called peer reviews, are usually conducted on project documentation early in the development cycle. The reviewers evaluate the contents of the documents from various groups. Each reviewer has his or her own perspective, expectations, and knowledge base.

A review is probably the best opportunity to publish assumptions for general scrutiny. Reviews are very good at uncovering possible logic flaws, unaddressed logic paths, and dependencies. All of these things will require testing. Tests determined through reviews can be added to the test inventory in the same way as any other tests. Typically, though, reviews, like inspections, are conducted on the paper documentation of a project.

Walk-throughs

Walk-throughs are usually group sessions that trace processes, both existing and proposed, in order to educate everyone of the current thinking. The documentation used in a walk-through may be high-level logic flows (bubbles on a foil or a whiteboard). Walk-throughs are also sources of tests for the test inventory.

In a RAD/Agile effort, the design and requirements may not be written down, but they can and are reviewed nonetheless. Some examples of non-paper documentation techniques that describe the way the system will work include story actors, metaphors, and day-in-the-life scenarios. These oral versions of the design and requirements of the project are continuously evolving and undergo continuous review under the scrutiny of the group. Many types of RAD/Agile efforts use reviewing techniques similar to those described previously to consider the way a software product will work or how a logic process will progress.

Path Analysis

There are many published techniques for conducting path analysis and path testing, also called *white box testing*. This type of analysis is systematic and quantifiable. Chapters 11 and 12 discuss the topic at length.

Data Analysis

There are many techniques published for conducting data analysis and data testing, also called *black box testing* and *behavioral testing*. This type of analysis is systematic and quantifiable. Chapter 13, "Data Analysis Techniques," discusses the topic.

Environment Catalog

The possible combinations and permutations of hardware and software environments in which a software system may be expected to run is virtually infinite.

Just because a software product runs perfectly in one environment does not mean that it will run at all in any other environment. All device drivers were not created equal. No two versions of the operating system are truly compatible, both upward and downward. Standards for data transmission, translation, and storage vary widely.

Note: The entire test inventory should be run against the software under test in _each_ test environment.

Verifying and validating that the software performs correctly in the hardware and software environments where it will be expected to run is the most demanding testing task of all. In all but the smallest applications, this amount of test coverage is impossible unless the testing is automated.

In the planning stage, testers must make a catalog of the environments they plan to test. Management is normally involved in the decisions about which environment combinations will be tested, because they approve the purchase of the hardware and software. The best source for selecting environments that _should_ be tested are the customer support records of problems. Unfortunately, problematic hardware and software environments are usually first identified and reported by customers.

Usage Statistics: User Profiles

It is common today for progressive commercial software makers to build automatic logging functions into their products, both for purposes of diagnostics when there is a problem and for gathering historical data to use in evaluating the functions and usability of their products. Historically, such logging functions have been used only in beta test sites and special situations. But the information that they provide is crucial to understanding how the customer uses the system. The understanding of how important this information is in a competitive market is best illustrated by considering the core features of the Web servers being marketed today. Makers of Web servers today have included very comprehensive logging abilities in their products. These logs run continuously in the production environment, giving the Web master instant access to usage statistics for every page and function in the system. This information can then be used to tune the Web on a daily basis.

User profile information provides historical data, or feedback, to the developers and testers about how the product is being used, misused, and not used. The most-used functions, options, and problems are usually part of this record. These records are often a source of tests for the current release, especially when new functions have been introduced or functions have been changed to accommodate the users.

When the users report a bug, the user profile information is the best chance of re-creating the bug for development to fix, and for the testers to regression-test the fix. User misunderstandings commonly show up in the user profiles, such as a sequence of actions taken by the user that caused an unexpected outcome. For example, the user did not realize the need to specify a location for a file, and so the file was not actually saved even though the user clicked on the OK button. Or, it was saved in some unknown location.

As valuable as these records are in adding tests to the inventory, they are more valuable for prioritizing the tests. This information is invaluable in determining which functions are used most and how they are used. This, in turn, helps testers determine where to devote test resources.

Profile information invariably leads to improved product features and usability. For example, a client/server application might produce over 200 reports. But usage statistics from the host show that only 15 to 20 of these reports were requested by the customers in the 12 months since release. Such information can have a profound impact on the projections for both the development and test schedules.

Another example of using usage statistics to improve a product is the evolution of the toolbar button. When toolbar buttons were first introduced, they were almost universally ignored by the users. There is a story from Microsoft that the beta test user profiles showed this nonuse. This information prompted an inquiry into why this timesaving feature was not being used. The answer was that users were uncertain what the buttons did and avoided them for that reason. That answer led to an explanation of each button being placed in the bottom row, or status line, of the window. When the mouse moved over the button, the explanation would appear. Human factors kept most people from seeing the information at the bottom of the window when their attention was focused on the toolbar button or menu at the top of the window. As a result, the buttons continued to be ignored. The next step in the evolution of the toolbar button was the inclusion of the explanatory text that opens next to the button. This latest innovation has led to widespread use of descriptive text for all active elements on the screen.

If the test effort has access to this type of usage data, it should be used to help prioritize testing, design the actual test scripts, and determine the order in which the tests should proceed. The use of user profile data in the prioritization of tests will be discussed in Chapter 9, "Risk Analysis."

Nonanalytical Methods

Nonanalytical methods are actually the most commonly used methods to design tests. However, when they are used without any analytical methods, the tests generated will probably not provide systematic or uniform coverage. Nonanalytical methods are most effective when used *after* analytical methods have been applied, to test assumptions made in the analytical tests, to do error guessing, and to design purely random tests.[3] A couple of the main types of nonanalytical methods are discussed in the sections that follow.

Brainstorming Sessions

Brainstorming sessions are good sources of test scenarios for the test inventory. The results of brainstorming sessions can range from highly structured sets of tests to chaos, depending on the rules by which they are conducted. The scenarios developed in brainstorming sessions typically exercise important functions in the system but are ad hoc in nature and do not ensure systematic or uniform test coverage. Typically, this type of test is also generated spontaneously as the test effort progresses through error guessing and assumption testing on the part of the tester.

An example of this type of test development are cases where a necessary dialog box will not open if the desktop is in a certain view. When testers discover a bug of this type, it is normal to add tests to verify that

---

[3] Random tests, usually generated and rerun by automated tools, are often called *monkeys*.

there are not other problems with the particular view. This is a normal corrective action when an underlying assumption—namely, that the software would function in the same way no matter what view it is in— is found to be in error.

Expert Testers

Typically, expert testers develop test scenarios that explore hot spots in problem areas such as module interfaces, exception processors, event processors, and routers. This type of testing is also used to probe critical security or data-sensitive areas in the system. While these scenarios are very important, again, systematic and uniform coverage is not ensured.

These tests are often designed to stress a particular module or component that is suspected of being buggy or to probe for vulnerabilities in components that must be demonstrably secure. An example of this first type of test would be to set up a series of actions to overload a queue in switch software, and then verify that the overload is handled properly. An example of the second type of testing is when the makers of software that provides system security, like a firewall, send their products to special consultants whose job is to find a way to break the security.

I do not have much to say about specific techniques for adding nonanalytical tests to the inventory. Nonanalytical tests represent an opportunity to exercise an *artistic* approach to testing. I have had plenty of experience creating these tests, as have most testers. They are spontaneous, ad hoc, often redundant, at least in part, and for the most part, inspirational in nature. Inspiration is capricious, and so are these tests. Children playing Pin the Tail on the Donkey use more consistent techniques than the nonanalytical techniques used to test software.

When nonanalytical methods are used without analytical methods, the test set generated will undoubtedly be seriously deficient. Formal path and data analysis techniques provide consistent and dependable tools for defining tests. But analytical approaches alone are not enough to ensure an excellent test suite either, given the current state of technology. The tester's creativity and artistic technique are still critical factors to building an excellent test set.

Summary

The performance or quality of the test effort is normally judged by the number of errors that occur *after* testing has been concluded—that is, after the product has been shipped to the users. The stringency of the definition of what is "adequate" varies with the criticality of the system under consideration. Generally, it can be said that an *adequate test effort* is one where few serious bugs occur in the product after it has been distributed to the user community. An adequate test effort requires adequate test coverage and adequate bug removal.

To determine the quality or adequacy of the test effort, we need to measure certain fundamental things to answer questions like "How big is *it*?", meaning the test effort, "How long will *it* take?", and "How much will be tested?" A test inventory is an excellent tool for answering these questions.

Determining the requirements for an adequate test effort requires that many factors be itemized, estimated, and totaled. The test inventory is an excellent tool for this job. The test inventory should be constructed using a combination of analytical and nonanalytical techniques to ensure the best overall coverage. Like the public grocery list posted on the refrigerator door, it will benefit from having the broadest possible input. When it is mature, the test inventory should contain a reference to every test that has been devised for the system. If a thorough analysis of the system is conducted, the number of tests on the inventory will far exceed the time and resources available to run them during the test effort. MITs risk analysis is used on the inventory to identify the most important tests and the optimal test coverage for the effort. The rest of this book gives you the theoretical and practical steps to develop a mature test inventory that will help you in each phase of your test effort.

In this chapter, I gave you the big picture of what the inventory is and what it can do for you and the quality of your test effort. The rest of this book deals with how to develop a test inventory that suits your needs, prioritize its items, negotiate for the resources you need to succeed, and finally, select and design tests. The first step is to construct a preliminary inventory. I will show you how I do this in the next chapter, "How to Build a Test Inventory."

CHAPTER 7

How to Build a Test Inventory

A well-crafted test inventory, like a grocery list, is as succinct as possible. Ideally, each item should fit on one line. All the description and detailed specifics of the test exist but are stored elsewhere, usually later in the test agreement or test plan. Each main topic or test category will have more detailed layers of tests beneath it.

My management always wanted all the information that they needed, and only the information they needed, on as few sheets of paper as possible. The first test inventory I ever submitted was a photocopy of the test description section of the table of contents of my test plan. It was about five pages long. Management liked it so well that I have never changed the practice. In project management this is called a *rollup*.

Starting with the Requirements

When I start an inventory, I begin with the development project requirement documents. These projects may be called by any number of names; the point is, I am looking for the level of project requirement that has a budget attached to it. I try very hard to make sure all budget items are accounted for on the inventory. I use these requirements to build a preliminary inventory. Next, I catalog all of the related development projects that I can identify under these requirements. Then I enumerate all the major functions and cross-reference them to their budgeted projects. It looks like this:

Requirement (with budget)

- Project under this requirement
  - Function under this project
    - Testable items under this function

There can be many testable items under a function, many functions under a project, and many projects under a requirement. When it is all rolled up, it just looks like a requirement. It's a lot like nested file folders on your hard drive. In fact, I have met many testers who store test cases in this type of structure.

Inventories from different projects can look very different. Following are two samples from the real-world examples discussed earlier. The first is a preliminary test inventory from the structured RAD example in Chapter 4, "The Most Important Tests (MITs) Method." At this point, it is only a list of the requirements; there is nothing to "roll down" yet. This is possible if it's a plan-driven project with formal budgeting procedures. If it is a RAD/Agile effort, you may need to be more creative, as we will see in the second example: a preliminary test inventory from a Web development effort also described in Chapter 4.

Sample Inventory from the Structured RAD Project

In this example, I describe a set of formal and politically correct procedures for building your test inventory and discovering the scope of your test effort. This method works well in large organizations where political and budget boundaries may be sensitive issues. It can scale from small to huge, and it is suitable for heavyweight as well as middleweight projects. This example is from a full system integration test effort in a large system, so the scope is extensive, as you will see in the coming chapters.

This system test effort differs from individual integration test and IT-conducted system tests in that it seeks to verify that critical business functions are operating properly across the entire system. The system test effort includes function, performance, and load testing. Rather than focusing on the new data flows through the system, it will focus on day-to-day business functions both before and after the system is subjected to the new data flows. In theory, very little function will change, but loads on various systems will be increased and new processes will be inserted in the system to handle the new data formats. As such, the final inventory will include extensive dependency and cross-reference information.

The test inventory is the tool used in this system test effort to identify the scope of the test effort and prioritize it based on each inventory item's risk potential. The inventory is intended to be an enumeration of the software system testable items that have been identified in the entire project. The initial test inventory was prepared from the available project documentation and is included in the master test plan. Initial priority ratings were applied to each item in the inventory based on the available project documentation. The inventory also contains the reference to the systems touched by a given item. This initial test inventory serves as a starting place for the Subject Matter Expert (SME) interview process.

The Billing System Preliminary Inventory

Table 7.1 is an excerpt from the preliminary test inventory prepared for the billing system real-world example discussed in Chapter 4. This excerpt included only the Project Development Requirement documents (PDRs) applying to one area of the billing system. It was prepared and sorted by the PDR. This example already includes a preliminary prioritization assigned by the test team based on the PDR documentation and budget.

This inventory was created in a spreadsheet using Microsoft Excel. One of the advantages of this representation is that the entire inventory can be sorted by any column. This sample is sorted by PDR, but it can just as easily be sorted by contact, size, or priority. Another advantage is that the spreadsheet makes it easy to apply formulas and keep track of totals.

The description and dependency sections need to be kept brief, less than 255 characters. The main reason is that you can't copy and paste an entire sheet that contains oversized fields. When you copy an entire sheet, all fields are truncated to 255 characters max; you have to copy larger fields individually, which is problematic and slow. Many more columns will be added to this inventory as the enumeration process continues, and too much text in the terse description becomes a formatting problem and a distraction. Use hyperlinks to related documents to carry details forward.

Table 7.1 Preliminary Test Inventory from the Billing System Example, Sorted by PDR

PDR	PROJECT DESCRIPTION	P	IT CONTACTS	DEPENDENCIES AND NOTES
MGT0026	AcqrdCo to ParentCo Property Management	1*		
MGT0027	Treasury System	1		
MGT0030	Convert AcqrdCo to ParentCo Expenditure Billing Sys	1		
MGT0033	Fixed Assets & Project Accounting	2		
MGT0034	Interface AcqrdCo to ParentCo Oracle General Ledger	4		
MGT0098	TAX	1.5		
MGT0145	Budgets—AcqrdCo Acquisition	1		
MGT0150	Convert AcqrdCo to ParentCo Risk Management	2		
MGT0201	Convert AcqrdCo to ParentCo Oper. Support/Environ	2		
MGT0202	Taxi and T&E Lodging	5		
MGT0203	AcqrdCo to ParentCo Car Repair Billing	3		
MGT0218	Convert AcqrdCo to ParentCo ORACLE Purch and Mat	2		
MGT0219	Convert AcqrdCo to ParentCo Accounts Payable Sys	1		

*P = Priority (1 = highest, 5 = lowest)

On the Project Web Site

When I create one of these inventories today, I like to do it in a collaborative Web site. Each PDR can then be a hyperlink to the actual documentation in a secure, single-source environment. Using the technology in dynamically generated Web pages allows me to create a completely traceable inventory that is linked to all its parent and child documents.

I use the Microsoft SharePoint Team Services Web site to support team collaboration and documentation for my projects. It is included free with Microsoft Office 2002; so many people already have it. It supports collaboration features on both PC and Mac systems and is discussed in detail in Chapter 8, "Tools to Automate the Test Inventory."

Table 7.2 shows the preliminary inventory from Table 7.1 after the addition of the notes from the interviews. This inventory is sorted first by contact and then by priority.

The List Builder function allows me to import a spreadsheet with one sheet in it. It automatically converts the range of fields I select into a dynamic list in my project database. Figure 7.1 shows the preliminary inventory with interview notes in list form. This one was imported from the spreadsheet shown in Table 7.2. I can then add fields, create custom views, and let the whole team update the list online by clicking on the Edit button, and I can export the entire list back out to a spreadsheet any time I want. Again, the field size cannot exceed 255 characters or else the import fails.

As indicated earlier, I have been experimenting with high-function Web sites as document automation tools for some time—with mixed results. Like any other form of automation, they require a change in the way people do their work, and that initiative requires incentive. Recently, I have proved enough savings from the use of a team site to make a very compelling case for management to demand these changes. See Chapter 8, "Tools to Automate the Test Inventory," on using a SharePoint Team Services Web Site in your test effort for more information on this emerging way of doing business.

Table 7.2 Preliminary Billing Inventory with the Interview Input, Dependencies, Environmental Description, and Test Requirements

PDR	Project Description	Test Area	Priority	Confirmed	Test Order	Test Number	Test Group	IT Contacts	Dependencies and Notes	EDI	EIS	FAS	HRIS	IIDS	Mercury	TMC	TWS	TWSNet	TYMS
MGT0030	Convert AcqrdCo to ParentCo Expenditure Billing Sys	G&A	2		1			SME1, Dev1, BIZPart1	Test together 0033 + 0030 + 0218. Dependent on MGT0026 shared file: Rents Receivable file with Payroll (MGT0207) PeopleSoft + GL MGT0034				x						
MGT0026	AcqrdCo to ParentCo Property Management	G&A	3		2			SME1, Dev1, BIZPart1	Works with MGT0030 shared file: Rents Receivable file with Payroll (MGT0207) PeopleSoft + General Ledger MGT0034				x						
MGT0203	AcqrdCo to ParentCo Car Repair Billing	G&A	3		2			SME1, Dev1, BIZPart1	Needs MGT - Car Maint. (the mechanical part) owner SME2 w/Payroll (MGT0207) PeopleSoft + GL MGT0034				x		x				
MGT0098	TAX	G&A	2		1			SME1, Dev1, BIZPart2	With Payroll (MGT0207) PeopleSoft + GL MGT0034	x			x						
MGT0218	Convert AcqrdCo to ParentCo ORACLE Purch and Mat	G&A	2		1			SME1, Dev1, BIZPart2	together 0033 + 0030 + 0218 w/Payroll (MGT0207) PeopleSoft + GL MGT0034	x									
MGT0027	Treasury System	G&A	4		2			SME1, Dev1, BIZPart2	With Payroll (MGT0207) PeopleSoft + GL MGT0034	x			x						

Table 7.2 *(Continued)*

PDR	Project Description	Test Area	Priority	Confirmed	Test Order	Test Number	Test Group	IT Contacts	Dependencies and Notes	EDI	EIS	FAS	HRIS	IIDS	Mercury	TMC	TWS	TWSNet	TYMS
MGT0034	Interface AcqrdCo to ParentCo Oracle General Ledger	G&A	4		2			SME1, Dev1, BIZPart2	With Payroll (MGT0207) PeopleSoft + GL MGT0034	×			×						
MGT0033	Fixed Assets & Project Accounting	G&A	5		2			SME1, Dev1, BIZPart2	Test together 0033 + 0030 + 0218 w/Payroll (MGT0207) PeopleSoft + GL MGT0034	×			×						
MGT0145	Budgets - Conrail Acquisition	G&A	5		2			SME1, Dev1, BIZPart2	With Payroll (MGT0207) PeopleSoft + GL MGT0034	×			×					×	
MGT0219	Convert AcqrdCo to ParentCo Accounts Payable Sys	G&A	5		99	X		SME1, Dev1, BIZPart2	Effectively Closed										
MGT0150	Convert AcqrdCo to ParentCo Risk Management	G&A	2		1			SME-Dev2, Dev3	Data conversion	×									
MGT0201	Convert AcqrdCo to ParentCo Oper. Support/Environ	G&A	2		1			SME-Dev2, Dev3	Data conversion	×				×		×		×	×
MGT0202	Taxi and T&E Lodging	G&A	3		3			SME-Dev2, Dev3	Manual work around available for split day.									×	

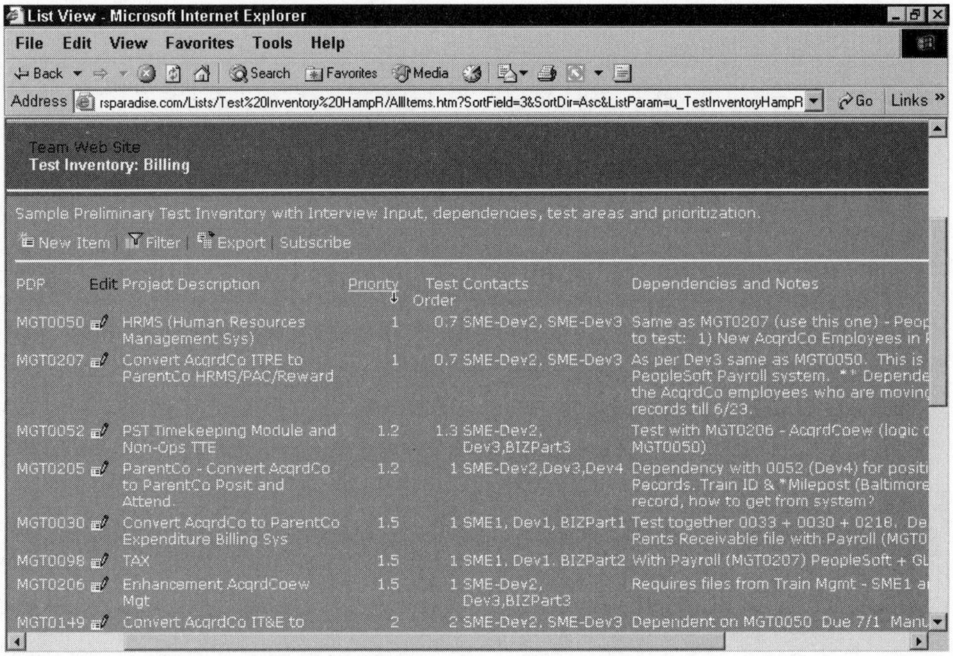

Figure 7.1 The inventory converted into a dynamic list on the project's Web site. (Powered by Microsoft SharePoint Team Services.)

Preliminary Inventory from a Web Project

The test inventory shown in Table 7.3 is an example of a preliminary or first-draft inventory from an early e-commerce application. This is how the inventory would look before any test analysis or design sessions. It is the second release of the product and has some categories that a new first-release product would not have, such as bug fixes.

Each of the main categories in the inventory was taken from a different project document or captured in a design meeting. If there is no suitable documentation, create a table containing every major feature and known or suspected facts about the software. These features may come from the marketing and design descriptions of the product, the user interface menus, or from the definitions of program procedures, functions, or object classes. As in the previous example, this preliminary inventory serves as the starting place for the SME interviews. The following paragraphs describe the main categories in the Web project inventory.

Table 7.3 Preliminary Inventory from a Web Project

Sample Application (Release 2.0)

BUG FIX INFORMATION

Fix for error #123 (see req. B477).

Fix for error #124 (see req. B501).

NEW FUNCTION (SEE REQ. <u>D071</u> AND <u>D072</u>)

New menu option #3: View mini clip.

Purchase option: Not available in some states.

Minimum order must be $30.00.

Method of payment limited to 2 credit cards.

STRUCTURAL/ENVIRONMENT INFORMATION

Enhancement-automatic detection for 50 modems. (Rel. 1 had auto-detect for 3 classes only).

Software installation is automatic at logon.

EXISTING APPLICATION BASE FUNCTION

Standard base function tests still apply:
All test suites for Version 1.0 will be run.

Our best system simulator.
(automated suite BSIM01 67% coverage of Release 1 Test Inventory for the Best Simulator functionality).

Message data flow checker
(automated suite DFCHECK 47% coverage of Release 1 test inventory for the data flow checker functionality).

Screen comparison— Pixel viewer
(automated suite PIXVIEW 77% coverage of Release 1 test inventory for the pixel viewer functionality).

ENVIRONMENT CATALOG

Operating Systems:

Client: Microsoft Windows 3.1 and higher, Win 95, Win 97, NT 3.51 with patches from #4 pack applied.

Host: To be determined.

Network: Under investigation by Net. Engineering plan due (?)

Hardware:

Computers: All machines on the operating system compatibility list.

Modems: All machines on the operating system compatibility list.

Bug Fix Information

This information would probably not exist in the first release of a product. In a new release of an existing product, there are almost always some bug fixes included in the release. The source documents here are the bug logs, the bug fix reports, and the product release notes.

New Function (See Req. D071 and D072)

This category comes from the design documents. The notes "See Req. D071 and D072" refer to specific requirements in the design document. If the project is a first-time implementation, all the functionality will probably be new. If it is a new release of an existing product, only a fraction of the functionality will be new.

Structural Information

These functions are closely related to the system rather than to the user interface. These are typically features that are not easily tested from the user interface and require separate attention. In most system test efforts, each of these categories has its own separate test inventory.

Application Base Function

This category is a listing of any existing test suites that will be used to reverify the existing functions in the system.

Environment Catalog

An environment catalog or inventory that lists the required hardware and software environments serves as the basis for this part of the test inventory. Testers usually identify a subset of all supported environments from the catalog for the test effort.

Identifying and Listing the Test Environments

What hardware and software must the system run on and with? Usually this information comes directly from the requirements documentation. Possible sources of these environmental requirements are development, in-house operations, and the client's operations group.

So far in the book, we have been discussing two of the main scenarios: the software that will deploy on a large, fairly static in-house system and the commercial software that will deploy to a large market and run in many environments. Many other scenarios are possible—for example, firmware, a small software product that will run in a finite number of environments.

Whatever your situation, you need to identify and list the environments that you will test during your effort. Each different type of scenario presents its own issues and challenges.

It doesn't matter whether the system is large or small. What is important is that in the real world, the test environment is never as big as production. However, in order to conduct meaningful testing, the integration environment must be in synch with production—or, at least, as close as possible. Thus, involvement with operations is vital, since that is where the expertise is. Hopefully, they will have adequate budget to create and support all the test environments that are needed.

I am a firm believer in the settling-pond approach to test environments. The settling-pond approach comes to us from wastewater management, a different but similar branch of engineering. The settling-pond approach uses a series of ponds to clean and purify wastewater. In the first pond, the heavy waste is encouraged to settle to the bottom, where it is pumped out. The top layer of fluid, now sans solids, is allowed to flow gently into the next tank for further cleaning. Cleaning may involve various activities, including the addition of aerobic entities and sanitizing chemicals. Each tank is its own environment, and each accomplishes a progressively more stringent clarification of the effluent by settlement. The settling-pond approach in testing is basically the same thing. It uses several test environments, each one cleaner than the last and more a mirror of the actual production environment. By the time the code gets to production, it has been well cleaned.

For example, at Prodigy, we performed module testing in a small, simulator-driven environment, and we performed our first integration tests in a shared integration environment. There was a lot of new code in the integration environment, so it was a fairly unstable place. Code might work one day and not the next. Once the application was thought stable and had passed its exit criteria, it was migrated to a cleaner integration environment where only tested, stable code was allowed. Finally, when it was ready to go to production, it was moved to a mirror environment for rehearsal and customer acceptance testing.

I still use this approach with all my Web-based applications. It is a very convenient way to test the application in the full production environment but still keep it private. It is also a good way to protect a functioning Web environment from new code. I make a backup mirror or, perhaps more correctly, a fall-back mirror, before new code is moved into production.

Note: Developers should not be allowed to control, modify, or even test in the tester's test environment. They must have their own.

Testing a Large System

If you are dealing with a large system, as in our real-world shipping example that we explored in Chapter 4, then the environmental definitions and requirements are probably already included in the PDRs. Operations is often way ahead of testers in the planning process. In this real-world shipping example in particular, the operations staff actually was the source of the environment information. They had purchased the equipment and scheduled its live dates before a test group was assembled. Development did not have the information; they relied completely on operations to supply them with the correct environments. In other large system projects that are deployed on the client's system, only the client will be able to tell you the environment requirements, and those requirements are probably different at each customer site.

If you are working on commercial software that will run in the real world, a separate analysis and definition step will probably be required when you enumerate the test environments for each customer. In my experience, performing customer-specific environmental evaluations has traditionally started by the software vendor publishing a list of supported hardware, software, and platform information to the customer. Then someone installs the software, and, finally, someone bulldozes through the system, fixing configurations, conflicts, and bugs as they are encountered.

Figure 7.2 shows the environmental definition for the real-world example. This screen shot is the Environment Catalog view of the billing inventory shown on the Web site, taken from the data shown in Table 7.2. Everything to the right of the column labeled EDI is an environment in the system—for example, EIS, FAS, HRIS, IIDS, Mercury, TMC, TWS, TWSNet, and TYMs. The X's at the left side of a column indicate that this particular project touches this environment in some way.

List View - Microsoft Internet Explorer

File   Edit   View   Favorites   Tools   Help

Back ▼ → ▼ ⊗ ⬆ ⬆ | Search Favorites Media | ▼ ⬆ ▼

Address s/Test%20Inventory%20HampR/Environment%20Catalog.htm?SortField=14&SortDir=Desc&ListParam=u_TestInventoryHampR ▼ Go Links »

Select a View: Sample Preliminary Test Inventory with Interview Input, dependencies, test areas and prioritization.

All Items   New Item | Filter | Export | Subscribe   Modify settings and

Project Dependencies

Environment Catalog

Edit	PDP	Project Description	Priority	Test Order	EDI	EIS	FAS	HRIS	IIDS	Mercury	TMC	TWS	TWSNet	TYMS
	MGT0207	Convert AcqrdCo ITRE to ParentCo HRMS/PAC/Reward	1	0.7				x						x
	MGT0205	ParentCo - Convert AcqrdCo to ParentCo Posit and Attend.	1.2	1				x					x	
	MGT0030	Convert AcqrdCo to ParentCo Expenditure Billing Sys	1.5	1				x						
	MGT0098	TAX	1.5	1	x			x						
	MGT0052	PST Timekeeping Module and Non-Ops TTE	1.2	1.3				x						
	MGT0026	AcqrdCo to ParentCo Property Management	3	2				x						
	MGT0203	AcqrdCo to ParentCo Car Repair Billing	3	2				x	x					

(Sort by HRIS)

Figure 7.2   Environment details provided during the second-level interviews.

This Web technology makes it very easy for the team to publish and maintain this information in a controlled environment. Any members of the team can be given authoring permission that lets them add, change, or delete any of this list information. Authors can even add columns to the list. The list concept also makes it very easy to sort or filter by any column. So it is very easy to pull a subset of items together—for example, all the projects that touch a certain system. When we combine this list with the list of tests, we can compile the list of tests that touch a system. We use this capability to build test suites on the fly as needed.

Testing Multiple Environments

If testing is automated, the entire test suite can be run against each environment each time code is turned over. In the Tester's Paradise sample application, a sample automated test effort found at the companion site to this book, www.testersparadise.com, environment testing is not mentioned directly in the overall count of tests because the test suite is automated and the test plan called for the test suite to be run simultaneously in all the test environments—hence, the assumption of 100 percent test availability. (The Tester's Paradise application is discussed further in Chapters 10, 12, and 13.)

Many projects today are funded by the organization that wants the product. So, you must first verify and validate the system in that first environment. Once the first customer is running, add the next environment to test; you already have the MITs tests in your suite.

If testing is manual, the prioritization of environments is critical, since there may not be sufficient time or resources to run the entire test suite against every environment. Consider Table 7.4. For example, if the test inventory contains 50 tests and takes 40 hours to run, every test environment you add to the test effort will require an additional 40 hours of test time, plus the time it takes to set up the test environment. In addition, when code fixes come in, they need to be tested in each of the environments.

Analysis and enumeration of test environments can be conducted using the same techniques as data sets, discussed in Chapter 13, "Data Analysis Techniques." An environment matrix is usually the easiest way to publish and track the environments that will be tested. A simple environment matrix is shown in Table 7.4. In this table, hyperlinks serve to link the environment name to the detail layers of the description. There are many ways to prepare an environment matrix. I present a different type in Chapter 8, "Tools to Automate the Test Inventory."

Adding Detail and Process Layers

The interview process is the most efficient method for reviewing, correcting, and enriching the test inventory and building the system-level process flows. The information gathered during the interviews is used to correct and refine the test inventory and to identify data dependencies and cross-project/intersystem dependencies.

The product of the interview process is a mature, prioritized test inventory that encompasses the entire system and includes the expert input of all the participants. The test inventory and its prioritized test items are used to build cost, sizing, and scheduling estimates during the planning phases. During the test effort, the test inventory becomes the test repository and test metrics database.

Table 7.4 Environment Description Matrix

ENVIRONMENT NAME	SERVER HARDWARE	OPERATING SYSTEM AND DATABASE	NUMBER OF USERS
C486-66-30O	2 Pentium 4 2.8-GHz, 120 GB HD	Windows XP Information Server, SQL Server	1
C486-33-30W	2 Pentium 4 2.0-GHz, 80-GB HD	Windows 2000 Advanced Server, SQL Server	1-50
C486-33-30W	2 Pentium 4 2.0-GHz, 80-GB HD	Windows 2000 Advanced Server, Oracle	1-100
C486-33-30S	To Be Determined 40-MB HD	Linux, MySQL	1-25
C486-33-30O	To Be Determined 40-MB HD	Unix, RDBMS	1-100
C486-33-30O	To Be Determined 40-MB HD	Unix, Informix	1-100
C486-33-30O	To Be Determined 40-MB HD	Unix, Oracle	1-100

Note: The number of possible combinations of hardware and software, users, and configurations often is larger than all other tests combined.

I have included the interview section here because it really is an integral part of building consensus and the agreement to test, along with determining the scope of the test effort. I use it to open management's eyes as to the size and complexity of what they are undertaking, as well as to educate myself and my team about what the project is and is not. The interview process or some other form of review needs to be conducted on the inventory before the analysis phases, which are discussed in Chapters 11, 12, and 13. Otherwise, your analysis will likely be a waste of time.

In addition to the project's coding requirements, it might also be appropriate for you to establish the environments that the system will run in during the interview process. However, I don't advise doing so during the interview if the number of environmental dependencies is extremely large or a political issue. I don't want the interviewee to become distracted from the core questions about his or her project.

Let's discuss two ways to approach this interview process: the traditional face-to-face interview approach and the modern Web-based collaborative approach. The preparation and materials are almost the same for both approaches. The difference is in the way we gather the information. The tried-and-true method using the interview process is described in the paragraphs that follow. The automated alternative is to prepare the materials electronically and place them in a high-function Web site. In this scenario, everyone is responsible for filling out the questionnaire as an electronic form, and you capture their responses in a database. I have tried for three years to use a Web site for this purpose and have only recently had any positive results that were actually preferable to the interview process. (I will talk about this project also.) Whichever method you choose, get support from upper management early in the process. If you don't, you will be pushing a big snowball uphill all by yourself. At any time it could overwhelm and crush you. Be especially cautious if this interview process is something new in your culture. If you opt for the interview approach, you will find instructions on how to perform the interviews in the following section, *The Interviews: What and How to Prepare.* Feel free to alter the process to fit your needs. Just keep your goals clearly stated and clearly in view.

The Interviews: What and How to Prepare

In the ideal case, I plan two levels of interviews for the system test planning effort: high-level interviews (duration: 15 to 30 minutes) and mid-level interviews (duration: 30 to 60 minutes). Interviewees are solicited from each of the project areas: IT, support, and system groups. Management may decide to go with just one set of interviews; I leave the choice to them. The trick is to do the best you can with what they give you.

Why Two Sets of Interviews?

The people I need to see are the SMEs. So why talk to the managers? The answer is, "because it is polite." I always offer management the choice and the opportunity to control the situation. That's what they are supposed to do, right?

Bona fide subject matter experts are few in numbers, expensive, and generally grossly overbooked. Development managers are especially protective of their wizards. In a bureaucratic shop, or worse, in a politically polarized situation, you will probably derail your effort if you try to go right to the SMEs. If you only rely on your personal charm, you will only get a subset of the SMEs into your interviews, and you could get into trouble. If you can't get management support, then by all means try the direct approach, but be careful.

The Expendable Tester Ploy

One of the values that I add to a test project when I come in as a consultant is that I am "expendable." That's part of the reason that my consulting rates go so high. I am sacrificed on a fairly regular basis. This may sound odd, but let me explain.

In a big project, there are lots of politics. They usually have to do with budget and deadlines (usually impossible to meet). Or worse, they involve projects that have already gone bad and someone is trying to put a good face on the failure. I am often charged with detecting such situations and failures.

The normal tester who works for this company doesn't have the clout, the budget, or the perspective to get through the opposition that a development manager/director or even vice president can dish out. And the tester shouldn't even try. Hence, one of my best uses as a contractor is to "test the water."

When I walk into a planning meeting with development and lay out this "best-practice" methodology for testing the system, it is likely that not everyone is delighted about it. Typically, there are many reasons for the participants to disagree with what I have to say. These reasons are usually related to budget, but they can also be about impossible delivery dates, and the ambition of employees who want to be recognized as "experts".

Asking regular employees to risk their pensions in an undertaking of this type is not fair or right. A shrewd manager or director (usually a vice president) knows a lot about these intrigues, but that person will always need to find out exactly what is going on "this time." So we engage in a scenario that is a lot like staking the virgin out in the wasteland and watching to see who comes to dinner.

I am normally sacrificed to an ambush in a routine meeting somewhere just before the actual code delivery date. And when the dust and righteous indignation settle, all the regular employees are still alive and undamaged. My vice president knows who his or her enemies are. And the developers have a false sense of security about the entire situation. Meanwhile, the now dead contractor (me) collects her pay and goes home to play with her horses and recuperate.

The message for you normal employees who are testers is hopefully that this information will help you avoid a trap of this type. In any case, don't try these heroics yourself, unless you want to become a contractor/writer. But do keep these observations in mind, as they can be helpful.

Prepare an overview with time frame and goals statements, like the one listed under the *Sample Memo to Describe the Interview Process* heading in Appendix C, "Test Collateral Samples and Templates." Also prepare your SME questionnaire (see the *Sample Project Inventory and Test Questionnaire for the Interviews* in Appendix C), and send both to upper management. Get support from management as high up as you can. Depending on your position, your manager may need to push it up on your behalf. Just remind her or him that it is in the manager's best interest, too. In a good scenario, you will get upper management's support before you circulate it to the department heads and all the participants. In the ideal scenario, upper management will circulate it for you. This ensures that everyone understands that you have support and that they *will* cooperate. Here are my general outlines for the middleweight to heavyweight integration effort in the real-world example.

My Outline for High-Level Interviews

I plan for high-level interviews to take 15 to 30 minutes. (See the sample in Appendix C.) This is just a sample. Your own needs may differ greatly, but make sure you have a clear goal.

My outline for this type of interview is as follows:

GOALS

1. Identify (for this expert's area):
   - The project deliverables
   - Owners of deliverables (mid-level interviewees)
   - Project dependencies and run requirements
     - Interproject
     - Cross-domain functions/environment
     - Database and shared files
     - Business partners' projects
   - System and environment requirements and dependencies
   - The location of, and access to, the most recent documentation

2. Get management's opinion on the following:
   - Ranking priorities (at the project level)
   - Schedules
     - Delivery
     - Dependencies
   - Testing

This next section was added after the preliminary inventory was built. These items were added based on what we learned during the preliminary interviews and the meetings that followed. I talk about the day-in-the-life scenarios later in this chapter.

3. Go through the day-in-the-life scenarios to understand and document, answering the following questions:
   - Where do the new projects fit? (If they don't fit, identify the missing scenarios.)
   - How do the systems fit together; how does the logic flow?
   - Which steps/systems have not changed and what dependencies exist?

My Outline for Mid-Level Interviews

I plan for mid-level interviews to take from 30 to 60 minutes. (See the sample in Appendix C and the section *Example Questions from the Real-World Example*, which follows. Your own needs may differ greatly from what's shown in the sample, but make sure you have a clear goal. Be sure to ask the developer what type of presentation materials he or she prefers, and have them on hand. See my discussion of the "magic" questions in the *Example Questions from the Real-World Example* coming up.

My outline for this type of interview is as follows:

GOALS

1. Find out everything possible about the project—what it does, how it is built, what it interoperates with, what it depends on, and so on. If appropriate, build and review the following:

- The logic flows for the projects and systems
- The test inventory
    - Enumerate and rank additional test items and test steps in the test inventory
    - Data requirements and dependencies
    - All systems touched by the project

2. Get answers to the following questions (as they apply):
- What will you or have you tested?
- How long did it take?
- How many testers did you need?
- What do you think the test group needs to test?

3. Identify additional test sequences.

4. Identify requirements for test tools.

5. Establish the environment inventory and dependencies, if appropriate.

Example Questions from the Real-World Example

From the real-world example, here are the questions that I asked in the interview questionnaire:

1. Are these your PDRs? Are there any missing or extra from/on this list?

2. Is the project description correct?

3. Which test area is responsible for testing your code and modules before you turn them over to integration test?

4. What is the priority of this project in the overall integration effort based on the risk of failure criteria?

5. Who are the IT contacts for each project?

6. What are your dependencies?

7. In addition to integrating this code into the new system, what other types of testing are requested/appropriate:
- Function
- Load

- Performance
- Data validation
- Other
- No test
- System test

8. What databases are impacted by this project?
9. What else do we testers need to know?

Conducting the Interviews

Schedule your interviews as soon after the statement is circulated as possible; strike while the iron is hot. Leave plenty of time between the individual interviews. There are a couple of reasons for this; one is to make sure that you can have time to debrief your team and record all your observations. Another reason is that you don't want to rush away from an expert that has more to tell you.

Prepare a brief but thorough overview of the purpose of the interview and what you hope to accomplish. I use it as a cover sheet for the questionnaire document. Send one to each attendee when you book the interview, and have plenty of printouts of it with you when you arrive at the interview so everybody gets one. Email attachments are wonderful for this purpose.

Be flexible, if you can, about how many people attend the interview. Some managers want all their SMEs at the initial meeting with them so introductions are made once and expectations are set for everyone at the same time. Other managers want to interview *you* before they decide if they want you talking to their SMEs. Every situation is different. The goal is to get information that will help everyone succeed. So, let the interviewees know that this process will make their jobs easier, too.

Keep careful records of who participates and who puts you off. If a management-level interviewee shunts you to someone else or refuses to participate at all, be sure to keep records of it. It has been my experience that the managers who send me directly to their developers are usually cutting right to the chase and trying to help jump-start my effort by maximizing my time with the SMEs. The ones that avoid me altogether are usually running scared and have a lot to hide. For now, just document it and move forward where you can.

How to Conduct the Interviews

Be sure that you arrive a little early for the interview and are ready to go so that they know you are serious. Hopefully, the interviewees have taken a look at the questionnaire before the meeting, but don't be insulted if they have not. In all my years of conducting this type of interview, I have only had it happen twice that I arrived to find the questionnaire already filled out. However, they usually do read the cover sheet with the purpose and goals statement. So make it worth their while. If you can capture their self-interest in the cover sheet, you have a much better chance of getting lots of good information from them. They will have had time to think about it, and you will need to do less talking, so you can do more listening.

Print out the entire inventory with all current information, sorted by priority/delivery and so on, and take it with you so you can look up other projects as well. Take a copy of the inventory that you have sorted so that the items relevant to the particular interview are at the top.

Give all attendees a copy of each of these materials, and have a dedicated scribe on hand, if possible.

Instructions for Interviewers

My short set of instructions to interviewers is as follows:

1. Be quick. Ask your questions 1, 2, 3—no chitchat. Set a time limit and be finished with your questions on time.

   Finish your part on time but be prepared to spend as much extra time as the interviewee wants. Go through each question in order and write down the answers.

2. Listen for answers to questions that you didn't ask. Often, the developers have things that they want to tell you. Give them the chance. These things are usually very important, and you need to be open to hear them. I will give you some examples later in this section.

3. Follow up afterward by sending each participant a completed inventory. Close the loop, and give them the chance to review what you wrote. Confirm that you did hear them and that what they told you was important. Sometimes they have something to add, and they need to have the opportunity to review and correct as well.

Another important reason for doing this is that often developers look at what other developers said and find things that they didn't know. Many integration issues and code conflicts are detected in this way. It is much cheaper to fix these problems before the code moves from development to test.

4. Let them hash out any discrepancies; don't propose solutions to their problems.

In the real-world example, interviews were scheduled with the directors of each development area. The directors were asked to name the developers from their areas who would participate in the second level of interviews. Some directors were pleased with the process; some were not. Only one of the seven directors refused to participate in the interview process. Two of the directors had their development leads participate in both sets of interviews. Operations, customer support, and several of the business partners also asked to take part in the interview process. Including these groups not only helped enrich the information and test requirements of the inventory, it also gained allies and extra SME testers for the integration test effort.

An interview was scheduled to take no longer than 20 minutes, unless development wanted to spend more time. We were able to hold to this time line. It turned out that several developers wanted more time and asked for a follow-up meeting. Follow-up interviews were to be scheduled with the development managers after the results of the preliminary interviews were analyzed.

Analyzing the Results: Lessons Learned

Refer back to Table 7.2, which, you'll recall, incorporates the notes from the interviews into the preliminary inventory from Table 7.1. This inventory is sorted first by contact and then by priority. Notice that under the Priority column, "P," several of the initial priorities have been changed radically. In this project it turned out to be a profound mistake for the testers to estimate the relative priority of the projects based on a project's documentation and budget. Not only were the estimates very far from the mark established by development, but the test group was soundly criticized by the developers for even attempting to assign priorities to their projects.

The lesson learned in this case was be prepared, be thorough, but don't guess. We learned that lesson when we guessed at the priorities, but learning this lesson early saved us when we came to this next item. Notice the new column, TS—that is, Test Order. I will talk about it in detail in the next section.

The next thing to notice in the table are all the dependencies. One of the unexpected things we learned was that when the dependencies were listed out in this way, it became clear that some of the SMEs were really overloaded between their advisory roles and their actual development projects.

And, finally, the columns with the X's are impacted systems. This is the environmental description for this project. Each column represents a separate system in the data center. The in-depth descriptions of each system were available in the operations data repository.

When the full post-interview test inventory was published, the magnitude of the effort began to emerge. The inventory covered some 60 pages and was far larger and more complicated than the earlier estimates put forth by development.

When I go into one of these projects, I always learn things that I didn't expect—and that's great. I can give management this very valuable information, hopefully in time, so that they can use it to make good decisions. In this case, we discovered something that had a profound effect on the result of the integration effort, and the whole project. Just what we discovered and how we discovered it is discussed in the next section.

Being Ready to Act on What You Learn

As you learn from your interviews, don't be afraid to update your questionnaire with what you have learned. Send new questions back to people that you already interviewed, via email, if you can. Give them the chance to answer at a time that's convenient in a medium that you can copy and paste into your inventory. Every effort is different, and so your questions will be, too. Look for those magic questions that really make the difference to your effort. What do I mean by that? Here are a couple of examples.

What Was Learned in the Real-World Example

In the real-world example, the most important thing that we had to learn was very subtle. When I asked developers and directors what priority to put on various projects, their answer wasn't quite what I expected. It took me about four interviews before I realized that when I asked,

> *"What priority do you put on this project?"*

The question they were hearing and answering was actually

> *"In what order do these projects need to be delivered, assembled, and tested?"*

What emerged was the fact that the greatest concern of the developers had to do with the order in which items were integrated and tested, not the individual risk of failure of any module or system.

This realization was quite profound for my management. But it made perfect sense when we realized that the company had never undertaken such a large integration effort before and the individual silos lacked a vehicle for planning a companywide integration effort. In the past they had been able to coordinate joint efforts informally. But this time just talking to each other was not enough. Each silo was focused on their own efforts, each with their own string Gantt on a wall somewhere, but there was no split day integration planning organization in place, only the operations-led integration test effort. So there was no overall critical path or string Gantt for the entire effort.

I added a new column to the test inventory, "Test Order," shown as the sixth column in Table 7.2. But it became clear very quickly that no individual silo could know all the requirements and dependencies to assign the test order of their projects in the full integration effort. This realization raised a large concern in management.

The beginning of the solution was started by inviting all interested parties to a required meeting in a large conference room with a big, clear, empty wall. Operations sponsored the meeting, and it was organized by the test group. We assigned a different color for each of the group silos. For example, accounting (which was the parent silo for billing) was assigned green, the color of money; documentation was gray; development was white; and so on. We printed each line from the preliminary inventory at the top of a piece of appropriately colored paper, complete with PDR, group description, IT owner, and dependencies columns.

About "Big Bang" Efforts

In this real-world example, upper management had promised their regulating agency that the transition from two companies to one company would be unde-tectable to the public and all customers. In this light it seemed that the best approach was to go to bed as two companies and wake up on as one company. This approach is called the "big bang" method. It is intended to minimize outages and aftershocks. Critical transitions are often performed using this approach—for example, banking mergers, critical system switchovers, and coups in small countries.

In a big bang, good planning is not enough by itself. Success requires that *everything* relating to the event be carefully choreographed and rehearsed in advance. Rehearsal is an unfamiliar concept to most developers, and so success usually depends on a specialized integration team with far-reaching powers.

After the prioritization fiasco, I had learned not to "guess." So rather than waste my time doing a preliminary layout on the wall that would let them focus on criticizing my group instead of focusing on their integration issues, I gave each director the stack of papers containing his or her PDRs as they arrived. We also bought a large quantity of 2-by-2-inch sticky pads in the silos' colors and gave each member of a silo a pad of stickies in their color.

We explained that the purpose of the meeting was to clarify the order in which the projects should be integrated and tested. And we invited the developers to stick their PDR project sheets on the wall in the correct order for delivery, integration, and testing. We also asked them to write down on the paper all the integration-related issues as they became aware of them during the meeting. Directors and managers were invited to claim the resulting issues by writing them on a sticky along with their name and putting the sticky where the issue occurred.

I started the meeting off with one PDR in particular that seemed to have dependencies in almost all the silos. I asked the director who owned it to tape it to the wall and lead the discussion. The results were interesting, to say the least. The meeting was scheduled to take an hour; it went on for much longer than that. In fact, the string Gantt continued to evolve for some days after (see Figure 7.3). We testers stayed quiet, took notes, and handed out tape. The exercise turned up over a hundred new dependencies, as well as several unanticipated bottlenecks and other logistical issues.

Figure 7.3   A string Gantt on the wall.

Fact: Integration is a matter of timing.

The "sticky meeting," as it came to be called, was very valuable in establishing where at least some of the potential integration problems were. One look at the multicolored mosaic of small paper notes clustered on and around the project papers, along with the handwritten pages tacked on to the some of the major projects, was more than enough to convince upper management that integration was going to require more that just "testing."

The experience of the sticky meeting sparked one of the high-ranking split day business partners to invent and champion the creation of the day-in-the-life scenarios, affectionately called "dilos." The idea behind the day-in-the-life scenarios was to plot, in order, all the activities and processes that a business entity would experience in a day. For example, we could plot the day in the life of a customer, a freight carrier, a customer service rep, and so on.

This champion brought in a team of professional enablers (disposable referees) to provide the problem-solving structure that would take all the participants through the arduous process of identifying each step in the dilos, mapping the steps to the PDRs and the system itself, recording the results, and producing the documents that were generated as a result of these meetings.

The dilos became the source of test requirements for virtually all system integration testing. They were used to plot process interaction and timing requirements. They also served as the foundation for the most important system test scenarios.

What Was Learned in the Lightweight Project

During the last set of interviews I did at Microsoft, the magic question was "What do I need to know about your project?" The minute I asked that question, the SME went to the white board, or plugged her PC into the conference room projector and started a PowerPoint presentation, or pulled up several existing presentations that she emailed to me, usually during the meeting, so that they were waiting for me when I got back to my office. I got smarter and put a wireless 802.11 card in my notebook so I could receive the presentation in situ, and I worked with the presentation as we conducted the interview. The big improvement was adding a second scribe to help record the information that was coming at us like water out of a fire hose.

The big lesson here is this: If you can use automation tools to build your inventory, do it. The wireless LAN card cost $150, but it paid for itself before the end of the second interview. The developer emailed her presentation to me in the meeting room. Because of the wireless LAN card, I got it immediately. For the rest of the interview, I took my notes into the presentation, cutting and pasting from the developer's slides into my questionnaire as needed. And I was able to publish my new interview results directly to the team Web site before I left the meeting room. After the meeting, I was finished. I didn't have to go back to my office and find an hour to finish my notes and publish them.

We have discussed automation techniques for documentation in a general way in this chapter. For specific details and picture examples, see Chapter 8, "Tools to Automate the Test Inventory."

Summary

It doesn't matter what weight your project is; you need a test inventory. It will help you at every stage of the test effort. In this chapter, I have shown you two examples of preliminary test inventories. We learned a great deal just assembling the preliminary test inventories. Neither one has a single test attached to it yet, and still it is valuable from the very beginning.

When you are building your test inventory, start with the requirements. Even if you don't have formal requirements, you can list what the product is supposed to do.

Be sure you identify and list the environments that you will have to test. In the heavyweight example, we needed to do a lot of planning to integrate the various projects in their test systems. But once there, the systems were fairly static. For example, we didn't need to test one application against four different RDBMS products. If you are working on a lightweight project, like a Web-based application, you will be more concerned with listing how many RDBMS products you need to test against. Remember, the number of possible combinations of hardware and software, users, and configurations often is larger than all other tests combined.

The product of the interview process is a mature, prioritized test inventory that includes the entire system. Ideally, it is built with the input of all the participants. The way you plan and conduct your interviews is a very important step in building a good inventory and getting an accurate prioritization of the items on it. The test inventory and its prioritized test items are used to build cost, sizing, and scheduling estimates during the planning phases. During the test effort, the test inventory becomes the test repository and test metrics database.

Expect some surprises and be ready to act on what you learn. It could give you the opportunity to add value early in the planning stages of the test effort—long before any testing is being done.

And finally, remember, integration is a matter of timing. Planning is probably not as useful as planning and rehearsing.

In Chapter 8, I show you the tools I use to construct my test inventories and automate my metrics calculation. As you will see, you probably already have these tools.

For Further Exploration

Before you go on to the next chapter, it's a good idea to try out your understanding of what you read in this chapter. These concepts are not difficult to understand, but fitting them into different types of projects requires a fair amount of creativity. Here is an opportunity for you to apply the concepts presented in this chapter before you go on to read about how to automate the construction of your inventory.

Imagine you are applying for a job as a test engineer at TestersParadise .com. You have just been presented with product descriptions for Product A and Product B. After reading through the descriptions, perform the following steps:

1. Construct a preliminary test inventory for each product.

2. Determine what is missing from these descriptions.

3. Determine what questions you would have for the designers and developers.

Product A

This product is a flexible Web conferencing system, or *forum*, which enables online discussions via the Web on intranets and the Internet. People can share information with each other using their Web browsers. The product provides a wide range of options for configuring discussions and managing access and security. The system can scale from hobby class Web sites, to enterprisewide systems, to online Web services. All the system administration and configuration is accomplished through the Web. In addition, Product A features:

- *A simple user interface with highly customizable layout.* This allows the user to easily adjust the format of each conference, including graphics, background colors, custom HTML headers and footers, and announcement text.

- *Unlimited conferences.* The user can create any number of conferences on the same system.

- *Threaded discussions.* The product uses an intuitive system of nested, threaded discussions that facilitates communication and increases the effectiveness of online interaction.

- *Advanced searching.* Users can use powerful searching tools to find messages or search for postings by author, date, keyword, or discussion area.

- *Flexible security.* The system provides highly configurable security options that meet the needs of a wide range of public and private conference configurations. It enables the use of transparent user identification with persistent cookies and email-back user verification.

- *Easy administration.* The administrator can administer the system via a Web browser. The system uses simple wizards to set up and configure all system and user settings.

Product B

This product is a Win2000/XP device driver for IrDA-compatible mobile computers. (IrDA stands for Infrared Data Association.) This driver provides a fast, reliable, and convenient way to exchange data wirelessly to or from your desktop computer with any IrDA-equipped laptop computer. You can access data and applications from local floppy or hard drives, access networked data, or print to any printer that is connected to your desktop computer or network. In addition, this product:

- Supports the Plug-and-Play standards.

- Supports IrDA IrLAP (Infrared Link Access Protocol) to keep your data safe and error-free.

- Supports IrDA infrared communications specification.

- Transmits and receives data at 115,200 baud with baud-rate switching capabilities.

- Uses standard PC serial (RS-232C) connections (9-pin or 25-pin).

As you can see, you could formulate any number of possible answers and questions about these projects. You can check your answers and compare notes with others online at www.testersparadise.com.

CHAPTER 8

Tools to Automate the Test Inventory

When I worked at Prodigy, each of my projects got its own 3-inch, blue, three-ring binder. The binder contained all the information required to understand, validate, and verify the project. Topics were separated by sheets with plastic topic tabs and annotated sticky notes of every color that stuck out from between pages at odd angles. The blue book was typically full to overflowing. The papers in it were a colorful hodge-podge of photocopies, faxes, and hand-drawn pictures. The formal ones were on quadrille grid paper, but many were on notepad paper and the odd napkin. The colorful part was not only due to the stickies but because most pages were liberally retouched in yellow, pink, and green highlighter.

The inventory figured prominently in the binder, as did the bug statistics and the list of open issues (closed issues were removed to a binder of their own to conserve space), delivery schedules, project dependencies, and lots of other test essentials. I took a lot of ribbing because I showed up at every meeting with one of those stuffed binders. But when anyone—manager, developer, tester, operations support, or even business partner—wanted to know something about the application or the system it was running in, he or she came to ask me to consult the blue book.

Today, my blue books live in my Web servers, under the regular scrutiny of my search engine. Now when someone wants to know something about the project, I direct him or her to the appropriate search page. Even though I can now keep more information than in the binder days, the type of information that I keep in Web sites hasn't changed much over the years, but I create it and maintain it a lot faster and with a lot less work. Where there were once sticky notes, today there are hyperlink menus. The colorful highlighter marks have been replaced by the search engine's transient gray highlight covering your search keywords in a document "hit." All in all, it's bigger, better, faster, and a lot smarter than the blue books, but when I go out consulting, most of the testers I meet are still trudging around with stacks of paper and no Web site to call their own.

Except for the time testers spend testing, most of their time is devoted to managing and preparing test documentation. Automation techniques for test documentation are both an excellent quality improvement opportunity and a potent tool for shortening the time required for documentation, and therefore, the test effort. My studies from 1993 to 1997 showed that document automation can reduce the time required to write the test plan, test scripts, and reports by as much as two-thirds.

My work with high-function Web sites from 1997 to 2003 has shown that Web-based automation can be used to automate the creation of many additional types of documents, such as test scripts, checklists, and status reports, as they are needed. This documentation is always up-to-date, and all parties are assured that they are getting the same document all the time, no matter where they are in the world. Perhaps even more importantly, the built-in search engine in the Web server allows the testers to find the information they are looking for in all those documents quickly.

The savings from this type of automation can be profound, and it can also serve to facilitate culture change in an organization. I have noticed that the speed with which testers deliver an answer to management has a direct relationship with their credibility. Of course, the correctness of the answer is also a factor, but I will leave that for a different discussion.

In this chapter, we discuss both types of automation in this feature. We also talk about the tools and the process that I use to evolve the test inventory. Again, I use different tools and different processes based on the needs of the project. The steps described are offered as guidelines and seed ideas only; they do not need to be followed precisely. Feel free to be innovative in the sources you use to begin your test inventory. Each of the tools discussed in this chapter has its strengths and weaknesses.

General rule of thumb: Use the sharpest tool in the shop for the job at hand.

Recently, a fellow tester asked me to evaluate a dedicated test tracking tool. The tool provided special document templates for most required test documentation, as well as customizable forms to be used to create and track tests. Finally, all documents could be stored in a specialized Web site. His group wanted to improve their efficiency, and they were willing to spend their own time to learn to use this tool set. The license for the 10-person test group would cost about $15,000.

I evaluated the tool and had my CS staff, who are my in-house testers, look at it as well. All of us had the same reaction: "Why spend money on a tool that just does what we already do with our Microsoft Office tools?"

Instead of telling the tester's group this, I asked what their goals were for the new tool, how quickly they thought they could convert to it, and what they thought the payback time would be for it. Then I asked them to consider what it would cost them to invest in their knowledge of Microsoft Office, which they already had installed, to learn how to create their own forms and document templates, store them in their own database, and use a SharePoint Team Services site for their specialized test Web site.

The answer surprised them. It turned out to be far more efficient for them to spend money on themselves to become educated on how to better use the tools they already had on their PCs. There were several additional benefits to the test department, as well as the improved efficiency of the next test effort. Chief among these was the prestige that came with deploying and capitalizing on one of the most useful and technically advanced Web sites in their company.

Sometimes the answer is simply to invest in learning how to use what you have better—learning to use more of its capability more efficiently. It makes you more valuable, too.

Note: Invest in yourself; learn to use the tools you have well.

Now let's look at this process using tools from the Microsoft Office Suite. For better or for worse, the Microsoft products are ubiquitous, and even high school kids today have training in the use of Word, Excel, and often PowerPoint. With the advent of the Web, there are more and more international projects being undertaken, and Office is there too, with internationalized dictionaries and even some modest translation capabilities. I apologize to those of you who use a different office product, word processor, spreadsheet, and so on. However, even though the specifics may vary, these instructions should give you the general direction in which to go.

The Evolving Test Inventory

The inventory precedes the test plan, or, in my case, the contract to test. When the inventory is fully fleshed and agreed upon, I can add the other items that the test plan needs in order to be acceptable. In the case of the heavyweight real-world example that we discuss throughout the book, the test plan was actually a master test plan that enumerated the test plans of the projects that it comprised and described how those projects would become integrated, verified, and validated. Its inventory contained all the functions and features of the projects it contained, appropriately rolled up to the high level. It was over 500 pages and contained references to over 1,000 related project documents. The project documentation for all the related projects filled an entire bookcase.

In a Web-based or other lightweight project, there is probably only one project. Its functions and features are enumerated in the inventory, as we discussed in Chapters 6 and 7. The inventory is the bulk of the test plan. It might be 10 pages long. I recently completed a project that used a PowerPoint slide deck and an Excel spreadsheet as the test plan; it was primarily made up of the test inventory. Most of the plan was built using FrontPage to create the links and deploy the slides. Most of the composition and information gathering was done online using our SharePoint Team Services Web site and its dynamic lists. The project was integrated, tested, and deployed with no major problems, on time and within the budget. It had project team members in four countries and three time zones, speaking three different languages. One of the biggest savings in the project was because we didn't even run up a long-distance phone bill.

> **Note:** The inventory document is a compilation that I will add to my test plan, or put another way, *the inventory is the foundation of my test plan.*

The Process in Brief

I like to start my test inventories in PowerPoint. PowerPoint is a good tool to help sketch the project quickly in an outline. This tool makes it easy to change the order and importance of any item or slide simply by dragging it wherever it should go and dropping it there. Even if there is extensive preexisting documentation, PowerPoint makes it easy to account for all the major pieces and produce an outline quickly.

In some projects, I am handed a stack of documents when I walk in the door; in others, I have to interview the developers, sales staff, and customer service to find out what the project entails. In either of these situations, I will probably construct the preliminary outline in PowerPoint and then export it to Word for embellishment and details. The heading levels that I apply to outline elements in PowerPoint are carried across to Word, and they allow me to import my rolled-up inventory items with no extra work. I use the outline view in both PowerPoint and Word to organize inventory items and to perform the rollup. And I can generate the short list that I will use in the columns of the inventory that I put into table form either in Word or Excel.

I can use Word's internal RTF fields to link project documents into my new inventory. But for the most part, I use hyperlinks for this purpose today.

Once the interviews are complete and I have my prioritization underway, I usually move the larger projects to a spreadsheet. You can simply copy and paste the columns from the Word table to the spreadsheet. For the expanded inventories that include cross-references to environments and functions, a spreadsheet is the tool of choice because it is so convenient to keep the various tables on individual pages in the spreadsheet workbook.

With the interactive data-sharing technology available today in the PC environment, it does not really matter which of these tools you choose. They each offer certain advantages, and you can pass your work back and forth between them with great facility. Don't be afraid of learning more about a Microsoft Office tool.

Finally, and most progressive of all, I can import my spreadsheets directly into my SharePoint Team Services Project Web site and allow the entire team to participate in the project. In the next sections, I will show you what the process looks like in each of these tools.

Inventory in PowerPoint

The preliminary test inventory used in the test estimation process normally starts with items from the project documentation—the requirement, function, and design specifications. I begin a list that includes all of these items that I know about, and I add new ones as they appear. Often, the inventory is built during design and review meetings. In any event, the process needs a starting place. I use PowerPoint more and more frequently as the tool to document this early "coming together" phase of the test inventory.

If the project documentation is not suitable, then a list of the primary functions and a list of all the menu options in the software is a good starting point. These functions can be taken from the user interface or source code listings, if necessary. Finally, the environment requirements need to be established and documented as discussed in Chapter 7, "How to Build a Test Inventory." In this type of effort, I would normally use PowerPoint to capture the initial test inventory and then import it into a Word document.

Figure 8.1 shows an example of this process. It features the sample inventory from the book. The outline view of PowerPoint is a good recording tool. I use it extensively in meetings to keep my notes.

PowerPoint is a powerful composition tool that is nimble enough to allow the user to keep up with a spirited design meeting. You can make structural changes interactively and then share your resulting outline with others. The outline is a properly formatted set of document headings, and you can easily move it to other document formats like RTF, Word's DOC, and HTML.

You can export the PowerPoint outline directly to Word by selecting *File*, *Send To*, *menu option*, and then selecting *Microsoft Word*. You then have several options that let you control the format of the exported information in your Word document.

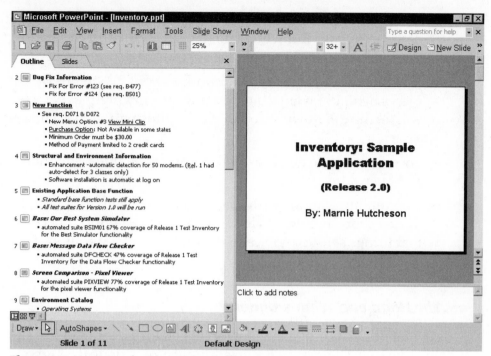

Figure 8.1   Inventory in PowerPoint Outline view.

PowerPoint's terse bullet-oriented makeup cannot carry the detail layers forward. This may not be perceived as a problem in a RAD/Agile shop, where there are no detail layers, but it can be crippling in a plan-driven environment. When you actually have data under these topics that you have to keep track of, you have outgrown PowerPoint, and it's time to move your outline to Word. Which brings me to my next topic: keeping my inventory in a document.

Inventory in a Document

For my verbose inventory document, I want to collect or link all the project information that I can into a single document, and I need the ability to get whatever view of that information that I want. After all, I am not creating the inventory because someone told me to. I am creating the inventory because it is my most powerful tool. As such, I need to be able to find anything quickly, and I need to view the inventory in as much or as little detail as necessary at that moment. For example:

- Initially, I need the high-level view; I don't want to get bogged down in details. But when I am trying to construct scenarios, I need to be able to find out what's under the hood.

- I need to move huge topics around without losing bits or leaving pieces behind. I want a single source for my high-level views that will let me dig down through all the information that I have if necessary.

- I need to include all types of documents, pictures, equations, tables, and even spreadsheets.

- For communications with others, such as meetings, I need to produce a short high-level view, and for my test effort, I need a view that brings selected topics to the foreground without losing all the other topics.

The Hood and What's Under It

As I mentioned, my management likes their information in short, succinct bursts. The man who was my vice president throughout all my years at Prodigy maintained that if you couldn't fit it into three to five bullets on a page, then you didn't understand it well enough to explain it to him. In all my years, I have kept this as a guiding principle. It has served me well.

Consequently, when I prepare for a report or status meeting, I want the shortest list possible—without losing the feeling that there is depth behind it. So I evolved a system to use the Outline view and the table of contents field in my verbose inventory document to do this.

Inventory in Outline View

I can show only the highest levels or I can show all the main topics and their subtopics just by selecting the heading levels that I want to display. A heading level 1 is the highest, usually the title of the chapter, and I typically don't go below 5.

The Office Tools: Collaboration and High-Function Web Sites

I use Microsoft Word to create and maintain my verbose inventory document. Word's superior table manipulation features, its ability to incorporate graphics and link multiple documents, and its superior built-in graphing tools make it ideal for these tasks. One other feature that has become very important is that these documents can be saved as Hypertext Markup Language (HTML) and put online in an internal private Web site, or intranet, to create a single-source test repository that is usable by people who don't have Microsoft Office.

Any of the major Windows-based word processors will probably perform most of the tasks described here. With Word, you can also send documents and receive them from the other Office tools like PowerPoint, and you can copy and paste tables to and from Excel. There is little or no conversion required on your part.

Today, I use Office 2002 because of its rich support for Web content and for the collaboration features it offers. At the time of this writing, most people are using Office 2000 and Microsoft Word for Windows version 6.0.

I use Microsoft SharePoint Team Services to power my test Web sites. The product is an add-on to the Internet Information Server that works in conjunction with the FrontPage server extensions to provide a host of Web components that interact with Microsoft SQL Server to create an automated interactive Web site. The SharePoint Team Services site also supports direct editing of Office documents by the Office 2002 applications. The site offers a rich set of project management tools, as well as document repositories. Figure 8.2 shows the home page of testersparadise.com, the Web site that supports this book. All the content on this page is generated dynamically. You add new announcements and events by simply filling out a form and submitting it. Team members who have contributor status can participate in all the interactive activities on the site.

Using Office 2002 and its support for SharePoint Team Services, I have been able to move my inventories to high-function SharePoint Web sites and include even more powerful searching capabilities across entire libraries of documents. The high-function Web sites also make it possible to include databases in my inventory, complete with stored queries and the ability to create ad hoc queries on the fly. I am currently using Microsoft SharePoint Server and Microsoft SharePoint Team Services Web sites to accomplish this. See http://www.testersparadise.com for examples.

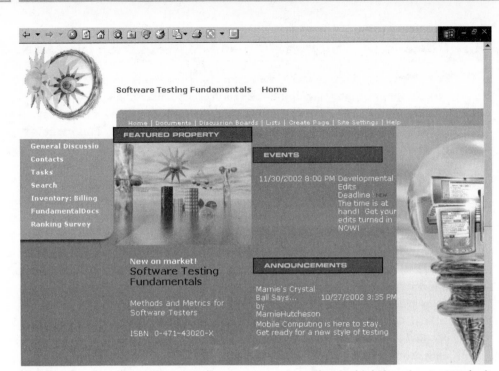

Figure 8.2 TestersParadise.com Home Page, an example of a high-function test Web site.

To start the test inventory document, I can either import my Power-Point outline as I just described or I can create my outline directly in Word. Figure 8.3 shows the inventory document in Outline View mode. This is the same inventory that we just saw in PowerPoint in Figure 8.1, after it has been imported into Word. If you click on any of the + signs, the text below the heading is revealed. Outline view in Word acts a lot like the rollup view in most project management tools. (If you are wondering why I don't just use a project management application for this work, see the sidebar, *Testing Is Not a Project—Or Is It?*) So, it is popular in status meetings. The problem is that you can't print it, which is probably why most people use PowerPoint to display this outline. However, if I need to print the rolled-up view (outline) of my inventory document, I use a table of contents. An example of this is coming up next.

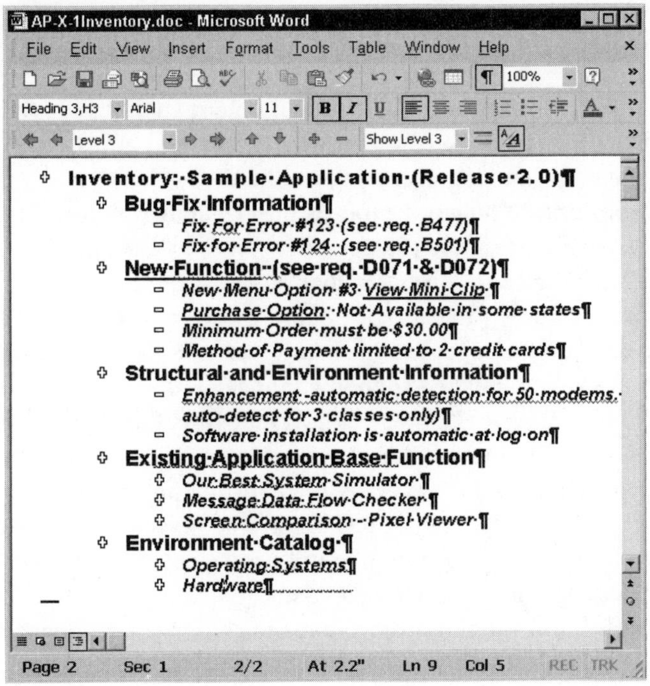

Figure 8.3 Inventory from a Web project as an outline in Microsoft Word.

Inventory in a Table of Contents

When you assign heading levels to your inventory items, it is possible to get a succinct listing of them in a table of contents, or TOC. To generate a TOC, put your cursor where you want the table of contents to appear in the document. In Microsoft, click on the *Insert* menu, choose *Field*, then scroll down to *TOC* and select it. Choose any formatting options you want, and click OK.

Figure 8.4 shows a table of contents complete with page numbers. I often take paper copies of the inventory in this form to status meetings. If there are issues that we need to discuss, I can add them as headings under the appropriate topic and print the table of contents with these items showing. My management has always enjoyed the brevity of this kind of presentation in meetings.

Testing Is Not a Project—Or Is It?

We should discuss project management tools for a moment so that you might benefit from my experiences trying to use them in software test efforts, and also so you will understand why I am not discussing any here.

Given that I am describing "rolling up" projects into a set of high-level items of work, many folks ask, why not just use project management skills and tools to "manage" the test effort? The short answer is that testing is not a project; it is a process. When a project is done, you check it off and go on. You almost never look back, except to celebrate. Budget has nice start and end dates to work with, and you can claim that you are finished spending money on that particular item. Testing, on the other hand, is never "done." The test may pass this time and fail next time. Consequently, we are never "done" testing; we simply stop at some point and ship the product. Budget is generally not satisfied because of this and several other factors discussed throughout this book. One reason why project managers don't want to touch a test effort is that it's too easy to end up looking bad. Ask any project manager if you don't believe me.

Consequently, a pure application of project management methods doesn't work any better than traditional software quality assurance methods. (Project management is a discipline that grew out of civil engineering.) This book is full of the project management methods that I have found workable in a test effort; however, the software tools are not so flexible. I spent two years trying to use two of the top project management software applications in my test efforts because they were required. Using them added a huge amount of documentation overhead to the test efforts, but worse than that, we couldn't share the information from the management tool with the documentation. So I had my outline (tasks) in one place and my detail layers in other places. It took a full-time administrator just to make sure that tasks were linked to their supporting documentation or point of origin—and, most especially, to somebody's budget.

I'm not saying it can't be done. I'm just saying that traditional project management tools have not been "sharp" tools when applied to test efforts. On a brighter note, the SharePoint Team Services Web sites offer strong support for project tools, like task lists. They also are good at sharing data, so you can import your task list from an Excel spreadsheet, and you can export it back out again so it can be used elsewhere. One final note, a product to watch for possible uses in a test effort is Microsoft Project, which is now Web-based. Who knows, it may end up bringing project management techniques to the test effort.

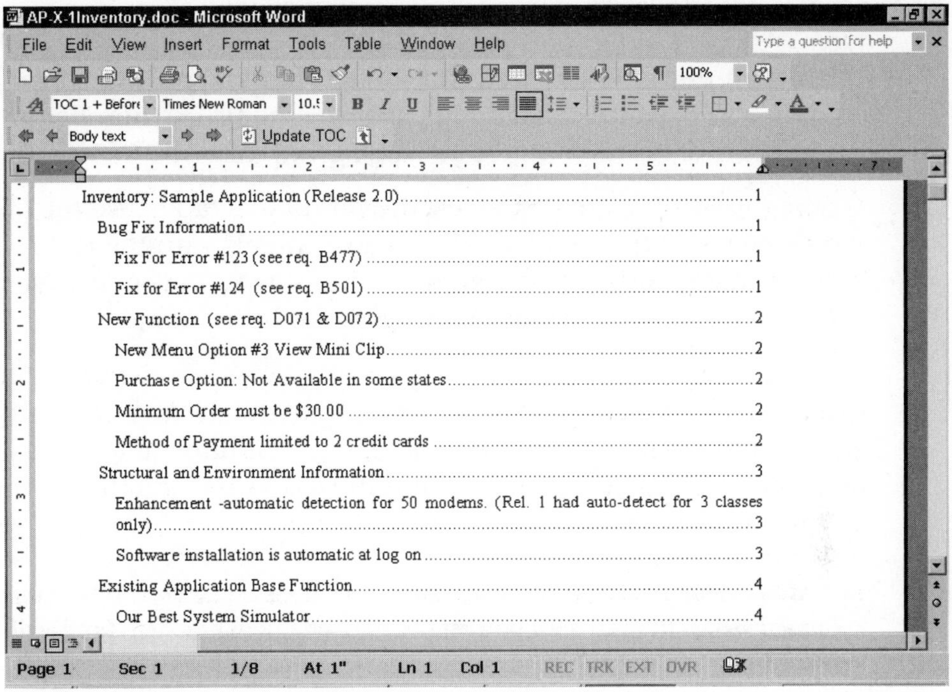

AP-X-1Inventory.doc - Microsoft Word

File Edit View Insert Format Tools Table Window Help

Page 1   Sec 1   1/8   At 1"   Ln 1   Col 1   REC TRK EXT OVR

Figure 8.4   The table of contents showing the inventory.

For the next step, creating a table to contain the inventory, it would be nice to just copy the items from the TOC, but unfortunately, in a Word document, the table of contents cannot simply be copied to another document and remain static during that process. It cannot because a TOC is a dynamically generated *field* where the headings in a document are collected.

One way to produce a permanent list from the table of contents field is to copy the table of contents and paste it into a new document. Use the *Save As* menu option to select the document type: Text with Line Breaks. This will remove the special field coding, leaving only the plain text of the categories. Close the text file. Repeat this procedure for each document that contains inventory items you want to gather. This process allows you to extract the inventory items so that you can do other things with them, like put them into a table or a spreadsheet. I will discuss building a table with them next.

Inventory in a Table

When you put your test inventory into a table, you can sort it by any column and perform calculations, like adding up the number of tests or the number of hours required to run a group of tests.

When you want to create the test inventory in a table, use the *Insert File* option to insert the plain text tables of contents into the test inventory document. Organize the categories in any way that makes sense, but keep each test item or category heading on its own line.

When you have assembled a list, select all of the inventory items and use the *Convert Text to Table* option under the *Table* menu to turn the entire listing into a one-column table. Add columns to this table as you need them. These columns will hold the individual counts for each row, or test, in the inventory.

✔ **Tip: If these topics are new to you, read the sections on document headings and automatic tables in your word processor user guide or online help for specific instructions.**

The New Function item in Table 8.1 is an example of functions taken from design documents. View Mini Clip is a menu option from the user interface. The two-credit-card limitation might have come from the interface or from some design or requirements document.

Notice the hyperlinks (underlined topics) in the functions that link to the requirement. The tests identified from these documents are usually high-level and general in nature, so they correspond to a category or type of test. Subsequent analysis will add tests to each of these categories. Often the categories evolve in the test suites. These categories usually appear as a *heading level one*, or the highest-level heading in the test inventory. Bug Fix Information in Table 8.1 is another example of using existing documents or references to existing documentation, such as the bug reports to define the testable item.

Table 8.1 Preliminary Inventory from a Web Project

SAMPLE APPLICATION (RELEASE 2.0)
<u>**Bug Fix Information**</u>
Fix for Error #123 (see req. B477)
Fix for Error #124 (see req. B501)
<u>**New Function (see req. D071 & D072)**</u>
New menu option #3: View Mini Clip
Purchase option: Not available in some states
Minimum order must be $30.00
Method of payment limited to 2 credit cards
<u>**Structural / Environment Information**</u>
Enhancement—automatic detection for 50 modems. (Rel. 1 had auto-detect for 3 classes only)
Software installation is automatic at logon
<u>**Existing Application Base Function**</u>
Standard base function tests still apply: All test suites for Version 1.0 will be run.
Our Best System Simulator
(automated suite BSIM01 67% coverage of Release 1 Test Inventory for the Best Simulator functionality)
Message Data Flow Checker
(automated suite DFCHECK 47% coverage of Release 1 Test Inventory for the Data Flow Checker functionality)
Screen Comparison—Pixel Viewer
(automated suite PIXVIEW 77% coverage of Release 1 Test Inventory for the Pixel Viewer functionality)
<u>**Environment Catalog**</u>
<u>**Operating Systems:**</u>
Client: Microsoft Windows 3.1 and higher, Win 95, Win 97, NT 3.51 with patches from #4 pack applied.
Host: To be determined.
Network: Under investigation by Net. Engineering plan due?
Hardware:
Computers: All machines on the operating system compatibility list.
Modems: All machines on the operating system compatibility list.

If you plan to construct your inventory using existing documentation, get *electronic copies* of the relevant specifications and requirements documents from your project. If electronic copies of the document are not available, consider faxing or scanning the documents and running character recognition software to produce an electronic copy. You have several choices on how to include your documents. You can use the include files method to link individual files into your document, or you can use hyperlinks within your document. Either way, if linked documents are updated, your document automatically reflects the changes. However, the Word Outline view and table of contents may not be useful to you, since Word does not follow hyperlinks when building these views. Therefore, your outline won't be easy to update automatically.

One of the major obstacles in document automation is the lack of a common standard for documentation. The developers and testers may use text files or a PC-based word processor, while the documentation group may use a publisher's tool such as Quark or an Adobe pdf file. Make sure that all the tools can produce a common high-level file format that supports the inclusion of graphics and tables. Acceptable examples in Microsoft Word document format are Rich Text Format (RTF), Standard General Markup Language (SGML), and HyperText Markup Language (HTML). I prefer HTML because it is easier to automate the creation and distribution of HTML files than it is with any of the other formats. HTML documents are small and can be easily distributed across networks and viewed on any platform that has an HTML browser.

Typically, project documents come in any number of formats. Start by converting any documents that are not in the correct format. Next, make sure that each document has a table of contents. Generate one if necessary. If the document was prepared in a text format or without heading level definitions, it will be necessary to apply the correct heading level style to the document's headings before a table of contents can be generated automatically. This operation is worthwhile because these headings will be used throughout the test effort.

Inventory in a Spreadsheet

When you begin to add environments and functions columns to your table, it can quickly grow beyond Word's capabilities. When this happens, it is time to copy your table to a spreadsheet. One of the great things about the spreadsheet is that you can add new pages (called sheets in Excel) as you need them. Figure 8.5 shows the inventory after it was copied into a new workbook. The inventory spreadsheet has sheets for the environmental catalog, functions, and test scenarios. All of these sheets are linked. The spreadsheet makes it possible to sort and filter the data. These features allow you to answer questions like, "What are the most important tests I can run to test EDI?" in seconds.

I always reserve budget in my projects for a spreadsheet specialist, a mechanic. By setting up the automatic calculations and shared data values, a good mechanic can create a spreadsheet workbook that instantly updates data on related sheets whenever you change anything in the spreadsheet. The workbook can also present the latest results in pivot charts, graphs, and whatever visualization is most effective for you at the moment.

When it comes time to test, I sort the test scenarios and filter the sheet to produce a list of the tests that have to be run to test a specific PDR, feature, or environmental aspect, such as a particular database. I can copy the resulting worksheet, print it, or publish it on the Web. My testers have a succinct list of tests that need to be performed.

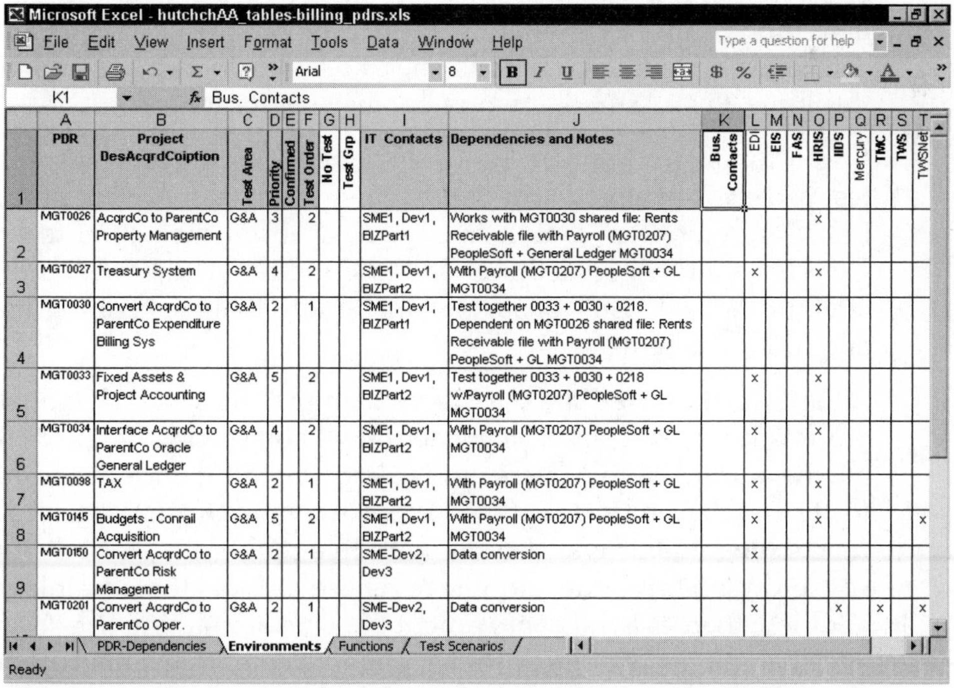

	PDR	Project DesAcqrdCoiption	Test Area	Priority	Confirmed	Test Order	No Test	Test Grp	IT Contacts	Dependencies and Notes	Bus. Contacts	EDI	EIS	FAS	HRIS	IIDS	Mercury	TMC	TWS	TWSNet
2	MGT0026	AcqrdCo to ParentCo Property Management	G&A	3		2			SME1, Dev1, BIZPart1	Works with MGT0030 shared file: Rents Receivable file with Payroll (MGT0207) PeopleSoft + General Ledger MGT0034					x					
3	MGT0027	Treasury System	G&A	4		2			SME1, Dev1, BIZPart2	With Payroll (MGT0207) PeopleSoft + GL MGT0034		x			x					
4	MGT0030	Convert AcqrdCo to ParentCo Expenditure Billing Sys	G&A	2		1			SME1, Dev1, BIZPart1	Test together 0033 + 0030 + 0218. Dependent on MGT0026 shared file: Rents Receivable file with Payroll (MGT0207) PeopleSoft + GL MGT0034					x					
5	MGT0033	Fixed Assets & Project Accounting	G&A	5		2			SME1, Dev1, BIZPart2	Test together 0033 + 0030 + 0218 w/Payroll (MGT0207) PeopleSoft + GL MGT0034		x			x					
6	MGT0034	Interface AcqrdCo to ParentCo Oracle General Ledger	G&A	4		2			SME1, Dev1, BIZPart2	With Payroll (MGT0207) PeopleSoft + GL MGT0034		x			x					
7	MGT0098	TAX	G&A	2		1			SME1, Dev1, BIZPart2	With Payroll (MGT0207) PeopleSoft + GL MGT0034		x			x					
8	MGT0145	Budgets - Conrail Acquisition	G&A	5		2			SME1, Dev1, BIZPart2	With Payroll (MGT0207) PeopleSoft + GL MGT0034		x			x					x
9	MGT0150	Convert AcqrdCo to ParentCo Risk Management	G&A	2		1			SME-Dev2, Dev3	Data conversion		x								
	MGT0201	Convert AcqrdCo to ParentCo Oper.	G&A	2		1			SME-Dev2, Dev3	Data conversion		x				x		x		x

Figure 8.5 The environment catalog sheet from the inventory spreadsheet.

Fundamental Principle: Never Rekey Data

The quality assurance process in software development is already in a position where it cannot keep up with development technologies.

Any process that requires the same data to be manually rekeyed into the system is badly flawed. Every time the same data is manually rekeyed, money is wasted. Every data entry point is a source of errors being introduced.

The cost of tracking and integrating review commentary increases with the number of reviewers.

Every time paper documentation is circulated, the potential for version control problems is expanded. The probability of outdated paper-borne information causing failure rises, and the cost of ensuring that everyone is on the same version increases.

Whatever tools and processes are selected, make sure that the documents are sharable and come from a single source.

Inventory in a High-Function Web Site

As I write this, I have to start by saying that putting your test collateral on a Web site is not always efficient. If the culture in your company does not embrace this technology yet, or if the control of Web resources is controlled by feudal Web lords, then I recommend you tread lightly on this topic. Rest assured; it won't be this way for long.

I tried to use traditional HTML document-based Web sites to aid my test projects for most of the 1990s. They were only "one-way" tools at best. At worst, they took resources away from the actual testing and gave the vultures something else to criticize. With few exceptions, a straight Web site isn't good for much more than publishing bug stats and test documents.

A high-function Web site is a different animal, however. The SharePoint Team Services Web site is a collaborative and interactive place. First of all, the administrative overhead is almost nothing once the administrator learns the product. It takes about five minutes to generate a fully functioning interactive Web site with five built-in levels of group security: browse, contribute, author, advanced author, and administrator. In addition, there is a full complement of pages containing lists (see Figure 8.6), including a document folder, announcements, events with a calendar, and a link list—all ready for your team to use. And, of course, you can create more if you need them.

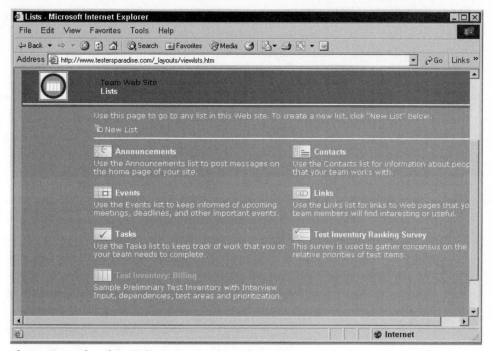

Figure 8.6 The SharePoint Team Services Lists page.

The Team Site is powered by SQL Server and several types of canned functionality with which you never need to worry. You customize the way your features work and administer your site using online forms. You don't need to know HTML, although it doesn't hurt, and you don't need to use a Web page creation tool like FrontPage, but that doesn't hurt either—especially if you want to customize your pages as I have for testersparadise.com. The List Builder tool is happy to absorb spreadsheets and allow you to create custom editable views of them.

Other features included out of the box are any number of forums; announcements; events, complete with calendar; and several built-in views, such as Today's Events, My Events, and All Events. The list enumeration page is shown in Figure 8.6. There is a contacts list that team members can add to, a link list where team members can add hyperlinks with explanatory text. The system provides several other canned lists, and you can create any number of custom lists.

List data is stored in an SQL Server database, so when someone edits the data on one of the views, it is updated in the database and the new value is automatically sent the next time anyone requests a list that contains that data. So there is no worry about propagating stale data from multiple data sources. SharePoint Team Services takes care of all the data updates and concurrency issues.

There is also a survey tool that allows you to create surveys on the fly. Surveys are a good consensus-building tool. For example, I like to use them when I establish priorities. (An example of this type of survey is in Chapter 9, "Risk Analysis.") All of these features can be created and modified by whatever groups the administrator chooses.

Figure 8.7 shows the PDR view of the inventory after the data was imported from the Excel spreadsheet. Notice the menu on the left side of the page; it shows three views available. These hyperlinks to other views are very much like the tabs on the bottom of the sheets in the spreadsheet. These views are easy to create, and you can create as many of them as you need from the data on the spreadsheet. I am often asked to create special views for different groups, like management.

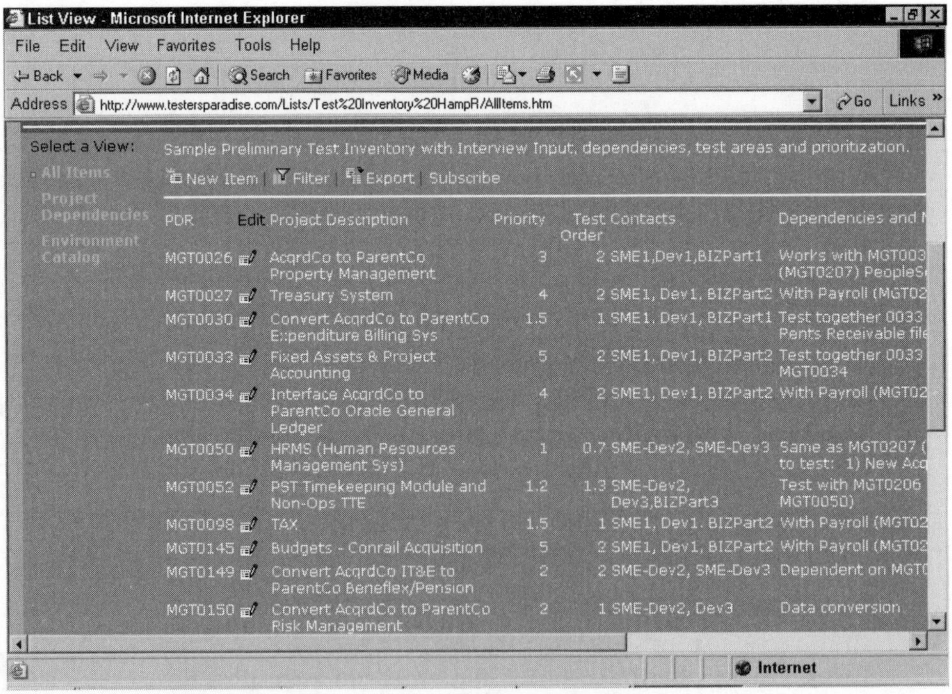

Figure 8.7 PDR view of the inventory in a Team Services list.

Figure 8.8 shows the Environment view of the inventory list. The user can sort any list view by any column simply by clicking on the column heading. The user can also filter the views so that only items meeting the filter criteria are displayed. For example, you can filter all PDRs by their group, display only the PDRs that use a particular environment, and so on. Users can also subscribe to a list and receive automatic notification via email when something changes on the list.

As nice as the lists are, it is much more difficult to keep running totals and perform other calculations in this canned environment; so the spreadsheet still offers some advantages. The good news is, permissioned users can export a list back to Excel 2002 and work on the data there.

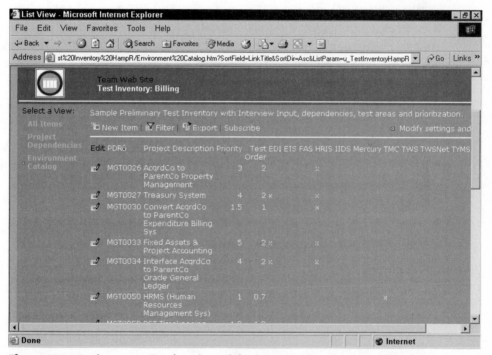

Figure 8.8   Environment Catalog view of the inventory in a Team Services list.

Summary

I have described the tools and the process that I use to automate the creation and maintenance of my test inventories. Obviously, different-sized projects require different treatments, as do the various development approaches. The approach I have described here is both flexible and scalable.

PowerPoint is a good tool to use when you want to create an outline. When your need for detail outgrows PowerPoint, move your outline to a Word document. Word allows you to develop both the terse outline for meetings and the detailed in-depth layers required to master the project.

When your working inventory gets too big for a Word table, move it to the spreadsheet. Don't be shy about hiring someone very knowledgeable in creating custom spreadsheets if you don't want to do this work yourself. The work they do for you will add hugely to the quality of your test contribution, and your credibility.

If you can move to a high-performance Web site without risking the farm and your reputation, do it. The sooner you start learning to leverage this incredibly powerful emerging technology, the better. A high-function Web site is not the answer to all your problems, but it's a good start. See www.testersparadise.com for some examples of what a SharePoint Team Services Web site can do.

Finally, do not be afraid to invest in yourself. Learn more about the tools you have, and don't be afraid of the new stuff. It requires some learning, but it can be worth it.

CHAPTER 9

Risk Analysis

"What are you going to test?" asked the vice president.

"The Most Important things," the tester replied.

"And how do you know what the most important things are?" asked the vice president.

Therein lies the tale. . . . Again, I was the tester in this conversation, and in truth the process of answering this question continues even today.

Engineers have been performing risk analysis for thousands of years. (It's been done ever since the first building fell down and the engineer's head rolled shortly thereafter.) It's interesting that some entrepreneurs in software testing houses are reinventing it as a marketing concept just when the heat is coming up under the *software engineers*.

To mitigate the risk of some event causing damage, you must first estimate the probability that the event will occur. This probability has to be translated into some quantity, usually represented as a percentage—for example, "There is a 50 percent chance that this will happen." Next, you need to determine the severity of such a failure. Severity is usually measured in currency, such as dollars, and loss of life. If the severity is minor, then even a high probability of occurrence may still be judged to cause a trivial problem.

If the severity of the failure and its probability of occurrence rise above a certain threshold, then it warrants preventative action. In engineering, a *standard* is put in place to ensure that the correct preventative actions are taken during construction so that if the event occurs, it will not cause the structure to fail. This standard is a rule.

In structures, the need for standards has long been understood, so we have building codes, which are sets of rules. Building codes ensure that all buildings are built to have enough structural integrity to withstand the demands that will *probably* be placed on them.

The probability that a thing will or won't occur can be calculated under certain circumstances—especially if you can answer a question like, "What was the outcome last time?" or "Do we know if the platform can really do what the maker claims it can?" If you can't provide a good measured answer to these questions up front, then you will need a strategy for dealing with the events that will occur later in the process. If the probability and severity cannot be measured, then they must be estimated. MITs risk analysis provides a formal method for both estimating up front and dealing with events as they unfold. In this chapter, we look at this formal approach to establishing risk and prioritizing the items on the test inventory.

MITs risk analysis uses both quantitative and qualitative analysis to establish a numeric value for risk based on a number of specific criteria. In the early planning phases of a test effort, this risk number is used to focus test resources to size the test effort. As the inventory evolves, the risk ranking plays an important part in actual test selection and optimal test coverage determination.

The Risk Analysis Process in Brief

I normally use MITs risk analysis for different purposes during different phases of the test effort. At the beginning of a project, I use risk analysis on the initial inventory to prioritize the items on the inventory. The process helps build consensus on test needs and focuses the test planning effort on the most important items. This helps me size the test effort and prepare my cost and time line estimates. I usually prepare an initial test schedule at this time to coincide with the order of the deliverables. This helps me plan my resource needs for the test system and testers over the course of the test phase.

In my case, this estimate, covered in Chapter 10, "Applied Risk Analysis," forms the basis of my contract or agreement to test. For a more traditional test role, it would form the basis of the test plan. In my case, this inventory, complete with risk ranking, will be presented to management for review and approval. In addition to using risk analysis to propose the appropriate test coverage, I may also use risk analysis on my test results in order to show management the value of the test effort, as in the case study later in the chapter, *Case Study: The 401(k) Web Project.*

In the next stage, path and data analysis, I will use risk analysis to select which tests to run and estimate the resource needs of the optimal test effort. In a heavyweight project, I will perform these first steps during the planning stage. I will use the MITs risk ranking and the number of tests identified to determine how many of the total number of tests identified for the item will be run. This is the percent test coverage that I will propose as optimal for the effort. I will repeat this process for each inventory item. Once I have identified the tests and calculated the number of tests required by the MITs risk rankings, I can complete a detailed test estimate. This process is discussed in detail as we proceed through Chapters 10 through 13.

In MITs, we use the risk index to determine how much we will test an item. Each item on the test inventory is ranked based on "how critical" a failure would be if it occurred in the item. The criticality of a failure in the test item is arrived at by applying a set of ranking criteria to the hypothetical failure.

The more critical a failure would be, the higher the MITs rank (the smaller the number) will be for the test and the more extensive the test coverage will be. For example, a rank of 1 results in 100 percent test coverage. A rank of 4 results in a 25 percent test coverage. This topic is covered in detail in Chapter 10, "Applied Risk Analysis."

If I am dealing with a lightweight project, I will probably do my path and data analysis on the fly when I get the first version of the application or system. Once I have identified tests for an item through my analysis, I record this number of tests for the item in the inventory. Then I calculate the actual percent test coverage achieved during the effort.

I use this number after the product has been shipped to calculate the performance of the test effort. This is a good metric to use when attempting to demonstrate the value added to the product by the test effort.

I mention this whole process here because I have seen too many testers balk at performing risk analysis, perceiving it as an unnecessary extra step. It is not extra, only the formalization is new—writing it down. If the tools used in this book are used, this step is not a hard one. But if testers don't understand that risk analysis has many uses, and that it will be reused throughout the test effort, they tend to ignore it. Risk analysis is a powerful technique that is useful throughout the test effort and beyond, into operations.

Benefits of Risk Analysis

In recent years, I have had better luck convincing managers of the value of risk analysis than testers. Conducting formal risk analysis on the project not only gives managers a more defensible position because they can demonstrate that they used a best-practice approach, but more importantly, it costs so little and provides a powerful tool that supplements traditional project management tools. It also gets everyone in the effort on the same page with respect to scope and priorities.

Ensuring Correct Focus for the Test Effort

A major part of the payback for performing MITs risk analysis is the assurance that testing is focused on the most important items. You will pick the best tests, perform fewer tests, and get a higher return on them than if you didn't perform risk analysis. And you will save the company more money.

You can have applications, systems, components, databases, even Web services (and apples and oranges and peas and spaceships) on your inventory—it doesn't matter, as long as each one is testable. Once any item has been added to the inventory, you can analyze it to whatever level necessary to identify its most important elements. For example, if the project requirements are on the inventory; they are testable. Under each requirement, there is some kind of program unit, system, module, or component; these are testable as well. (There also may be manual processes, like faxing or data entry.) Under each program unit are paths and data; these will have tests associated with them. What is the rank of these tests? How much will you test them? Which ones will you test first? The MITs risk analysis answers these questions.

In a plan-driven effort, these tests can be planned in advance, through analysis of the requirements and the actual functionality. Theoretically at least, you can rank these items based on the requirements and then use path analysis and data analysis to design the tests for them. And you can do so without having seen the software.

Publishing Testers' Assumptions

One of the great benefits of this MITs system is that it is published. Publishing the risk matrix is a type of assumption publishing. Ranking documents the assumptions of the testers. Everyone has the chance to review and comment. If faulty assumptions are not pointed out, it is not the fault of the tester. And other groups can also use the information.

Sometimes, however, it is hard to live with that publicity. In the real-world shipping example from Chapter 7, we testers were criticized by developers for applying risk-ranking criteria to their projects, but their vehemence and righteous indignation served to energize them into providing not only the ranking but the test order as well. This leaves testers with an excellent tool and guide map through a huge project.

Promoting Reuse by Other Groups

One of the classic test waste scenarios happens when project personnel are changed. The new people don't know the application, or the tests, or what does what. So they tend to ignore the existing test collateral and invent their own. Since they don't know anything, the new collateral usually lacks maturity and depth of the existing material. The company has just paid good money to take a step backward and lose time as well.

The first question that someone new usually asks is "Which tests should I run to find out X?" The variable X can be replaced by virtually anything. If your test collateral can't provide an answer as simple as this, then you have failed to pass on your legacy and the new tester will probably start from scratch.

With MITs, all you need to do to answer the question is filter and re-sort your inventory by the test category that includes X and then by the

MITs rank. They don't have to know anything about the application; all they have to do is look at the ranked test inventory in order to know where to start. Adding new categories to the test inventory to answer questions like this is one of my most important jobs. It shows the depth and value of the tests in the inventory, serves as the basis for funded new test development, and gets my tests reused.

This system works so well that other groups can also benefit from the tests. Operations is almost always the first beneficiary of the test inventory after the testers. They can use it to quickly identify just the tests that they need to create system-targeted diagnostics suites. Figure 9.1 shows the spreadsheet inventory from the real-world shipping example. It shows the "Day in the Life of a Car" test cases sorted by test order and priority. Notice that the view also shows the environments touched by each scenario.

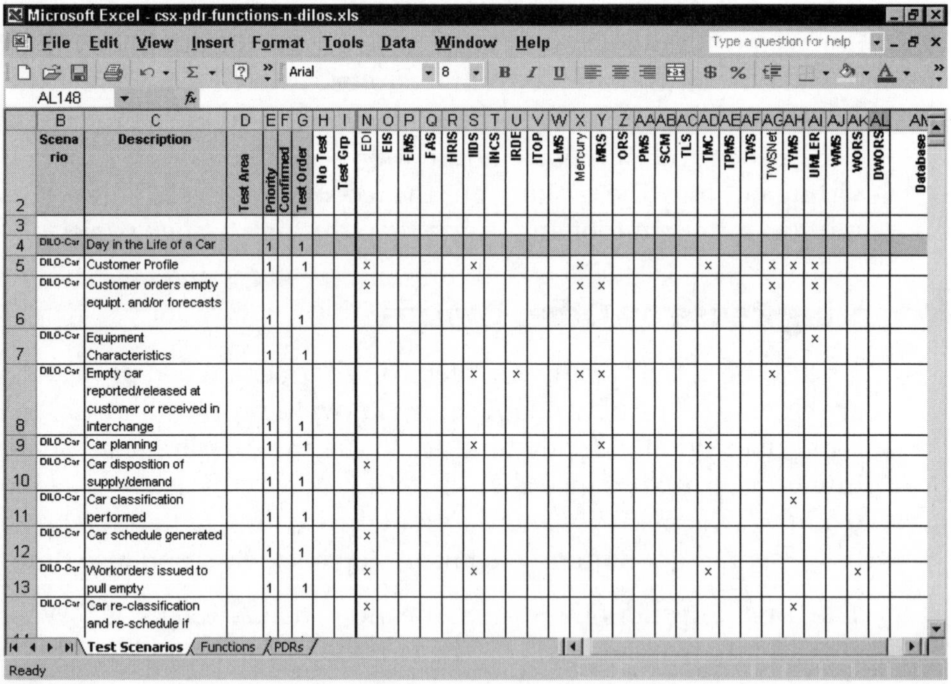

Figure 9.1 The spreadsheet inventory showing the "Day in the Life of a Car" test scripts, sorted by test order and priority.

Providing a Powerful Project Management Tool for the Test Effort

By itself, the inventory is a very nice parts list, useful for keeping track of items. When you add a priority to those items, the inventory becomes a powerful tool for answering all kinds of important questions. If you take one additional step and add a sequencing field like "Test Order," you have created a project management tool that is uniquely applicable to the test effort.

How the Inventory Can Be Used

In the real-world shipping project, development and operations both benefited from the inventory. One of the biggest reasons was that careful attention was paid to identifying the environmental requirements of each PDR and major function. So the inventory could be used as a checklist by operations when preparing test systems for various stages of testing. For example, systems managers were planning a day-long meeting to determine the order in which they needed to bring their test systems online. We testers arrived at the meeting with several different printouts, like the one shown in Figure 9.2.

Figure 9.2 shows the Web-based inventory and the environment catalog for the real-world case study of the shipping company. This listing shows the environmental catalog portion of the inventory; it has been filtered by the HRIS column. Notice the small funnel icon below the HRIS column heading, to show all items that touch the HRIS system. The list was then sorted by priority and finally by test order. Also notice the small arrow beneath the "Test Order" column heading. The questions answered by the view in Figure 9.2 are "What PDRs impact the HRIS system, and what order will I have to prepare for them?" and "What are the other systems that will need to be ready?"

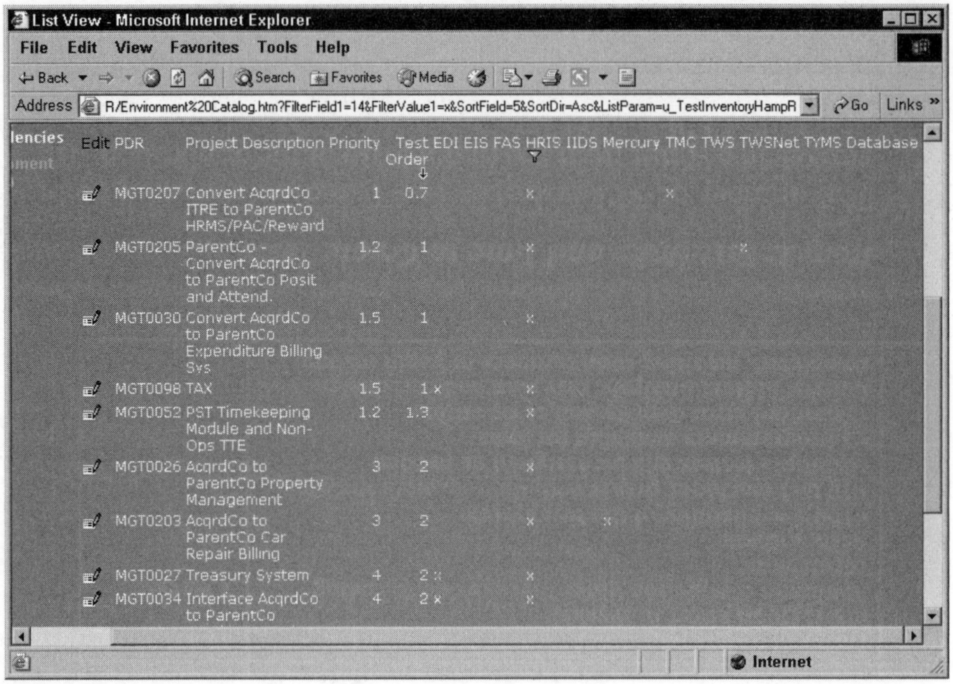

Figure 9.2 The shipping company's inventory showing the test order of the most important tests for the HRIS system.

The process of filtering and sorting took less that a minute, and the resulting list shows not only the most important inventory items for this system but also the order in which they will be tested. The managers were finished with their meeting in less than an hour, and they requested several additional views of the inventory. The inventory became one of the most frequently consulted (and quoted) documents in the integration effort.

Building the Inventory on-the-Fly

The real-world shipping project was plan-driven. But the prioritized inventory is a valuable management tool in a RAD/Agile effort as well. You just don't construct it in quite the same way. In a RAD/Agile effort, since you will probably be handed some software to test with little or no idea what it is or what it will do, you will probably build your inventory as you go.

As soon as you have access to a functioning application, you can identify major functionality, prioritize it, and record it on your inventory. Once you have explored a function (inventory item), you can add the detail layers to your inventory. Sooner or later, features coalesce and become stable. If you have been building your inventory as you go, you will have an up-to-date report of everything that you have tested at all times. So when management wants to know if it's shippable, you have good answers in your hand. See *Case Study: The 401(k) Web Project* later in this chapter for an example.

A mature test inventory in a RAD/Agile effort also fuels the user guide and instructions to customer service. It is the definitive source for how things really work. In many RAD/Agile development efforts today, my title is actually technical author, not tester.

If you are involved in a RAD/Agile effort, you won't have a lot of time to plan, measure, or estimate, but you do want to be prepared, because you will be expected to be ready to test. If you are involved in a plan-driven project, it will be necessary and expected that you measure, plan, and estimate the size of the test effort in advance so that it can be budgeted and fitted into the time available. This brings us to the fundamental difference between the two development strategies and how they relate to risk.

Project Management Strategies and Risk

Spending money for information, or MFI, is generally considered to be part of the plan-driven management strategy. Reserving money for flexibility, or MFF, is considered to be part of the RAD/Agile management strategy. In the real world, I have observed that there is a balance between MFI and MFF in all projects. Moreover, testing is a critical element of both strategies. So, whether management wants to plan a little or a lot, they still need to know what and where the risks are. I find it ironic that whether management believes that they need testers to determine risk or not, managers use their own type of risk analysis to determine how to divvy up their budget in order to balance their MFI with their MFF. This managerial risk analysis is usually established informally using a "gut feel" approach, which is just another flavor of the I-feel-lucky approach.

Examples from the Real World

The plan-driven management is willing to spend MFI to mitigate risk when the outcome is uncertain, as with new technologies or systems. It is used for unpredictable and "all or nothing" scenarios, when we don't know actual usage patterns or system limits. These are things that can be measured or simulated in advance of development. That way, there is time to change course before the project hits the wall. Oddly enough, the best example I ever saw of good use of MFI was in a RAD project.

Real-World Money for Information

My RAD client was developing a specialized messaging server to run on a new carrier class unified communications platform. From the beginning, we were suspicious that a core server component, built by a third-party provider, would not scale to meet the required service levels. The MITs risk analysis showed that the successful performance of this single core component was the single most important factor to the success of the entire product development effort. Because of this information, my RAD client was willing to spend quite a bit of money trying to establish the real-world limits of this core system—before they invested heavily in developing their own server.

It was fortunate that they did invest in a good MFI test effort, because the core system did seem to scale, but it proved to be fatally flawed in a way that no one expected: It was built on a nonstandard protocol that was incompatible with the standards used by most carriers. The MFI test effort to establish the credibility of the core system probably saved this RAD division's financial life. The platform was never deployed. Their development efforts would have been for nothing, and all their investment would have been lost.

This was an extreme use of MFI. Normally, risk analysis conducted by the testers doesn't venture into the "actually test it and find out" stage. The more common use of MITs risk analysis is to identify the areas that testing should concentrate on.

On the other end of the spectrum, and in the interest of balance, is one of the best examples of MFF that I ever saw. It was accomplished by a plan-driven development manager from an office supply company. The office supply company had purchased an e-commerce engine from a heavyweight third-party vendor that promised to ease their transition from client/server to an HTML-based service running on a Web server. We look at this real-world scenario in the next section.

Real-World Money for Flexibility

The office supply company had implemented and integrated most of the system and had begun user testing by the customer service department when they realized that they had major performance problems in the browser. While they were trying to establish exactly what was causing the problems, both major browser makers released new versions, and it was discovered the system did not work on either new browser.

My company had been commissioned to perform the user acceptance testing and a human factors review on the product for one of the office supply company's business partners. I looked at the code that was being sent to the browsers and quickly realized that the system was one enormous applet that simply took over the browser. Their "Web" pages were not HTML, but rather, huge scripted files that were being processed by the applet in the client machine. Further, the third-party front-end bypassed the Web server and all things Internet, and relied entirely on its own monolithic proprietary application to process every screen for every client.

This client system that was supposed to be browser-based contained almost no HTML. Instead, it was packed with Visual Basic (VB) code. Apparently, the third-party programmers didn't bother to learn any HTML. For example, one screen that displayed query results in a table used over 70 lines of scripted code to set the font for the table and a background color for the table's heading row. This feat can be accomplished in one line of HTML with two style definitions: font and background color. Once I had seen the code, it was clear why there were performance problems.

The browser incompatibility problem had a similar cause. To take control of the browser, these developers had written specific code instructions to the browser. The newer releases of the browser did not accept this code, and so the applet did not work at all. My company's client failed the product, and our report was passed along to the office supply company, where it caused a firestorm in the office supply company's development group.

The development manager from the office supply company handed the third-party contract to his legal department with a sticky note on it reading, "Get our money back. This isn't HTML and it isn't a Web application." Then, he came to visit my test team. He said he wanted to see how we tested the product, and he wanted to borrow a book on HTML. He spent several hours with us going over our test results. When he left, he took several books and the names of some reputable Web programming consultants.

My company completed its testing and human factors review for the business partner, and some very good consultants joined the office supply company's development team. The consultants took the functional requirements and the results of our user acceptance testing and human factors reviews, and they turned out functioning screens within three weeks. This was just about the time frame we had estimated for the bug fixes to be turned around.

Meanwhile, the office supply company's own developers did some crash learning on integrating their own systems, which they knew well, with the standards-based Web server's Internet Server Application Programming Interface (ISAPI). The system was finished on time, and the business partners were very happy with its features and the maturity of its workflow.

If you are wondering where the money came from, the rewrite actually cost less than the original contract with the heavyweight third-party vendor. The developers at the office supply company learned some new skills, and the office supply company bootstrapped itself into the Web on its own.

So contrary to popular myth, RAD/Agile developers can plan, and plan-driven developers can change the plan. Understanding risk and being ready to deal with the outcome, or better still, avoid failures altogether, is independent of the development methodology. It's just good management.

Agile and plan-driven teams use different approaches. Agile will set up to absorb late-breaking changes; plan-driven teams will try to plan for them early by charting contingencies. We testers don't need to be much concerned with how the developers design; all we need to know is what *it* is supposed to do. Once you have your inventory to keep track of the testable bits, you can prioritize them and reprioritize them at will. I will talk about this again in *Case Study: The 401k Web Project* later in this chapter.

MITs helps the plan-driven effort predict where the difficulties will be because it is a formal methodology that supports a thorough and flexible analysis of project elements. This approach helps the Agile project retain flexibility because it uses as much or as little collaboration and measurement as befits the project at hand, and it produces visible results very quickly. MITs also makes it is easy to rebalance the focus of the test effort quickly. Even though this falls into the MFF category, it is popular with sensible managers from all parts of the development rainbow.

As with the inventory, the risks will be different depending on the type of project. However, the tools you, the tester, need to succeed are pretty much the same in both types of projects. In the end, it doesn't matter which development methodology is in use. Risk is risk, and the better the project risks are understood, the better they can be mitigated.

MITs Risk Analysis

In MITs, the process of estimating risk involves identifying "what" the risk is and "how much" is required before action will be taken to mitigate that risk. These answers are provided through performing quantitative and qualitative analysis.

We discuss these topics throughout the rest of this chapter. In the next phase, actual test selection, the risk analysis ensures that the selected test set has the highest probability of packing the biggest punch, smallest test set, highest yield. We discuss this in the following chapter, "Applied Risk Analysis."

Quantitative and Qualitative Analysis

Both quantitative and qualitative analysis came from chemistry. They go back before the Renaissance in Europe. You probably remember reading about efforts to turn lead into gold. Well, that's where these methods started. Chemistry is what happened to alchemy when the I-feel-lucky approach to turning lead into gold gave way to methods and metrics.

What are quantitative and qualitative analysis? Let's examine dictionary-type definitions:

Qualitative analysis.   The branch of chemistry that deals with the determination of the elements or ingredients of which a compound or mixture is composed (*Webster's New World Dictionary*).

Quantitative analysis.   The branch of chemistry that deals with the accurate measurement of the amounts or percentages of various components of a compound or mixture (*Webster's New World Dictionary*).

Risk analysis deals with both understanding the components of risk and the measuring of risk. Recognizing "what bad things might happen" is not "risk analysis" until you quantify it. You could limit yourself to one or the other of these two forms of analysis, but if the object is to provide a solution, you are missing the boat.

Next, you have to quantify what are you willing to do to keep it from failing. "Try real hard" is not an engineering answer. It contains no measured quantity. But it's the one we've been hearing from software makers. Getting real answers to these questions does not require "art." It requires measurement. And it requires that management allocate budget to the test effort to do so.

For instance, if you are going to make cookies, it isn't enough to know what the ingredients are. You need to know how much of each thing to use. You also need to know the procedure for combining ingredients and baking the cookies. These things taken together create a recipe for the successful re-creation of some type of cookies. If the recipe is followed closely, the probability for a successful outcome can be estimated based on past performance.

For this risk cookie, my "ingredients" are the criteria that are meaningful in the project, such as the severity, the cost of a failure, and the impact on customers, users, or other systems. There are any number of possible criteria, and each project is different. I start my analysis in a project by identifying the ones that I want to keep track of.

One of the easiest things to quantify is cost. We usually use units of time and currency to measure cost. Even if what is lost is primarily time, time can have a currency value put on it. Management seems to understand this kind of risk statement the best. So, it's the one I look for first.

After identifying the risk criteria that will be used to evaluate the items in the inventory, I want to determine the correct amount of priority to give each one, both individually and in relation to one another. I use an index to do this.

The MITs Rank Index

The MITs Rank Index is normally a *real* number between 1.0 and 4.0. A rank index of 1 represents the most severe error. A Severity 1 problem usually is described using terms like shutdown, meltdown, fall down, lethal embrace, showstopper, and black hole. Next is a rank of 2; this represents a serious problem, but not one that is immediately fatal. A rank index of 3 is a moderate problem, and a rank index of 4 is usually described as a matter of opinion, a design difficulty, or an optional item.

Rank indexes are real numbers, so a rank index of 1.5 could be assigned to a risk criteria. The decimal part of the index becomes important when we use the MITs rank index to calculate test coverage. This topic is covered in detail in Chapter 10, "Applied Risk Analysis."

Weighting an Index

Several types of weighting can be applied in addition to the rank index; for example, two additional factors that are often considered when assigning a rank index are the cost to fix the problem and the time it will take to fix the problem, or the time allowed to resolve an issue. The time allowed to resolve an issue is a normal part of a service level agreement, or SLA. This item will become increasingly important in Web applications, since hosting and Web services are both provided with SLAs. Failure to adhere to an SLA can become a matter for loss of contract and litigation.

Table 9.1 provides a simple index description and some of the criteria that might be used to assign a particular rank. Like everything else in MITs, you are encouraged to modify it to meet your own needs. However, the index should not become larger than 4 in most cases, because it translates into such a small percentage of test coverage that the benefits are normally negligible.

Table 9.1 MITs Rank Index Description and Criteria

Rank = 1	*Highest Priority*
	Failure: Would be critical.
	Risk: High; item has no track record, or poor credibility.
	Required by SLA, has failed to meet an SLA time or performance limit.
Rank = 2	*High Priority*
	Failure: Would be unacceptable.
	Risk: Uncertain.
	Approaching an SLA time or performance limit, could fail to meet an SLA.
Rank = 3	*Medium Priority*
	Failure: Would be survivable.
	Risk: Moderate.
	Little or no danger of exceeding SLA limits.
Rank = 4	*Low Priority*
	Failure: Would be trivial.
	Risk: May not be a factor.
	SLA—Not applicable.

The Art of Assigning a Rank Index

In some cases, there is one overriding factor, such as the risk of loss of life, that makes this an easy task. When there is such a risk, it becomes the governing factor in the ranking, and assigning the rank index is straightforward and uncontested. The rank index is 1.

However, in most cases, assigning a rank index is not so straightforward or obvious. The normal risk associated with an inventory item is some combination of factors, or risk criteria. The eventual rank that will be assigned to it is going to be the product of one or more persuasive arguments, as we discussed in Chapter 3, "Approaches to Managing Software Testing."

The rank index assigned to a MITs ranking criteria may be a subtle blend of several considerations. How can we quantify multiple ranking criteria? It turns out that assigning a rank index is something of an art, like Grandmother's cookies. A lump of shortening the size of an egg may be the best way to describe the risk index that you should apply to a potential failure. For example, consider the following problem from my testing of the 401(k) Web Project (discussed later in the chapter):

> *One of the errors I encountered caused my machine to lock up completely while I was trying to print a copy of the 401(k) Plan Agreement document from a downloaded PDF file displayed in my browser. I was supposed to review the document before continuing with the enrollment process. When the machine was rebooted, the PDF file could not be recovered. I tried to download the file again, but the system, thinking I was finished with that step, would not let me return to that page. I could not complete the enrollment because the information that I needed to fill out the rest of the forms was contained in the lost PDF file.*

I reported this failure as a Severity 1 problem because, in my opinion and experience, a normal consumer would not be willing to pursue this project as I did. Remember, this was not the only blockage in the enrollment process. As far as I am concerned, an error that keeps a potential customer from becoming a customer is a Severity 1 error. Developers did not see it this way. As far as they were concerned, since the file wasn't really lost and no damage was really done, this was a minor problem, a Severity 3 at most.

Fortunately, the MITs ranking process allows us to balance these factors by using multiple ranking criteria and assigning them all a rank index, as you will see in the next topic.

The MITs Ranking Criteria

Over the years, I have identified several qualities that may be significant factors in ranking a problem or the probability of a problem.

Identifying Ranking Criteria

The following are qualities I use most frequently in ranking a problem or the probability of a problem:

- Requirement
- Severity
- Probability
- Cost

- Visibility
- Tolerability
- Human factors

Almost every different industry has others that are important to them. You are invited and encouraged to select the ranking criteria that work for your needs. The next step is to determine the appropriate rank index for a given ranking criteria.

Assigning a Risk Index to Risk Criteria

The way that I determine the rank index for each ranking criteria is by answering a series of questions about each one. Table 9.2 shows several questions I ask myself when attempting to rank. These are presented as examples. You are encouraged to develop your own ranking criteria and their qualifying questions.

The only danger I have experienced over the years with risk ranking happens if you consistently use too few criteria. If you use only two criteria for all ranking, for example, then the risk analysis may not be granular enough to provide an accurate representation of the risk. The worst fiasco in risk-based testing I ever saw was a project that used only two criteria to rank the testable items: probability and impact. These two criteria did not account for human factors, or cost, or intersystem dependencies. It turned out that these factors were the driving qualities of the feature set. So, the risk analysis did not provide accurate information.

Table 9.2 MITs Risk Criteria Samples

Required	
Is this a contractual requirement such as service level agreement?	Must have = 1 Nice to have = 4
Mitigating factors: Is this an act of God?	
If the design requirements have been prioritized, then the priority can be transferred directly to rank.	
Has some level of validation and verification been promised?	

Table 9.2 *(Continued)*

Severity	
Is this life-threatening? System-critical?	Most serious = 1
	Least serious = 4
Mitigating factors: Can this be prevented?	

Probability	
How likely is it that a failure will occur?	Most probable = 1
	Least probable = 4
Mitigating factors: Has it been previously tested or integrated? Do we know anything about it?	

Cost	
How much would it cost the company if this broke?	Most expensive = 1
	Least expensive = 4
Mitigating factors: Is there a workaround? Can we give them a fix via the Internet?	

Visibility	
If it failed, how many people would see it?	Most visible = 1
	Least visible = 4
Mitigating factors: Volume and time of day intermittent or constant.	

Tolerability	
How tolerant will the user be of this failure? For example, a glitch shows you overdrew your checking account; you didn't really, it just looks that way. How tolerant would the user be of that?	Most intolerable = 1
	Least intolerable = 4
Mitigating factors: Will the user community forgive the mistake?	

Human Factors	
Can/will humans succeed using this interface?	Fail = 1
	Succeed = 4
Mitigating factors: Can they get instructions or help from Customer Service?	

Combining the Risk Factors to Get a Relative Index

MITs does not require that you apply a rank index to all of your criteria for every item on the inventory, so you don't have to apply a rank to inappropriate qualities. The MITs ranking process uses the average of all the criteria that have been assigned a risk index. Figure 9.3 shows a sample ranking table from the Tester's Paradise inventory (discussed in Chapters 8, 10, 12, and 13).

Tester's Paradise (Release 2.0)	Inventory Items	Tests	S	P	C	C/CS	R	AVG R	
Bug Fix Information	Fix For Error #123 (see req. B477)	7	1	-	-	-	1	1.00	
	Fix for Error #124 (see req. B501)	4	3	4	3	-	-	3.33	
New Function	New Menu Option #3 View Mini Clip	4					1.6	1.60	
(see req. D071 & D072)	Arrange Payment(Path)	5	1	2	1	1		1.25	
	Method of Payment (Path)	11	1	2	2	1	2	1.60	
	Method of Payment (data)	12	1	2	1	1		1.25	
	Purchase Option: Not Available in some states (data)	50					1	1.00	
	Minimum Order must be $30.00 (data)	3	1				1	1.00	
	Method of Payment limited to 2 credit cards (Data)	12	1	1	1	2	1	1.20	
Structural / Environment Information	Enhancement -automatic detection for 5 modems. (Rel. 1 had auto-detect for 3 classes only)	5					1	1.00	
	Installation is automatic at log on	1					1	1.00	
	Total New Tests with average rank:	114						1.38	
Existing Application Base Function	Our Best Simulator (automated suite BSIM01)	65					1.00	1.00	

Figure 9.3 Sample ranking index for Tester's Paradise.

Notice that the different items don't all have risk indexes assigned for every criteria. For example, if the risk is concentrated in a requirement, as in the structural item, installation is automatic at logon. Therefore, there may be no need to worry about any of the other criteria. But the risk associated with an item is normally a combination of factors, as with the New Functions category, where most of the risk factors have been assigned an index value.

Note: When a ranking criteria has been assigned a rank index, I say that it has been "ranked."

In this sample, each ranking criteria that has been ranked is given equal weight with all other ranked criteria for that item. For example, the item Method of Payment (data) has four ranked criteria assigned to it; the average rank is simply the average value of $(1 + 2 + 1 + 1)/4 = 1.25$. It is possible to use a more complex weighting system that will make some criteria more important than others, but I have never had the need to implement one. This system is simple and obvious, and the spreadsheet handles it beautifully. The spreadsheet transfers the calculated average rank to the other worksheets that use it. If a change is made in the ranking of an item on the ranking worksheet, it is automatically updated throughout the project spreadsheet.

In some projects, like the real-world shipping project, it is necessary to rank each project for its importance in the whole process, and then rank the items inside each inventory item. This double layer of ranking ensures that test resources concentrate on the most important parts of a large project first. The second internal prioritization ensures that the most important items inside every inventory item are accounted for. So, in a less important or "risky" project component, you are still assured of testing its most important parts, even though it will be getting less attention in the overall project. This relative importance is accomplished through the same process and serves to determine the test coverage for the item.

Using Risk Ranking in Forensics

After the product ships or goes live or whatever, there is an opportunity to evaluate the risk analysis based on the actual failures that are reported in the live product or system. Problems reported to customer service are the best place to do this research. I have had the opportunity several times over the past years to perform forensic studies of various products and systems. There is much valuable information that I can use when I develop criteria for the next test effort by examining what was considered an important or serious problem on the last effort.

Mining the customer support records gives me two types of important information. First, I can use the actual events to improve my analysis in future efforts and, second, I find the data that I need to put dollar amounts in the cost categories of my risk analysis. If I can use this real-world cost information when I rank my tests and evaluate my performance, then I can make a much better case for the test effort. This last point is well illustrated in this next case study, the 401(k) Web Project.

Case Study: The 401(k) Web Project

I recently reviewed a new Web application for a fiduciary trust company. The company had been assured by their eXtreme developers that testers are unnecessary in Web projects. Since the risk of project failure would be measured in millions of dollars in lost business, they thought it a good idea to risk a few hundred on a second opinion. This turned out to be a good risk for them and a really good example for this chapter.

The Application

The only information I was given was that this was a long-awaited Web-based application that would provide 401(k) retirement plans for self-employed small-business people. Up until this new product line, the benefits of a 401(k) retirement plan had been the exclusive province of large businesses. Not only had there not been any opportunity for self-employed persons to have a 401(k) program, but there was also a significant number of now self-employed persons whose 401(k) retirement plans had been frozen in the 401(k) plan of their last major employer. People with their 401(k) plans in this situation couldn't contribute to them or borrow from them. These assets were effectively unavailable to their owners until they rolled them into an IRA, which could accept contributions but from which they could not borrow. The other option was to close the fund and remove their money, and pay a significant penalty and income tax on the amount.

This new product would allow self-employed people to set up and administer their own 401(k) plan. It would also allow them to transfer in their lame duck 401(k) holdings, and contribute to and borrow against the plan. The response to the plan offering was expected to be huge.

My Testing

No specific requirements were stated, so I adopted the fundamental risk requirements for all fiduciary dealings: No money can be created or destroyed (or lost or prematurely withdrawn). The main risk, if any of these conditions should occur, could include financial instability, audits by government agencies, criminal proceedings, and high-stakes litigation. I approached the assignment armed only with my ID, my newly issued password, my Internet-connected PC, and a blank document open in Word.

My first test was to log on and enroll in the plan. The logon failed to complete because of a security breaching procedure in the application code. This objectionable procedure was rejected by the security settings in the browser, creating an endless logon loop where the logon succeeded but no other page could be displayed. This caused the system to redisplay the logon page. However, no error message was displayed, and normal users would have been completely stymied. And there were more errors.

Within a few hours, I had identified three fatal errors in the application and two fatal errors in the process. In four hours of testing, I logged 20 issues. Of these, 15 required a call to customer service to resolve, and 5 were of a nature that would cause the customer to lose confidence in the institution. I found all of these issues by simply trying to enroll in the program.

Reporting My Results

It was a simple matter to keep track of the number of minutes spent on the phone with CS and the developers—215 minutes—and, of course, my time spent testing, talking, and reporting. The total came to 8 billable hours. I created an inventory of the features that I tested, the logic flow map of enrollment, and a bug report complete with pictures. The logic flow map clearly showed two of the fatal errors. These could have been detected in a design review.

Most of the issues were first reported over the phone, but I prepared a report enumerating all of them, which was widely circulated among the developers and the agents.

Reproducibility and Savings Estimates

The thing that makes this effort so important for demonstrating risk and its associated costs is that all of my issues were 100 percent reproducible. They were going to occur during *every* enrollment. So every customer was going to experience them. Consequently, calculating the value of testing or the risk of not testing in terms of dollars saved was doable, and the results were impressive and defensible.

Developers have long disputed this kind of cost savings statement on the basis that you can't be sure how many users will be affected. If you have to wait until you have collected actual usage stats from production before you can justify an estimate, the gun is a long time cold and it is hard to get a hearing.

Calculating the Value of Testing

The first step was to calculate the cost of their test effort. There were no expenses, so the invoice was for time only:

The cost of my testing: 8 hours × $125 per hour = $1,000

The next step was to calculate how much cost was incurred by the company for supporting the customer, me, through this process. I asked what their support costs were for call-in customers on a per-minute basis; the average estimated cost was $5 per minute. That figure includes all the costs associated with handling a call—floor space, telecommunications, salaries, benefits, and so on. This gives a typical cost per (computer-literate, Web-savvy) customer of:

215 minutes per customer × $5 per minute = $1,075 per customer

So, they would probably make back their investment on testing the first time a customer did not have to call customer service to get through the process of setting up their plan. This estimate doesn't take into account all the potential customers who would not become customers because of the number of issues they would have to resolve in order to set up their plan. Nor does it take into account the ones who would simply fail, give up, and go away without calling customer service.

Next, I asked how many customers they expected to sign up in the first month. (I ignored the cost to fix the bugs and assumed for the sake of estimation that all the bugs I found would be fixed within the first month.) The company had planned a mass mailing to 40,000 targeted prospective customers. They expected a record response to the long-awaited new plan, so estimates went as high as 20 percent response to the mailing, or 8,000 customers for the plan. (A 5 to 10 percent response would be the normal estimate.) So, I calculated a range from a 5 percent response, or 2,000 customers at the low end, to a 20 percent response, or 8,000 customers at the high end.

For simplicity, I will round off the estimated customer support cost per customer to get through the plan setup stage (calculated in the preceding text) to $1,000 per customer. The savings in customer support alone, due to testing this one feature, is somewhere between

$$\$1,000 \times 2,000 \text{ customers} = \$2,000,000$$

and

$$\$1,000 \times 8,000 \text{ customers} = \$8,000,000$$

Note: **Conversely and conservatively, the risk of not testing is somewhere between $2 million and $8 million *in the first month*.**

If no testing is done, this range represents the budget that they had better have ready for customer support if they want the product to succeed.

Without a test effort to warn them of these problems in advance, the company would have discovered these issues in public and in volume. Yet they had not thought it necessary to spend even 1 percent of this potential loss on a test effort. This is typical of the I-feel-lucky approach to software development that I talked about in Chapter 3. It is also proof that this approach to software development is still very much in use.

Managers at the company didn't believe that a test effort would be worthwhile. They didn't believe because testers don't normally measure these things, and so the value of testing remains a mystery at best. Testers must learn how to demonstrate the value of their efforts, and they must pursue every opportunity to demonstrate this value.

Some Thoughts on This Project

This was a small application. I walked into it cold and broke it, many times. Or rather, I discovered many places where it was broken or disconnected, and I reported them to the maker. There was no planning and no estimation done. I just started exploring. The effort certainly saved the company millions of dollars. But there are some problems in this example.

The first problem is that in a larger project this would not be possible. While I could manage the complexity of this one function in my head and in my notes, in a larger project, there are too many complexities to succeed using this method. Like my friend in the maze in Chapter 11, "Path Analysis," I need a string to help me find my way. The next point is that this was an ad hoc effort; a one-time deal (also covered in Chapter 11). Again, ad hoc efforts don't work on a large scale, which brings me to the next problem.

The biggest thing wrong with this whole scenario is that it gave management the wrong message, even though it was unintentional. I cannot believe the naïveté and myopia that encumbers the managers who somehow reasoned that by testing one-tenth of the application, I had discovered most or all of the bugs and they were now safe to proceed with the deployment.

Summary

I use my risk analysis for many different purposes before, during, and after the test effort. A ranked inventory is a powerful tool for answering important questions about the test effort and the product. If you take one additional step and add a sequencing field like "Test Order," you have created a project management tool that is uniquely applicable to the test effort.

In the scheme of things, risk analysis costs very little to perform and provides a powerful project management tool for the test effort. It also ensures that everyone in the effort understands the project's scope and priorities.

Risk analysis is not a science; at this stage it is mostly an art. However, by using MITs risk analysis, you can select ranking criteria that are appropriate and pertinent to your project and use them to make your inventory a very powerful tool in your test effort. There are other benefits as well.

We discussed several benefits of conducting risk analysis in this chapter. It can be an invaluable tool for improving the test effort, but performing risk analysis has many benefits besides better testing. Other groups benefit as well from this process, particularly operations.

Risk analysis is valuable in both the plan-driven and RAD/Agile efforts. Understanding risk and being ready to deal with the outcome is independent of the development methodology. It's just good management. The case study showed how I use risk analysis and forensic data to demonstrate the value provided by testing in terms of the money saved by testing.

In this chapter, I described a formal approach to establishing risk and prioritizing the items on the test inventory, MITs risk analysis, which uses both quantitative and qualitative analysis to establish a numeric value for risk, based on a number of specific criteria. In the early planning phases of a test effort, this analysis is used to focus test resources on the most important parts of the project and to size the test effort.

Once the risk analysis has been completed and tests have been identified, MITs risk analysis is used as the basis for determining the test coverage that should be given to an item, as you will see in Chapter 10, "Applied Risk Analysis."

Applied Risk Analysis

The first time I told my management that I would not be testing 100 percent of the project, they were shocked and outraged. There ensued a lively discussion. I found myself with a lot of explaining to do. But once I had showed them my inventory with its hundreds of test scenarios, they were ready to hear about my process for ranking the requirements and tests so that I would only run the most important tests, even if that represented only 67 percent of the inventory, rather than 100 percent.

The managers were much more amenable to the 67 percent test coverage once I had walked them through my test sizing worksheet and they became acquainted with how long it would take the test team to actually perform those tests. Finally, my management was particularly pleased when, many months later, I was able to report to them that these most important tests had found and caused to be removed 90 percent of all the bugs ever found in the software, before it went to production.

I used my inventory ranking worksheet and my test sizing worksheet to explain the facts of testing to my management all those years ago. It still works today. The biggest difference is that back when I started, my worksheets were written and calculated by hand on a quadrille pad. Today they are automated in an Excel spreadsheet. Back then I spent a lot of effort and time to produce these worksheets; today they take only a small amount of effort, and they give me answers so fast that I can keep up and even get ahead of most RAD/Agile developers. In fact, in many Web projects, my worksheets end up being the only piece of development collateral extant.

The ranking worksheet shows the relative importance and the recommended test coverage for the inventory item. The sizing worksheet takes those quantities and combines them with project level constants to grind out an estimate of the time and resources that will be required to perform the recommended test coverage of the most important tests. Or, from another viewpoint, the worksheet tells you how much remains to be done.

These worksheets are very popular with the bean counters. The ranking worksheet and the sizing worksheet have often proved to be the only record of how big the project is, how extensive the test effort should be, and why. The bean counters understand the worksheet; it turns data into information. This information answers many of their favorite questions, like the ones discussed in Chapter 1, "The State of Software Testing Today." These include the following:

What does the software do?   The inventory contains the requirements, if they exist; the feature list; the environment catalog; and so on.

What are you going to do to prove that it works?   A tester reads this as, "What are you going to test?" and "How are you going to test it?" The risk analysis and MITs ranking identifies exactly what needs to be done to prove that *it* works and how I plan to test *it*. It also answers the question, "How big is *it*?"

What will it cost?   The worksheet allows me to answer this question, both by estimation during planning and in actuality during the test effort as the estimates are replaced with actual measured quantities.

Usually the auditors don't want to know how I got the inventory; they just pick it up and run with it. Oddly, in all my years of testing, the developers in the real-world shipping project, discussed in Chapter 7, are the only ones who have ever seriously challenged my risk analysis.

Again, every project is different, and each sizing worksheet is likely to be different as well. I have developed a new flavor of sizing worksheet in almost every project I have ever done. But I almost always start with the same Excel spreadsheet template. The point is, I could not give management the quality answers that I do without an inventory and a sizing worksheet.

> **Note: The worksheet is the place where all those numbers, those measurements I have been recording, become valuable information. This information can be used to make decisions.**

This chapter talks about how to use risk analysis on the inventory to produce answers to the questions in the preceding list. You will find ways to build a preliminary sizing worksheet and use it in test estimation. Then you will learn how to continue to use the inventory and sizing worksheet as you refine your estimates and add the most important tests to the inventory.

As in previous chapters, these techniques are discussed in terms of how they apply to various development approaches.

Applying Risk Analysis to the Inventory

During the planning phase, we want to be able to produce quick estimates of the number and type of tests that we will need to perform. I use a method that yields a quick estimate of the MITs for this process. I will then use this estimated MITs total in the sizing worksheet to estimate the optimum time frame, and resources required, for the test effort.

Part of the payback for a good risk analysis is that you pick the best tests, perform fewer tests, and get a higher return (higher bug find rate) on them. When I begin constructing test cases, I examine the paths and data sets in greater detail. I will use the more rigorous approach to calculate the MITs total.

In my spreadsheet-based inventory, a sizing worksheet begins with inventory items already discussed in chapters 8 and 9. In this next step, we will add the inventory risk analysis and the test coverage estimates that it yields. Once you enter an inventory item or a test item into one of the spreadsheet inventories, its name, average rank, and the number of tests associated with it are carried automatically to all the worksheets. So, for example, if you change the rank of an item or the number of tests associated with the item, the number of MITs, or the recommended test coverage, all the estimates for resource requirements are automatically updated for you. You can download this sample spreadsheet, which I developed for the Testers Paradise Application Version 2.0, to help you get started, at www.testersparadise.com.

The Test Estimation Process

Consider the information in Table 10.1. This is the first page of the spreadsheet.[1] It is the ranking worksheet that contains the project information, the preliminary high-level inventory, a number of tests for each item, and the rank of each item. In this worksheet, the ranking criteria are S for severity, P for probability, C for cost, C/CS for cost for customer service, and R for required.

Table 10.1 Sample Preliminary Inventory with Ranking

Tester's Paradise (Release 2.0)	Inventory Items	T #Tests Identified	S	P	C	C/ CS	R	AVG R
Bug Fix Information	Fix For Error #123 (see req. B477)	7	1				1	1.00
	Fix for Error #124 (see req. B501)	4	3	4	3			3.33
New Function	New Menu Option View Mini Clip	4					1.6	1.60
(see req. D071 & D072)	Arrange Payment (Path)	5	1	2	1	1		1.25
	Method of Payment (Path)	11	1	2	2	1	2	1.60
	Method of Payment (data)	12	1	2	1	1		1.25
	Purchase Option: Not Available in some states (data)	50					1	1.00
	Minimum Order must be $30.00 (data)	3	1				1	1.00
	Method of Payment limited to 2 credit cards (Data)	12	1	1	1	2	1	1.20
Structural/ Environment Information	Enhancement – automatic detection for 5 modems. (Rel. 1 had auto-detect for 3 classes only)	5					1	1.00
	Installation is automatic at logon	1					1	1.00
	Total New Tests with average rank:	114						1.38
Existing Application Base Function	Our Best Simulator (automated suite BSIM01)	65					1.00	1.00
Standard base function tests still apply:	Message Data Flow Checker (automated suite DFCHECK)	61					1.00	1.00
All test suites for Version 1.0 will be run	Screen Comparison – Pixel Viewer (automated suite PIXVIEW)	76					1.00	1.00
MITs Totals - All Tests	Tot tests & average rank =	**316**						1.31

[1] I simply selected the cells I wanted in the spreadsheet and copied them, then pasted them here in my Word document.

Which Comes First? The Analysis or the Plan?

For many years I covered the analytical test analysis topics, path analysis and data anaylsis, before I discussed risk analysis. But in that time, I have found that in practice more testers can put risk analysis into practice and get real value from it more quickly and easily than test analysis. As a result, I put the risk analysis topics before the test analysis topics in this book. If you have to go back to testing before you finish the book, you can at least take the risk topics and the worksheet with you.

However, it is not possible to discuss all the great uses for a worksheet without having some tests to count. So for the purposes of finishing the discussion on risk analysis, I am going to pretend that you have already identified some tests under each inventory item. The next three chapters present good methods for counting how many tests actually exist, along with other good tools for you to use in the actual selection process.

In each of the next three chapters, I will continue to add tests to the inventory as I explain path and data analysis.

This project is a typical middleweight project with some Agile programming on the Web front end and some well-planned database and business logic modules in the back.

There are many ways of determining the risk index associated with each ranking criteria, as we discussed in the previous chapter. The worksheet calculates the average rank of each inventory item. This becomes the base rank used in the estimation process. But before we move on to this next step, we need to examine where the tests associated with each inventory item came from.

Where Do the Tests Come From?

The worksheet lists a number of tests associated with each inventory item. The notations (Path) and (Data) next to certain inventory items refer to the type of tests being counted. I will cover both path and data analysis in detail in the next three chapters, where I will show you some very powerful and fast techniques for estimating and counting the number of path tests and data tests you will need in your test effort.

Suffice it to say, you can be as general or as specific as you like when you estimate the number of tests for each of these preliminary inventories. I always estimate certain types of tests; as with everything else in MITs, you are invited to customize this list to suit yourself. The following are my test sources:

Most Important Nonanalytical Tests (MINs). These are the tests that come from the Subject Matter Experts. They tend to dig deep into the system and focus on hot spots. They are often ad hoc in nature and do not provide any type of consistent coverage.

Most Important Paths (MIPs). These are the logic flow paths through a system. They form the basis for user-based function testing and allow the tester to verify and validate functions end to end. Chapters 11 and 12 deal with path analysis.

Most Important Data (MIDs). These are the data sets that must be validated and verified. Chapter 13 deals with techniques for counting and choosing your test data.

Most Important Environments (MIEs). There are two types of environmental testing. The first type is illustrated in the real-world shipping example from Chapter 7, where it was important to identify the various parts of the system that were used by the inventory test items (see Figure 7.2 and Figure 8.9 for examples of this type of environment). In this case, we use the test inventory to track what tests use what environments. This type of environment test is incorporated into various test scripts as a matter of course. The second type of environment testing is unique because it involves multiple environments that the software must run on. This is the more common scenario in RAD/Agile development efforts, where the application will be expected to run on several types of platforms, hardware, operating systems, databases, and so on.

This type of test is unique in this list, because while the other three types of tests tend to turn into test scripts, testing these environments requires that you run all your scripts on each environment. This is shown in the following equation:

$$\text{MITs} = (\text{MINs} + \text{MIPs} + \text{MIDs}) \times (\text{MIEs})$$

For this reason, this type of testing has an enormous impact on the time it will take to complete testing, and that is why the test environments get their own pages in my spreadsheets.

Clearly, the more accurate the number of tests identified at an early stage, the better the quality of the resulting estimate of the resources required to conduct the test effort. Once this worksheet has been filled out, the next step is to update the MITs Totals worksheet with these values.

The MITs Totals Worksheet

Up until now I have talked about risk in general terms, as it relates to a requirement or a feature—the high-level view. If I am analyzing the requirements and feature list, I will identify smaller and smaller testable bits through analysis. Those testable items are ranked and recorded in the inventory. Eventually, I will add up the most important tests in each category and put the totals in the sizing worksheet so that I can count how much time they will take to accomplish.

In my spreadsheet, the base values are automatically transferred from the Ranking worksheet to the MITs Totals worksheet, where the estimated test coverage and MITs tests are calculated as shown in Table 10.2. In this table, you see a preliminary estimate of the test coverage and the number of MITs that need to be run.

The first section of Table 10.2 deals with the new test items in Release 2. The middle section lists the tests from the previous release, and the last section contains the MITs totals. We will talk about this last section first.

The first thing to notice about the last section of Table 10.2, the last four lines, is that a total of 315 tests have been identified. But there are two different totals for the MITs. These are listed in the third from the last line.

MITs by the Rank Average Method

The first MITs value, 201 tests, coverage of 64 percent, is the average value of the total of all the tests divided by the average rank of all the tests:

$$\text{Minimum MITs} = (\text{MINs} + \text{MIPs} + \text{MIDs}) / \text{Average Rank}$$

This is the absolute minimum number of tests that we could run. It is not the recommended value, and it may be completely hypothetical; however, it does give management a low-end value to use in the resource negotiations.

Table 10.2 Data from the MITs Totals Worksheet

Tester's Paradise (Release 2.0)	Inventory Items	T #Tests Identified	Rank	%Cov (100/ Rank)%	PastPerf Past Performance	TI Tests Identified /Rank = Number of tests to run
Bug Fix Information	Fix For Error #123 (see req. B477)	7	1.00	100%	75%	7.00
	Fix for Error #124 (see req. B501)	4	3.33	30%	95%	1.20
New Function	New Menu Option #3 View Mini Clip	4	1.60	63%		2.50
(see req. D071 & D072)	Arrange Payment (Path)	5	1.25	80%	NA	4.00
0	Method of Payment (Path)	11	1.60	63%	NA	6.88
0	Method of Payment (Data)	12	1.25	80%	NA	9.60
0	Purchase Option: Not Available in some states (Data)	50	1.00	100%	NA	50.00
0	Minimum Order must be $30.00 (Data)	3	1.00	100%	NA	3.00
0	Method of Payment limited to 2 credit cards (Data)	12	1.20	83%	NA	10.00
Structural/ Environment Information	Enhancement –automatic detection for 5 modems. (Rel. 1 had auto-detect for 3 classes only)	5	1.00	100%	NA	5.00
0	Installation is automatic at logon	1	1.00	100%	NA	1.00
0	Total New Tests, Average Rank, Average Test Coverage, MITs by Summation	113	1.38	72%	MITS SUM	100.18
	TotalTests/avg of rank values and MITs by Summation	82.00			--->	101.00
Existing Application Base Function	Our Best Simulator (automated suite BSIM01)	65		67%	97%	43.55
Standard base function tests still apply:	Message Data Flow Checker (automated suite DFCHECK)	61		47%	90%	28.67
All test suites for Version 1.0 will be run	Screen Comparison – Pixel Viewer (automated suite PIXVIEW)	76		77%	94%	58.52
	Tot New + Old tests =	315	avg. %	64%		231.74
MITs Totals - All Tests	min MITs = T × %Cov =	201.00			MITs =	232.00
Minimum % test coverage	min MITS / T × 100 =	201.00		64%		
Proposed % test coverage	(TI / T) × 100 =			74%		232.00

MITs by the Summation Method

The second MITs value, 232 tests, with a test coverage of 74 percent, is the recommended value for the MITs in this test effort. This value is the sum of the MITs for each item divided by its rank index. This is MITs by the summation method. The formal equation is shown in the following equation:

$$MITs = \sum_{i=1}^{i=tsi} Ti / Ri$$

where:

T = All tests for the item

R = Rank of the item

tsi = Total selected items

The summation method always gives a more accurate picture of how many tests will be needed, since it is more granular by nature. In my sizing worksheet, it provides the high end for resource negotiations.

If I am preparing a simple high-level (pie-in-the-sky) estimate, it will use requirements and features as the ranked test items. The work estimates will be very approximate. If I can include the count of actual tests identified for the project and use the MITs by summation method, then I can create a much more accurate estimate of resource requirements.

This means I have a better chance of negotiating for enough resources to actually succeed in my test effort. This is why I perform path and data analysis on the test items before I present my sizing estimates. Don't worry, though. If the development methodology in your shop does not give you time to plan and analyze, the worksheets are still powerful measurement and reporting tools.

Risk-Based Test Coverage and Performance

In the MITs method, the proposed test coverage, shown in column 5 of Table 10.2, is based on the number of tests identified for the item and the average rank index of the item. The past performance metric shown in column 6 is a measure of how good the MITs test coverage was. It is unfortunate that you have to wait until the product has been in production for some time before you can get the performance measure, but it does help you improve your work in the future.

The middle section, Existing Application Base Function, comprises the tests that were developed for the previous release. Notice that these tests found from 90 to 97 percent of the bugs before this previous release went into production. Especially noteworthy was the test suite for the Data Flow Checker. It only provided 47 percent test coverage, yet this suite found 90 percent of bugs in the release. Not much had been changed in these existing functions, so there seems to be no reason to make any changes in these test suites.

Rerunning test suites from previous releases is normally used to make sure that nothing got broken in the process of putting the new code in place. Unfortunately, they are the first thing management likes to cull out when time pressure builds.

A good test sweep for Release 1 can then be a starting point for subsequent releases. Microsoft likes to call this a "smoke test"; I like to call it a diagnostic suite. The point is that a test suite of this type can outlive the code it was originally written to test. So don't lose track of where you put these older tests if you are forced to forego them in one test cycle. You may well want them back at some point.

One final note before we move on to examining the sizing worksheet: Keep in mind that the rank of tests can change from one release to the next, as well as during a release. For example, maybe a low-ranking block of tests finds an astounding number of bugs. We'd want to up the ranking for it the next time we run it. Eventually, when the system stabilizes, you might want to go back to original ranking on that block of tests. This also assumes that assumptions for Release 1 are also valid for Release 2, which is not always the case.

The Sizing Worksheet

The sizing worksheet, as I use it here, is first and foremost the tool I use to calculate how much the test effort will do, based on the risk analysis, and how much that will cost in terms of testers, test time, regression test time, and test environments.

The sizing worksheet will contain relative percentages, like test coverage. It will contain time taken, and if you are lucky and very clever, it will contain the cost of doing and not doing certain tests. It will contain assumptions; these should be clearly noted as such. It will also contain estimates, which should be clearly distinguished from actuals.

Some Thoughts about Test Coverage

How much of what there was to test did you test? Was that "adequate"? I saw a reference to an IEEE guideline that said that minimum test coverage should be 80 percent. I want to know: "80 percent of what?" If there is no immutable method for counting all the tests that exist, what benefit are we gaining by testing some fixed percentage? How do we know that the 80 percent that was tested was the right 80 percent? It is ironic that Pareto analysis suggests that 20 percent of the code generally causes 80 percent of the problems. How does this method ensure that we will test any part of the most-likely-to-fail 20 percent?

Unfortunately, there is no magic number for test coverage. The adequate test effort is made so by selecting the correct tests, not by running a particular number of them. Further, you can only find the magic 20 percent problem center with good risk analysis techniques.

During the test effort, estimates are replaced by the actual effort times. The worksheet becomes the tracking vehicle for project deliverables. As we test, we replace the estimates with real time, so when we estimate the next test effort, we have actual times to compare the estimates with. This improves our estimates.

Once my ranking is complete, the totals on the MITs Totals worksheet populate the sizing worksheet. Table 10.3 shows my sample test sizing worksheet. Most of the numbers in the third column are either linked values from the MITs Totals worksheet or they are calculated in their cells here on the sizing worksheet. I will point out some of the highlights of this sample.

Item 1: MITs Tests and Coverage

The total number of tests that have been identified in this application is 315. After MITs analysis, the recommended test coverage is 74 percent. This means that I am going to size the test effort for 232 tests—the high end of the estimate. From this starting point, the rest of the worksheet is dedicated to calculating how many hours it will take to run 232 tests, create automated tests, report and track bugs, and so on.

If I have to, I can fall back on the minimum MITs number, but I really don't like to underestimate the test effort at this time.

Table 10.3 Tester's Paradise Test Sizing Worksheet

Item	Tester's Paradise (Release 2.0)	
1	Total Tests for 100% coverage (T) from MITs Totals row on Test Calc. Sheet	**315**
	MITs Recommended number of scripts	**232.00**
	MITs Minimum number of scripts from MITs Totals Sheet	208.00
	MITs estimate for recommended coverage — all code	**74%**
	MITs estimate for minimum required coverage — all code	66%
	Number of existing tests from Version 1	130.74
	Total New Tests identified	113
	Number of tests to be created	101.00
2.	Average number of keystrokes in a test script	50
	Est. script create time (manual script entry) 20 min. each-> (total new tests × 20/60) = person-hours total	32.58
3.	**Est. Automated replay time** total MITs (including validation) 4/60 hours/script = replay hr./cycle total (For each test environment)	**15.47**
	Est. manual replay time for MITs tests (including validation) × 20/60) = hours/cycle (For each test environment)	**77.33**
4.	LOC Approx. 10,000 C++ language, 2,000 ASP	12,000 lines
	Est. Number of errors (3 error/100 LOC) = 400	400 errors
5.	Number of code turnovers expected	4
	Number of complete test cycles est.	5
6.	Number of test environments	6
	Total Number of tests that will be run (against each environment) 4 complete automated cycles = Total MITs × 4	**928**
	Total Tests - all environments in 5 cycles × Total MITs × 6 environments	**6960**
7.	Pre-Turnover: Analysis planning and design	80 hr
	Post-Turnover:	
8.	Script creation & 1st test cycle (manual build + rerun old suites) = Hours	41.30
	4 Automated Test cycles (time per cycle × 4) × Running concurrently on 6 environments (in Hours)	**61.87**
	Total: **Script run time with automation** Running concurrently on 6 environments (1 manual + 4 automated) = **weeks** to run all tests through 5 cycles on 6 environments	**7.22**

	Total: **Script run time all Manual** (5 manual cycles) = weeks serial testing for 6 environments - Best Recommendation for automating testing!	58
9.	Error logs, Status etc. (est. 1 day in 5 for each environment) weeks	1.73
	Total: Unadjusted effort Total Run Time + Bug Reporting (in Weeks)	8.95
10.	**Factor of Safety adjustment = 50% Total adjusted effort (Total effort in Weeks)**	**13.43**
11.	**Minimum completion time: 7 weeks due to coding constraints** **Assumptions:** **• 100% availability of the test system.** **• 10 test machines preset with the req. environments.** **• Multiple testers will be assigned as needed** **• 3 Programmers available for fixes** **• Standard error density and composition** **Current Status: Analysis, test plan and test design completed. Awaiting code turnover to begin testing.**	**7 weeks**

Item 2: Test Units and Time to Create Tests

The number of 50 keystrokes was based on average number of keystrokes in a script from the first release of the application. The estimate of how long it would take to capture a script, 20 minutes, was also based on historical data.

Caution: Check yourself carefully on this estimate. One of the most interesting and amusing boo-boos that I have ever been asked to find a way out of came from a very mature and professional test organization. This group had performed a full MITs evaluation, complete with factor of safety, only to find when they began creating tests that their time to create estimate was underestimated by two-thirds. Happily, we were able to speed the test creation just a bit, shave the number of MITs by 5 percent, and make up the difference from the factor of safety.

You will need to specify your own definition for "test" units. In this example, the units are keystrokes. This is because all of these tests are driven from the user interface. The average number of keystrokes per script was established based on the test scripts developed in the first release of the application. But you may have data sets, or message types, or all sorts of other units. Just add as many rows as you need and keep adding up the totals.

You can add more rows and columns to your own worksheet as you need. For example, these tests are all driven from the user interface and entered via keystrokes. If you have tests that run from batched data files, you will add a row that contains your estimate of the time required to perform the batch testing.

Item 3: Time to Run Tests and Create Automated Tests

Again, this estimate needs to be as accurate as possible. Keying in scripts is hard and thankless. I use a team-oriented approach to ensure that everyone keeps moving and that morale stays high. I believe in providing free soda, pizza, and whatever else it takes to make my people feel good about doing this boring, repetitive work. A tester who is awake creates better scripts than one who is bored to death.

Notice that the estimated replay time for the automated tests was 15.47 hours, or just under two days per cycle. This was the time it would take the entire test suite of 232 tests to run to completion on one machine. The same tests would take 77.33 hours to run manually.

Item 4: Estimate the Number of Errors That Will Be Found

This project had about 12,000 lines of code and script. The company maintained bugs per KLOC (thousands of lines of code) statistics; three errors per KLOC was the magic number, so we used it. It's very hard to estimate how many errors you will actually find, but if you can estimate based on historical data, you at least have a target. We never took it too seriously, but sometimes it was helpful.

Do be careful, though. I was on a project once where the development manager wanted us to stop testing the product after we had found the "estimated" number of bugs. We were not finished testing; we were still finding bugs at the rate of several each day. Nonetheless, I had my hands full convincing her that we were not finished testing.

Item 5: Code Turnovers, Test Cycles

Four code turnovers were expected during the test effort. So the team was expecting to process one or two major deliveries and two or three bug fix deliveries. Because the effort was automated, the testers were expected to run the entire automated test suite every time code was turned over. This meant running every automated script as many as five times.

This was a completely different approach from running a manual test effort. In a manual effort, you can hardly hope to run most tests more than once. In this effort, we found that testers had time on their hands once they started running the automated tests, so instead of just going back and rerunning tests, they were actually refining the existing tests and creating better, higher-quality tests. They would take two or three old tests, pull them out, and replace them with one high-quality test. Over the course of the test effort, the number of tests actually dropped because of this refinement.

Building the new scripts was counted as part of the first test cycle, killing two birds with one stone. The new automated test scripts were built and tested at the same time. This counted as the first test cycle. The plan was to run the following four test cycles in a fully automated mode.

Item 6: Test Environments and Total Tests

Every test needed to be verified and validated in all six environments, so the test room was set up with all six machines. This meant that in two days of automated test runs, 928 test scripts were run on each of the six machines. This was when we found that the administrative overhead was higher than our estimate of having to spend one day out of five doing administrative and bug reporting tasks. (See Item 9.)

This meant that 6,960 tests would be run over the course of the test effort, in five cycles against six test environments. Because the effort was automated, this was doable. It would not have been possible to test to this standard if the tests were being run in a manual mode. The bug reporting effort was larger than expected, however.

Item 7: Planning Time

I don't usually spend more than two weeks planning my test efforts, but I may spend the entire test cycle designing and refining tests. It just depends on how the code arrives, how many test environments I have, and any other relevant particulars for the effort. Also, I like to have this planning time finished before I present the sizing worksheet to management. It simply goes down better. Of course, this in not possible in a really large project, but it usually is possible in a Web application project.

If "plan" is one of those four-letter words that is not politically acceptable in your shop, then you can always absorb your planning time in the estimate of the time required to run your tests, or by adding an extra test cycle.

Item 8: The Case for Test Automation

One of the most noteworthy things about Table 10.3 is the comparison between the total number of hours it would take to run a mostly automated test effort, 15.47, compared to the number of hours it would take to run a manual test effort, 77.33. You can see that there is a good case here for automating the test scripts from this new release. It is this kind of analysis that allows you to make good recommendations about what to automate and when to do it.

In a manual effort it would have taken 58 weeks to run all five test cycles. The automated tests could be run in under eight weeks by fewer testers.

Item 9: Administration, Documentation, and Logging Time

In our shop we usually spent about one day in five bug-logging. This seems to be pretty normal. However, it turned out to be low in this effort, for the reasons that I stated previously, in Item 6. We needed our factor of safety to help us survive this low estimate during the effort.

Test results have to be analyzed, bugs have to be reported, questions have to be answered about what happened, tests have to be reconstructed to understand just went wrong, and failures need to be reproduced for developers. These are a few of the administrative tasks that kept the testers busy in between test runs. In this effort, managing the multiple test environments required more time than we anticipated.

Item 10: Factor of Safety

Notice that there is a 50 percent safety factor built into the overall time required to conduct this effort. Now if your management says, "What's this factor of safety?", you can say it's to cover the unforeseen and unplanned activities that happen every day, like meetings, kids getting sick, telephone and computer systems going down—this is just real life. As I said before, 50 percent is very low; this is where everyone is focused on this test effort. We used it up making up for our low bug reporting and administration estimate.

Item 11: Constraints, Assumptions, and Status

This next box looks pretty innocuous, but it is where everything hits the wall. The minimum completion time is seven weeks, due to coding constraints. This is the quickest we could get it done. We expect to find 400 errors here. It takes time to fix errors. This is the part management loses sight of most often: the time it takes to fix the bugs. See the section coming up, *Don't Forget the Developers to Fix the Bugs*, for a real-life example of this.

The main assumption in this effort was 100 percent availability of the test system. I am happy to say this wasn't a problem in this particular project, but it normally is a major dependency.

The head tester, Joseph, a quiet, gentle person who couldn't kill a spider, had completed his analysis, test plan, and test design when this proposal was presented to our senior vice president. His test environments were ready, baselined, and fully mirrored. This tester was waiting for his code.

Negotiating the Test Effort

After many years testing, this is still my favorite example of how a good tester can succeed. Joseph had successfully negotiated for 12 weeks to complete the automated test effort in the tables. When the first cycle was automated, his actuals looked so good that he rescaled his sizing worksheet and it looked like everything would still fit into the 12 weeks. Then someone in marketing promised a vice president somewhere that they would deliver the application in four weeks.

I was asked to join the test team that went to tell our vice president what he had to do to get this delivered in four weeks. As always, I was ready to play the sacrificial tester in case things went bad.

"So how can we get this done in four weeks?" the vice president asked the tester, Joseph. "You only have three testers; we can give you 10 good folks from customer service and editorial to help you test. That will do the trick, won't it?"

Joseph wasn't ruffled. "We planned on having six machines running. It takes one machine 16 hours to run the entire suite. If we doubled the number of machines, we could cut that in half." This made sense to the vice president.

Joseph continued, "I wouldn't mind having one other trained tester, but I would decline your kind offer of these guys from editorial because they don't stick to plan and we can't reproduce what they break. We end up spending all our time with them, instead of getting our testing done.

"What we really need is lots of developers to fix the bugs we find right away. If we can run a test cycle in a day, we need the bugs fixed as fast as we can find them. The programmers we have can't possibly give us fixes for 400 bugs in four weeks."

The VP was surprised, but he agreed. The product was delivered in four weeks, and it was very stable. The lesson here is, don't forget the time required to fix the bugs found by testing. This is a common problem in test efforts—mostly because testers don't control this issue.

Don't Forget the Developers to Fix the Bugs

I have encountered this problem several times in my career, enough times to spend a few words on it here. The following example is the best example I ever saw of this situation, because it happened to a very mature and contentious development shop. It just goes to show that we can all get sucked into this mistake.

This was a heavyweight project for a major telecommunications company that came dangerously close to failure because management did not keep sufficient developers ready to fix the bugs that the testers found.

The testers had prepared a full complement of test collateral, including a very good estimate of how many bugs the effort would find, what severity they would be, and so on, but they didn't take the next step and build an estimate of how much time and how many developers it would take to fix all these bugs. So when the project was marked complete by the development managers, they moved all but one of the developers to new projects in different countries.

When I joined the project, I built a worksheet straight away. The lone developer was kind enough to contribute estimates of how much time it would take to fix each logged bug with a severity of 2 or higher. The testers had a good inventory; I simply added a sheet to it. The new sheet was basically the test script worksheet with an environment matrix. Each bug was recorded under the test script that uncovered it. I added two columns to the sheet; one was for the severity of the bug, and the other was the time-to-fix estimate. This worksheet showed management not only how many developer hours would be required to fix these serious to critical bugs, but which requirement, features, and environments the developers should be familiar with. It also showed testers where they could expect to be regression testing the most.

Initially, management supplied developers who were not assigned to any project at that time to fix the bugs. These developers spent precious weeks not fixing bugs, but, rather, trying to understand the system. Management was finally persuaded to bring back key developers specifically to address issues in the code they had written. The developers who had written the code were able to fix the bugs, and the deadlines for system delivery were met, but meanwhile, their new projects fell behind.

It seems absurd that something so important as fixing the bugs found by testing could fall through the cracks. I attribute this problem mostly to a failure of project management techniques in general. When I have seen this failure, it has always been traceable to the fact that there was no task on the project plan for fixing bugs after the code was delivered. This is especially true and problematic in large integration projects where integration issues are not discovered until well after the code has been turned over.

In these cases, the developers who wrote the code have invariably been assigned to their next project, leaving no one who is familiar with the code to fix the bugs. In such circumstances, the time and the cost needed to fix the bug are both significantly higher than when a bug is fixed by the original author.

On a slightly different note, I have to say that not everyone has this problem. There is a new development methodology called eXtreme programming that has gone in quite the opposite direction. Rather than forget that time and developers are required to fix the bugs that testers find, they are counting on it.

The eXtreme Project

Software makers are still trying to off-load the cost of validation and verification onto the user. The latest example of this is eXtreme programming. After close inspection, I have decided it is simply the latest iteration of the I-feel-lucky approach to software development. eXtreme uses a frontal assault on the concept of testing. The RAD approach was to pretend to do formal testing, while what is really going on is a bit of cursory exploration by the testers before letting the customers test it. eXtreme asserts that they are so good that no testing is necessary. This means that no time or effort is wasted before turning it over to the customer, who will begin testing in earnest, whether they mean to or not. What the method does do *extremely* well is pander to the classic A-type compulsive personalities, giving them full permission to run amuck while keeping the financial auditors at bay until it is too late to turn back.

If eXtreme succeeds at all in fielding a viable product, it is due to the Money for Flexibility (MFF) strategy that goes along with this approach and the full dress rehearsal that they are giving the software while the first sacrificial customers test it. The successful eXtreme projects that I have seen keep a full contingent of developers at the ready when they roll out the software to a select few customers. This gives them the lead-time that they need to fix all the major issues before too many people see the thing.

The Contract to Test

The sizing worksheet is an important tool in establishing the contract to test. When I write a contract, the first thing I do is estimate the test effort. Then I write the test scripts for some of the buggier areas and compare the two. I can then go in to sign the contract feeling better about my estimate. A test sizing worksheet is used to prepare estimates of the resources required to carry out the test effort.

The worksheet is an important communications tool both in the estimation and in the negotiation phase. It shows management why I couldn't do what they wanted. It protects the customer. If management doesn't understand how big the thing is, they don't understand why you can't test it in 24 hours. In the resource negotiations process, the worksheet, along with the rank and test calculations sheets, serves as the basis for the contract to test between parties.

Once the negotiations are concluded and the contract to test is formalized, this part of the process is completed. The next step is to actually identify tests under each inventory item. Now let's imagine that you are going to actually start designing, collecting, and discovering tests.

Risk Criteria for Picking Tests

As with requirements and functions (discussed in the previous chapter), where criteria must be applied when ranking them, you also need to apply additional criteria when selecting the most important tests. In general, each of the criteria that I use is related to a type of analysis or some other process that defines tests. In this next section, I talk about the tests, the analysis methods I use to identify them, and the criteria I use to rank them. Ultimately, it is the rank of the tests that determines exactly what will be tested and what will not.

There are an infinite number of things that could be tested even for a small, shrink-wrapped application. There can be a hundred permutations on simply resizing a window. It is not generally cost-effective to try and test everything that can be tested. I want to pick the most important tests, and I do that by applying criteria to each test to measure its relative importance. I want to select the tests that fulfill the following requirements.

Validating and Verifying the System Requirements

In traditional commercial software development endeavors (heavyweight to middleweight projects), the requirements are the basis of communication throughout the entire project. They must be well planned and clearly stated. It is a straightforward process to plan tests that verify system requirements when the requirements are well documented. Testers in a traditional software development effort must verify that the system meets the requirements. They were normally detached from the validation of requirements.

In a RAD/Agile effort, the requirements are changing faster than anything else, and they are rarely well documented. This makes it difficult to plan verification tests. Development delivers a function important to end users, and the RAD test team response is, "Oh, that's great, but can we make it do this, too?" Communication is direct; the requirements are embodied in the product. Testers in a RAD/Agile effort are more concerned with answering the validation question, "Does the system do the right things in an acceptable way?"

Exercising the Most Important Functions in the System

Exercise the least understood and the riskiest internal functions of the system—the tests that exercise the most important code or logic paths and data, along with all the interfaces, including module, system, database, network, and business rules. These tests often come together through path analysis (see Chapters 11 and 12), but they also can come directly from the design and requirements.

Exercising the Most Important Paths and Data

From the perspective of the user, the most used functions and data are the most important paths to be tested. These path and data tests are in addition to those identified previously as system function needs. See Chapter 11, "Path Analysis," Chapter 12, "Applied Path Analysis," and Chapter 13, "Data Analysis Techniques," for details on this type of test.

Giving the Most Bang for the Buck

If a test suite provides 50 percent test coverage and finds 97 percent of the errors ever found in the system, then the test coverage provided by this test suite is probably adequate. That's the kind of quality I want to target.

Tests that delve into the areas where the level of confidence is lowest are always a good bet. You are going to want to look very closely at the newer, riskier things. You will want to get way down in the code and make sure you test absolutely everything. Unfortunately, for RAD/Agile efforts, we usually only have time to make sure the function holds together under the best set of circumstances, and then we have to move on.

The test budget gets more bang from the bucks spent on scripts that pack the largest number of the best tests into the most optimized sequence. This type of test usually evolves over time and is the product of several test cycles. Another possible source for this type of test is an expert tester. In either case, these are usually the tests that will be used again and again. If possible, they should be automated. These test scripts are commonly used to form high-power *diagnostic suites* or *basis suites.*

Note: When testers get into the code, there are always more paths to test than originally estimated.

The number of tests associated with each inventory item will continue to grow as you proceed to analyze them, whether that is before or during testing. The reason that I keep my totals on their own worksheet is that it allows me to add columns for the actual number of tests that I end up running. This allows me to carry both the estimated totals and the actual totals through the project. By keeping tabs on the estimates and the actuals, I can baseline the project, measure bloat, and establish factors of safety for the next project. Even in a RAD/Agile effort, this is important, because if the actual numbers deviate too far from the budgeted estimates, I can alert management early—instead of waiting until we are out of money.

This capability of providing constant status information is very compatible with the MFF approach. Without this type of information, testers must approach the test effort as if it were a pie-eating contest. They simply start testing when the product arrives and keep banging away on it until someone ships it. I hate to say it, but I believe that is a big part of the reason that testing has such a bad reputation today. The testers never know how big it is so that when the management asks, "What did you test?" they can say, "We tested it all." From their point of view, they tested everything that they knew about; the problem is that they never really saw the whole thing. No one talks about the heaps of pies that weren't dealt with before the "ship it" whistle blew.

Summary

In this chapter, I walked you through the process of implementing an automated test inventory complete with test totals and a sizing worksheet. I showed you how I use this information to construct a test sizing worksheet that I use to negotiate the particulars of the test effort.

Using the sizing worksheet, testers and managers are in a position to make well-informed decisions about trade-offs between test coverage and test resources. It is an enormous aid in budget negotiations because I can change the rank of test numbers and environment numbers and see the effect immediately, then show the effect to management.

In the last chapter, we discussed how to establish the risk criteria and ranking index for the items on your inventory from the high level. In this chapter, I showed you how I use that analysis to focus my test efforts on the most important areas. I discussed the criteria that I use to pick the right tests to fulfill my estimated test coverage and provide an adequate effort.

There are many types of tests in the inventory. In the next three chapters, we discuss path and data analysis techniques that will help you quickly identify the most important tests for your test scripts.

CHAPTER 11

Path Analysis

"The path not tested is certain to blow up when the users get the product."
—One of the few certainties of testing

A *labyrinth* or *maze* is a perplexing arrangement of pathways designed in such a way that anyone entering has great difficulty finding the way out. The paths through a software system are a maze that the software tester must navigate, not just one time, but many times while the software system evolves and changes. Certainly, this is a daunting task, but software testers are not the first people to grapple with it. The subject of maze traversal has been on people's minds in one way or another for a very long time.

The Legend of the Maze of the Minotaur

About 4,000 years ago, the wealthy seafaring Minoans built many wonderful structures on the island of Crete. These structures included lovely stone-walled palaces, probably the first stone paved road in the world, and, reputedly, a huge stone labyrinth on a seaside cliff called *The Maze of the Minotaur*.

The Minotaur of Greek mythology was a monster with the head of a bull and the body of a man, borne by Pasiphaë, Queen of Crete, and sired by a snow-white bull. According to legend, the god Poseidon who sent the white bull to Minos, King of Crete, was so angered by Minos' refusal to sacrifice the bull that Poseidon forced the union of Queen Pasiphaë and the beast. Thus the monster Minotaur was born. King Minos ordered construction of the great labyrinth as the Minotaur's prison. The beast was confined in the maze and fed human sacrifices, usually young Greeks, in annual rituals at which young men and women performed gymnastics on the horns of bulls and some unfortunate persons were dropped through a hole into the labyrinth's tunnels. The sacrifices continued until a Greek Hero named Theseus killed the Minotaur.

The Minoans did give their sacrifices a sporting chance. Reportedly, there was another exit besides the hole that the sacrifices were dropped through to enter the maze. If the sacrificial person was able to find the exit before the Minotaur found them, then they were free.

It was rumored that a bright physician from Egypt traversed the maze and escaped. The Egyptian succeeded by placing one hand on the wall and keeping it there until he came upon an exit. This technique kept him from becoming lost and wandering in circles.

The Egyptian's technique—always branching the same direction—is called an algorithm. An *algorithm* is any special method of solving a certain kind of problem. This algorithm does not guarantee that the path followed will be the shortest path between the entrance and exit. The length of the path traversed could be quite long, depending on where the exit is relative to the entrance. Note in Figure 11.1, which shows a maze with an exit, that the right-hand path, marked by the dotted line, is significantly shorter than the left-hand path, marked with the dashed line.

The technique used by the fabled Egyptian will only work if the maze structure has certain characteristics, namely:

- There cannot be any pits or traps to fall into along the way. (No Minotaur can block the way.)
- The exit must be along a wall where it can be detected in the dark by a hand.
- The hole in the roof will not be found unless some landmark is erected on the spot.
- The exit must be along a wall that is connected to other maze walls, meaning that it is not on an island, as shown in Figure 11.2.

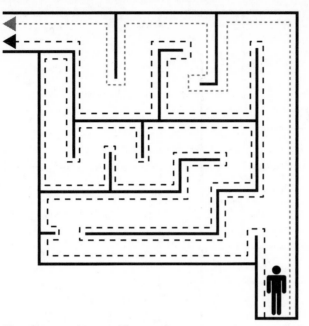

Figure 11.1 Maze with an exit.

If the maze conforms to these rules and if one sure path is all that's required, then the Egyptian's algorithm will always work. This technique is systematic and reproducible. It does not matter which hand you use as long as you do not change hands after you start. This is the simplest maze problem and possibly the most fundamental general technique for finding a solution.

If the maze has no exit, the Egyptian's algorithm would eventually lead him back to the entrance. In a no-exit maze, the left-hand and right-hand paths are the same length; one is simply the reverse of the other.

Undoubtedly, there are nitpickers in the readership saying, "Ahh, but the entrance is also an exit." Under some circumstances, the entrance could be a viable exit, given the proper tools. Say, for instance, the person inside the maze had an accomplice on the outside who was willing to provide him with a rope or a ladder, as Theseus did (more on him in a minute). It is worth mentioning the case where a person is dropped into an enormous maze and the first wall that comes to hand is part of an island with no exit on it. If this person uses only the one-hand-on-the-wall method, she will probably never find an exit. If this person marked her starting point, she would eventually determine that there was no available exit and would probably try a different method, such as wandering away from the island.

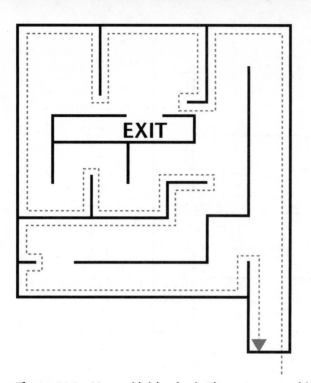

Figure 11.2 Maze with island exit. The entrance to this maze cannot be used as an exit.

Trying to find a path to the exit by wandering through the maze does have a chance of success. In fact, wandering the maze actually has a better chance of finding an island exit than the one-hand-on-the-wall method.

Trying to find a path through a maze by wandering through it, without a method, is often called *ad hoc testing*. The term *ad hoc* is often used interchangeably with *random* in software testing, but the two terms are not the same. Ad hoc testing may or may not be random, and it may or may not be systematic. Ad hoc means for a specific case only. An ad hoc test is a one-time-only test. The maze-traversing efforts of the Egyptian and Theseus were ad hoc, because neither one of them ever returned to do it again. In testing practice, the one-time-only criteria is too often used to justify not keeping any records and possibly not using any algorithms. After all, why invest in records or methods when the test will never be repeated? Because of this rationale, most ad hoc testing that is done is *not reproducible*.

The one-hand-on-the-wall method is systematic and reproducible. If the maze has not changed, the one-hand-on-the-wall method will always follow the same path. The tester can always turn around, put the other hand on the wall, and retrace steps to the entrance. This method is only ad hoc if the sacrificial person never has to go back into the maze again once he has found a way out. Unlike the Egyptian, software testers are dropped back into the maze regularly—every time there is new code.

Thus, the one-hand-on-the-wall method is not random; it is systematic, because each branch taken is based on static criteria—that is, always branch right or always branch left. Random simply means without specific order. Random tests *can be reproducible*. Tests that are generated at random can be documented or *mapped* and later reproduced. This brings us to the maze-traversing method used by Theseus, the Greek who slew the Minotaur.

Theseus was determined to stop the sacrifices to the Minotaur, and for that reason, he volunteered to enter the maze. Minos' daughter Ariadne had fallen in love with Theseus. She gave him a ball of thread, which he tied to the entrance of the maze and unwound as he wandered through the maze. Theseus found and killed the Minotaur, rounded up the sacrificial men and women, and followed the thread back to the entrance, where Ariadne lowered a rope for Theseus and the sacrifices to climb to freedom.

The technique that Theseus used to find the Minotaur was *random*, because he did not use a systematic method, such as putting one hand on the wall to determine his course. He simply followed his instincts till he found the Minotaur. Theseus' technique was ad hoc, because Theseus traced the path to the Minotaur only one time. The technique used by Theseus will work for any path in any maze with virtually any structure. If the string is not disturbed, the path can also be retraced at a later time, making it a reproducible random path.

Theseus succeeded and escaped the Minotaur's maze because he used the thread as a documentation tool that automatically kept track of the turns he made, allowing him to retrace his path back to the entrance. Clever testers typically use a *key trap tool* as their "ball of string." Testers may hope that they will never have to replay the test captured as they went; but if something breaks, they can at least try to reproduce the test.

An undocumented ad hoc test may be adequate if the test never needs to be repeated, but it falls short when the test finds a bug (which is, according to many experts, the whole reason for testing). To diagnose the bug, someone will have to reproduce it. If there is no repeatable method or *string trail,* then reproducing the problem can be virtually impossible. Even when such bugs do get fixed by development, when the fixes are delivered to test, the testers are not in a position to verify them because there is no way to retrace the path.

This is the core of what is wrong with ad hoc test efforts. The sacrificial testers are trying to get through the maze by running through it as fast as they can go—random and ad hoc—rather than using a systematic approach and marking their trail. If a tester is lucky enough to find the exit and if the director asks, "What did you test?", the answer is just about guaranteed to be, "I tested *it.*"

By contrast, in the testing conducted in the prop-up-the-product-with-support scenario, discussed in Chapter 3, the support person gets to play the part of the hero Theseus and rescue the poor sacrificial customers from the monster bug in the maze. The support person's mission is clear: a bug exists and must be removed. Support does not need to know anything else about the maze. The most important distinctions between test and support personnel are that:

- The folks in the test group must go looking for bugs, while the users bring bugs to the folks in support.
- The folks in support are often empowered to fix the bugs they find, while the folks in the test group are not.

Note: In software testing, we need to be able to *identify* and *count* the paths through the maze.

We use algorithms to identify and map paths, but we also need to be able to calculate the number of paths that exist in a given maze based on the properties of the maze. As the maze grows larger and the number of branching corridors increases, the potential for multiple paths to the exit also grows. If the maze does not conform to some rules, like the ones necessary for the Egyptian's method, then the number of paths through a maze can be virtually infinite, impossible to trace or map algorithmically and impossible to determine by calculation.

Webster's New World Dictionary defines a *system* as a set or arrangement of things related or connected so as to form a unity or organic whole. A *structured system* is a system or subsystem that has only one entry point and one exit point. The concept of structured programming was introduced many years ago to help limit the number of paths through a system and thereby control the complexity of the system. Essentially, structured programming gives the sacrificial testers a sporting chance, by guaranteeing that there will be only one way in and one way out of the maze, and no trapdoors or pits.

The fundamental path question for software testers is this: "How many paths are there through this system?" This number is, effectively, one of the two primary measures of "How big *it* is." If we can't establish this parameter, we have no benchmark to measure against. We have no way to quantify how big the project is, and we cannot measure what portion of the total we have accomplished. We will not be able to give a better answer than "I tested *it*."

The one-hand-on-the-wall approach alone does not answer the question, "How many paths are there?" The selection criteria are limited to all branches in a single direction. Random testing does not answer this question either. When paths are selected at random, there is no guarantee that all possible paths will be selected. Some paths will probably be selected more than once, while others won't be selected at all. To map all the paths through a system, the tester will need to follow a systematic set of algorithms.

Determining the number of paths through a maze *empirically*, by trial and error, can be very unreliable. Algorithms can be combined in order to trace all paths, one at a time, but this is time-consuming and virtually impossible to carry out in a large real-time system. In complex systems, a tester using these methods may never be able to prove that all possible combinations of paths have been traced. For the purpose of identifying paths, we introduce the concept of *linear independence*.

Linear Independence

Consider a line that is independent of other lines. For paths, this means only one trace or traversal for each path is counted. In a structured system with one entrance and one exit, where the object is to proceed from the entrance to the exit, this is the same as saying the following:

For any structured system, draw each path from the entrance of the system to the exit. Only count the path the first time you walk on it. In the process of traversing all the paths from the entrance to the exit, it may be necessary to retrace some path segments in order to reach a path segment that has never been traversed before, or to reach the exit. But a path through the system is linearly independent from other paths only if it includes some path segment that has not been covered before.

When a person becomes lost in the maze, he or she can potentially wander through the maze retracing steps until he or she dies. The paths followed by the wanderer are not linearly independent. A programming example of paths that are not linearly independent is a program that loops back to retrace the same path through the system, repeatedly. In that example, the total number of possible paths is potentially infinite. The program can get stuck in a loop until someone kills it. Another example is a logon screen with no functional cancel button, meaning the user cannot leave the logon screen until a correct and valid password and user ID have been entered. This will cause an infinite loop for any user who does not have a valid password and ID.

The path traces caused by looping, feedback, and recursion are only counted once as linearly independent paths, even though they may be retraced over and over again as different paths are traced through the system. In a program, how many times a loop is traced, along with how many times a recursive call is made, is controlled by *data*. When we build our test cases, we will add data sets to our linearly independent paths in order to exercise the data boundary conditions and the logic paths accessed by them. Some paths will be traversed many times because of the data that will be tested. The purpose of this exercise is to calculate the number of paths necessary to cover the entire system.

Let's take a look at two structures that are common in programming and some methods for counting the paths through them: the case statement and a series of required decisions.

The Case Statement

The *case statement* is particularly important for software application testers because it is the structure used in menus. Figure 11.3 shows a typical case statement structure. The maze analogy is a single room with several doorways in which every doorway leads eventually to the exit. The user has as many choices as there are doors. Where the program goes next is determined by the user's selection. The user makes one choice at a time and can always come back to the menu and make a different choice.

Linear Independence

As shown in Figure 11.4, there are five linearly independent paths through this example. We can identify them by *inspection*, tracing them visually one at a time. The first two paths, Paths 1 and 2, could be found using the left- and right-hand-on-the-wall method. Paths 3, 4, and 5 are the other linearly independent paths through this maze. Note: Traditionally, the exit arrow pointing down is the *true* condition.

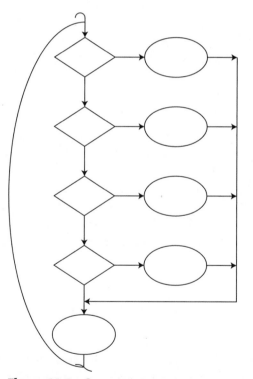

Figure 11.3   Case statement structure.

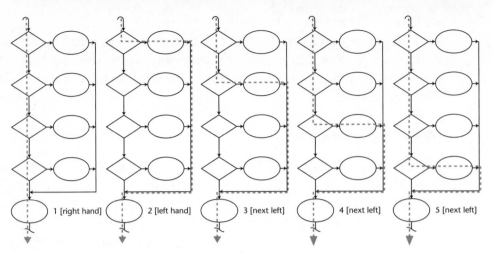

Figure 11.4 Five linearly independent paths.

We can also find the five paths by using the following algorithms.

ALGORITHM 1, PATH 1

1. Enter the system.
2. At every branch, select the *true* condition for each decision (right-hand) path until the exit is encountered.

ALGORITHM 2, PATHS 2, 3, 4, 5, AND 1

1. Enter the system.
2. Select the true (right-hand) path until the first branch where the false (left-hand) path has not yet been selected.
3. Take the false (left-hand) branch.
4. Thereafter, always select the true (right-hand) path until the exit is encountered.

Anyone who has studied data structures will recognize this method of traversing a tree structure. It is systematic and reproducible. Using this algorithm, the tester can reliably identify every path through this system. Other algorithms can be used to solve this problem. By using the systematic approach, we are sure of what we have done when we finish, and we can count the number of paths that go end-to-end through the system.

Algorithm 2 will find all five paths. Path 1, the all true (all right-hand) path will be found last, after all the false (left-hand) branches have been exercised. The reason it is presented with the shortest path as the first path identified is because this shortest path should be the most important path in this system from a tester's perspective. It is the quickest way out of the maze. If, for example, this same logic flow was behind the logon component of a vast and wonderful network, the most important path to both user and tester is the correct logon scenario. If this simplest and most direct true path does not work, what good is any other path?

In software, other criteria are used to define paths besides linear independence. Statement coverage and branch coverage are two examples and are described in the following paragraphs.

Statement Coverage

Statement coverage is a method of path counting that counts the minimum number of paths required to walk through each statement, or node, in the system. This number may or may not be the same as the linearly independent paths. In this example, the case statement, only paths 2, 3, 4, and 5 are required to satisfy 100 percent statement coverage. Note that a tester who only uses statement coverage as a basis has no requirement to exercise path 1, which is possibly the most important path.

Branch Coverage

Branch coverage is a method of counting paths that counts the minimum number of paths required to exercise both branches of each decision node in a system. In the case statement example, all five linearly independent paths are required to satisfy 100 percent branch coverage.

The case statement is a straightforward example. Now we will look at an example that is more complex.

In the case statement, the number of paths required for 100 percent coverage:

Statement coverage = 4
Branch coverage = 5
Linearly independent path coverage = 5
Total paths = 5

A Series of Required Decisions

This construct is important because it is common and it serves to illustrate how quickly the number of paths can become uncertain and confused. Figure 11.5 is a visual representation of such a construct. In this type of maze, each branching path leads back to the main path. There is only one branch that leads to the exit. The number of possible combinations of path segments that one could combine before reaching the exit becomes large very quickly. This is the type of processing that goes on behind some data entry screens. For example:

Are the contents of the first field valid? If they are, check the second field. If not, branch to the exception and then check the second field. Are the contents of the second field valid? If they are, check the third field. If not, branch to the second field's exception and then check the third field, and so on.

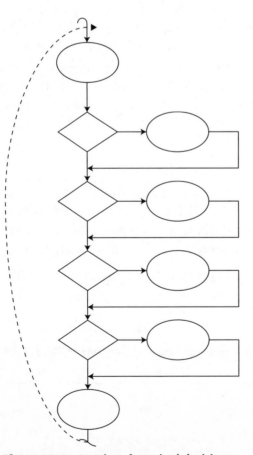

Figure 11.5 A series of required decisions.

When we use the left-hand method in Figure 11.6, we discover that we have already walked through each statement or node of the system in only one path traversal. Thus, 100 percent statement coverage can be accomplished in a single path. Branch coverage can be accomplished in two paths by exercising Path 1, the right- hand or all-true path, and Path 2, the left-hand or all-false path.

This means that the tester who performs only 100 percent statement test coverage is missing 50 percent of the branch conditions. The tester performing only 100 percent branch test coverage is missing all the paths where true and false data conditions are mixed. Example: We have already discussed two paths through this maze; how many paths are there in *total*?

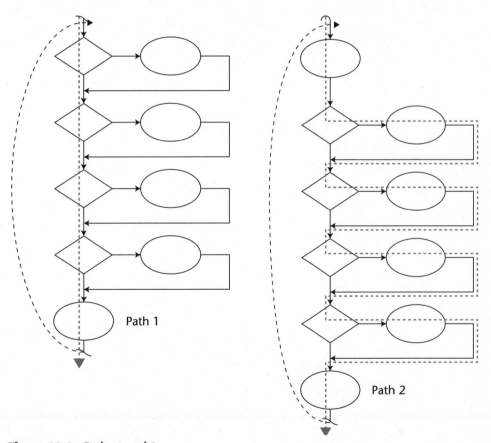

Figure 11.6   Paths 1 and 2.

If-then-else-structure paths for 100 percent coverage:

Statement coverage =1
Branch coverage = 2
Linearly independent path coverage = 5
Total path coverage = 16

If we select only one branch at a time, we will find four linearly independent paths. Notice that Paths 1, 3, 4, 5, and 6 all traverse some path segments that have been traversed by the others, but each includes some path segment that is unique to that particular path. All of the right-hand or true paths are exercised across these four paths. Each left-hand or false path segment is covered one time. Paths 1, 3, 4, 5, and 6 are linearly independent from each other. Each contains path segments that are not covered by any of the others. Path 2 is not linearly independent from Paths 3, 4, 5, and 6 (see Figure 11.7).

If we select *two* branches at a time, we will find six more paths (see Figure 11.8).

If we select *three* left branches at a time, we will find the last four paths (see Figure 11.9).

This series of decisions, with four decision or branching nodes, has 16 paths through it. These paths represent all the combinations of branches that could be taken through this maze. If all of these 16 paths are exercised, several of the path segments will be retraced many times. A typical program contains *hundreds* of branching nodes.

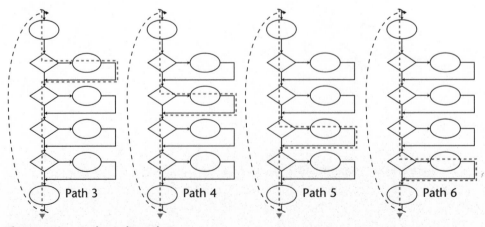

Figure 11.7 Paths 3 through 6.

We have been discussing program logic at the code level. We could just as easily be discussing the logical interaction between many programs in a software system. Both of the preceding examples were structured systems.

Note: **100 percent path coverage is beyond the resources of ordinary test efforts for all but the smallest software systems.**

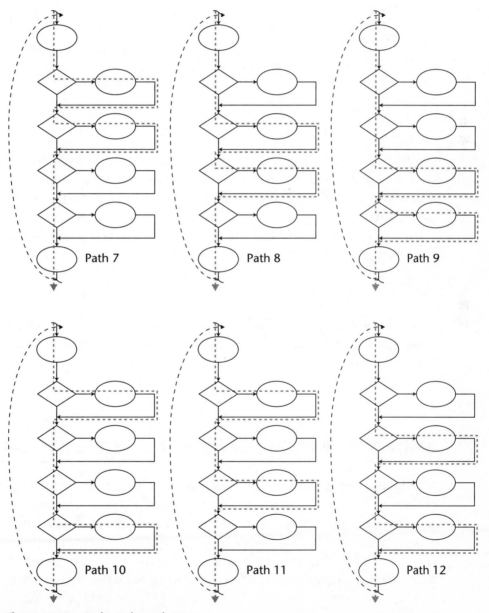

Figure 11.8. Paths 7 through 12.

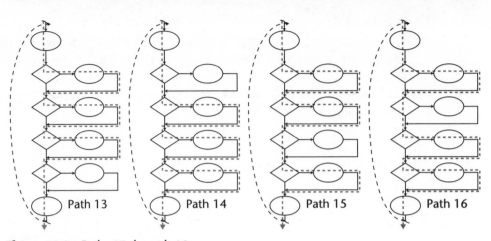

Figure 11.9 Paths 13 through 16.

Given that a software system contains hundreds of logic branches, the number of paths in even a small software system is huge. Two things should be clear from this example. First, when we map every possible path, it becomes clear that while many paths segments are covered repeatedly, others may only be touched once. We won't have time to test them all. Second, even if we have time to test them all once, we won't have time to retest them all every time new code is turned over. We need to use rational criteria in order to pick our test sets.

Note: It is not feasible to count the paths through such a system empirically or by inspection. What is really needed is a way to *calculate* the number of paths that exist in the system.

Calculating the Number of Paths through a System

The tester needs a systematic way of counting paths by calculation—before investing all the time required to map them—in order to predict how much testing needs to be done. A *path* is defined as a track or way worn by footsteps, and also a line of movement or course taken. In all following discussions, path can refer to any end-to-end traversal through a system. For example, *path* can refer to the steps a user takes to execute a program function, a line of movement through program code, or the course taken by a message being routed across a network.

In the series of required decisions example, each side branch returns to the main path rather than going to the exit. This means that the possible branching paths can be combined in $2 \times 2 \times 2 \times 2 = 2^4 = 16$ ways, according to the fundamental principles of counting. This is an example of a 2^n problem. As we saw, this set of paths is exhaustive, but it contains many redundant paths.

In a test effort, it is typical to maximize efficiency by avoiding unproductive repetition. Unless the way the branches are combined becomes important, there is little to be gained from exercising all 16 of these paths. How do we pick the minimum number of paths that should be exercised in order to ensure adequate test coverage? To optimize testing, the test cases should closely resemble actual usage and should include the minimum set of paths that ensure that each path segment is covered at least one time, while avoiding unnecessary redundancy.

It is not possible today to reliably *calculate* the total number of paths through a system by an automated process. Most systems contain some combination of 2^n logic structures and simple branching constructs. Calculating the total number of possibilities requires lengthy analysis. However, when a system is modeled according to a few simple rules, it is possible to quickly calculate the number of *linearly independent paths* through it. This method is far preferable to trying to determine the total number of paths by manual inspection. This count of the linearly independent paths gives a good estimate of the minimum number of paths that are required to traverse each path in the system, at least one time.

The Total Is Equal to the Sum of the Parts

The total independent paths (IPs) in any system is the sum of the IPs through its elements and subsystems. For the purpose of counting *tests*, we introduce TIP, which is the total independent paths of the subsystem elements under consideration—that is, the total number of linearly independent paths *being considered*. TIP usually represents a subset of the total number of linearly independent paths that exist in a complex system.

$$\text{TIP} = \sum_{e=1}^{e=tot} IP_e$$

TIP = Total enumerated paths for the system

e = element

IP = Independent paths in each element

What Is a Logic Flow Map?

A *logic flow map* is a graphic depiction of the logic paths though a system, or some function that is modeled as a system. Logic flow maps model real systems as *logic circuits*. A logic circuit can be validated much the same way an electrical circuit is validated. Logic flow diagrams expose logical faults quickly. The diagrams are easily updated by anyone, and they are an excellent communications tool.

System maps can be drawn in many different ways. The main advantage of modeling systems as logic flow diagrams is so that the number of linearly independent paths through the system can be calculated and so that logic flaws can be detected. Other graphing techniques may provide better system models but lack these fundamental abilities. For a comprehensive discussion of modeling systems as graphs and an excellent introduction to the principals of statistical testing, see *Black-Box Testing* by Boris Beizer (John Wiley & Sons, 1995).

The Elements of Logic Flow Mapping

→	**Edges**	Lines that connect nodes in the map.
In / No / Yes (decision diamond)	**Decisions**	A branching node with one (or more) edges entering and two edges leaving. Decisions can contain processes. In this text, for the purposes of clarity, decisions will be modeled with only one edge entering.
In / Out (process oval)	**Processes**	A collector node with multiple edges entering and one edge leaving. A process node can represent one program statement or an entire software system.

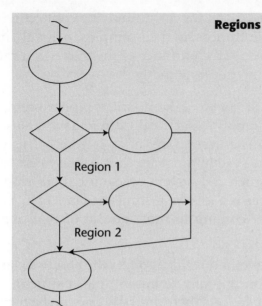

Regions A region is any area that is completely surrounded by edges and processes. In actual practice, regions are the hardest elements to find. If a model of the system can be drawn without any edges crossing, the regions will be obvious, as they are here. In event-driven systems, the model must be kept very simple or there will inevitably be crossed edges, and then finding the number of regions becomes very difficult.

Notes on nodes:

- **All processes *and* decisions are nodes.**
- **Decisions can contain processes.**

The Rules for Logic Flow Mapping

A logic flow map conforms to the conventions of a system flow graph with the following stipulation:

1. The representation of a system (or subsystem) can have only one entry point and one exit point; that is, it must be modeled as a structured system.

2. The system entry and exit points do not count as edges.

   This is required to satisfy the graphing theory stipulation that the graph must be strongly connected. For our purposes, this means that there is a connection between the exit and entrance of the logic flow diagram. This is the reason for the dotted line connecting the maze exits back to their entrances, in the examples. After all, if there is no way to get back to the entrance of the maze, you can't trace any more paths no matter how many there may be.

The logic flow diagram is a *circuit*. Like a water pipe system, there shouldn't be any leaks. Kirchoff's electrical current law states: "The algebraic sum of the currents entering any node is zero." This means that all the logic entering the system must also leave the system. We are constraining ourselves to structured systems, meaning there is only one way in and one way out. This is a lot like testing each faucet in a house, one at a time. All the water coming in must go out of that one open faucet.

One of the strengths of this method is that it offers the ability to take any unstructured system and conceptually represent it as a structured system. So no matter how many faucets there are, only one can be turned on at any time. This technique of only allowing one faucet to be turned on at a time can be used to write test specifications for unstructured code and parallel processes. It can also be used to reengineer an unstructured system so that it can be implemented as a structured system.

The tester usually does not know exactly what the logic in the system is doing. Normally, testers should not know these details because such knowledge would introduce serious bias into the testing. Bias is the error we introduce simply by having knowledge, and therefore expectations, about the system. What the testers need to know is how the logic is *supposed* to work, that is, what the requirements are. If these details are not written down, they can be reconstructed from interviews with the developers and designers and then written down. They must be documented, by the testers if necessary. Such documentation is required to perform verification and defend the tester's position.

A tester who documents what the system is actually doing and then makes a judgment on whether that is "right or not" is *not* verifying the system. This tester is *validating*, and validation requires a subjective judgment call. Such judgment calls are always vulnerable to attack. As much as possible, the tester should be *verifying* the system.

The Equations Used to Calculate Paths

There are three equations from graphing theory that we will use to calculate the number of linearly independent paths through any structured system. These three equations and the theory of linear independence were the work of a Dutch scholar named C. Berge who introduced them in his work *Graphs and Hypergraphs* (published in Amsterdam, The Netherlands: North-Holland, 1973.) Specifically, Berge's graph theory defines the cyclomatic number $v(G)$ of a strongly connected graph G with N nodes, E edges, and one connected component. This cyclomatic number is the number of linearly independent paths through the system.

We have three definitions of the cyclomatic number. This gives us the following three equations. The proofs are not presented here.

$$v(G) = \text{IP} = \text{Edges} - \text{Nodes} + 2 \quad (\text{IP} = E - N + 2)$$
$$v(G) = \text{IP} = \text{Regions} + 1 \quad\quad (\text{IP} = R + 1)$$
$$v(G) = \text{IP} = \text{Decisions} + 1 \quad\quad (\text{IP} = D + 1)$$

Even though the case statement and the series of required decisions don't have the same number of total paths, they do have the same number of linearly independent paths.

The number of linearly independent paths though a system is usually the minimum number of end-to-end paths required to touch every path segment at least once. In some cases, it is possible to combine several path segments that haven't been taken previously in a single traversal. This can have the result that the minimum number of paths required to cover the system is less than the number of IPs. In general, the number of linearly independent paths, IPs, is the minimum acceptable number of paths for 100 percent coverage of paths in the system. This is the answer to the question, "How many ways can you get through the system without retracing our path?" The total paths in a system are combinations of the linearly independent paths through the system. If a looping structure is traversed one time, it has been counted. Let's look at an example.

Refer to the looping structure shown in Figure 11.10. All three equations must be equal to the same number for the logic circuit to be valid. If the system is not a valid logic circuit, it can't work. When inspections are conducted with this in mind, logic problems can be identified quickly. Testers who develop the logic flow diagrams for the system as an aid in test design find all sorts of *fuzzy* logic errors before they ever begin to test the system.

When it is not possible to represent a system without edges that cross, the count of the regions becomes problematic and is often neglected. If the number of regions in a model cannot be established reliably, the logic flow cannot be verified using these equations, but the number of linearly independent paths can still be calculated using the other two equations.

Most of the commercially available static code analyzers use only the number of decisions in a system to determine the number of linearly independent paths, but for the purposes of logic flow analysis, all three equations are necessary. Any one by itself may identify the number of linearly independent paths through the system, but is not sufficient to test whether the logic flow of the system is valid.

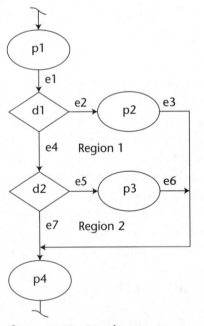

$$\text{nodes} = d + p = 2 + 4 = 6$$
$$\text{edges} = 7$$
$$\text{decisions} = 2$$
$$\text{regions} = 2$$

$$\text{Independent Paths} =$$

$$e - n + 2 = 7 - 6 + 2 = 3$$
$$d + 1 = 2 + 1 = 3$$
$$r + 1 = 2 + 1 = 3$$

Figure 11.10 Looping structure.

Twenty years ago, several works were published that used definitions and theorems from graphing theory to calculate the number of paths through a system. Building on the work of Berge, Tom McCabe and Charles Butler applied cyclomatic complexity to analyze the design of software and eventually to analyze raw code. (See "Design Complexity Measurement and Testing" in *Communications of the ACM*, December 1989, Volume 32, Number 12.) This technique eventually led to a set of metrics called the McCabe complexity metrics. The complexity metrics are used to count various types of paths through a system. In general, systems with large numbers of paths are considered to be *bad* under this method. It has been argued that the number of paths through a system should be limited to control complexity. A typical program module is limited to 10 or fewer linearly independent paths.

There are two good reasons for this argument. The first is that human beings don't handle increasing complexity very well. We are fairly efficient when solving logic problems with one to five logic paths, but beyond that, our performance starts to drop sharply. The time required to devise a solution for a problem rises geometrically with the number of paths. For instance, it takes under five minutes for typical students to solve a logic problem with fewer than five paths. It takes several hours to solve a logic problem with 10 paths, and it can take several days to solve a logic problem with more than 10 paths. The more complex the problem, the greater the probability that a human being will make an error or fail to find a solution.

The second reason is that 20 years ago software systems were largely monolithic and unstructured. Even 10 years ago, most programming was done in languages like Assembler, Cobol, and Fortran. Coding practices of that time were only beginning to place importance on structure. The logic flow diagrams of such systems are typically a snarl of looping paths with the frayed ends of multiple entries and exits sticking out everywhere. Such diagrams strongly resemble a plate of spaghetti—hence the term *spaghetti code*, and the justifiable emphasis on limiting complexity. The cost of maintaining these systems proved to be unbearable for most applications, and so, over time, they have been replaced by modular structured systems.

Today's software development tools, most notably code generators, and fourth-generation languages (4GLs) produce complex program modules. The program building blocks are recombined into new systems constantly, and the result is ever more complex but stable building blocks. The structural engineering analogy to this is an average 100-by-100-foot, one-story warehouse. One hundred years ago, we would have built it using about 15,000 3-by-9-by-3-inch individually mortared bricks in a double course wall. It would have taken seven masons about two weeks to put up the walls. Today we might build it with about forty 10-foot-by-10-foot-by-6-inch pre-stressed concrete slabs. It would take a crane operator, a carpenter, and a welder one to two days to set the walls. A lot more engineering goes into today's pre-stressed slab, but the design can be reused in many buildings. Physically, the pre-stressed slab is less complex than the brick wall, having only one component, but it is a far more complex design requiring a great deal more analysis and calculation.

Once a logic problem is solved and the logic verified, the module becomes a building block in larger systems. When a system is built using prefabricated and pretested modules, the complexity of the entire system may be very large. This does not mean that the system is unstable or hard to maintain.

It is simplistic to see limited complexity as a silver bullet. Saying that a program unit having a complexity over 10 is *too* complex is akin to saying, "A person who weighs over 150 pounds is overweight." We must take other factors into consideration before we make such a statement. The important factor in complex systems is how the paths are structured, not how many there are. If we took this approach seriously, we would not have buildings taller than about five stories, or roller-coasters that do vertical loops and corkscrews, or microprocessors, or telephone systems, or automobiles, and so on. If the building blocks are sound, large complexity is not a bad thing.

> **Note:** **Complexity is not a bad thing. It just requires structure and management.**

Summary

Software is a maze and software testers have problems that are not unlike those of the men and women who were dropped into the Maze of the Minotaur in ancient Crete. While software testing is not normally considered life-threatening, it is fraught with other perils. Those dropped into the Maze of the Minotaur were only expected to enter the maze one time, while software testers must keep going back into the maze until they are sure that they have checked it thoroughly.

There are several types of paths through a software system, as illustrated in the case statement and the independent decisions examples. How many of each type of path exist in a system is dependent on the configuration of decisions and processes within the system. Each type of path can be counted. Following are the four types discussed in this chapter:

- The number of paths required to exercise each statement.
- The number of paths required to exercise each logic branch.
- The total number of paths possible through the system.
- The number of paths required to ensure that each path segment is traversed at least once—that is, the linearly independent paths.

Software testers need to know how many paths they are dealing with so they can estimate how long their effort will take. Being able to calculate the number of paths through the maze is far preferable to determining the number empirically, by trial and error.

The tester will also need a map of the maze. The logic flow map, or diagram, introduced in this chapter, is a simple way to create a map of any structured system. Modeling systems using logic flow diagrams offer several benefits. When the system is modeled according to the rules of logic flow mapping, three equations are available to calculate the number of linearly independent paths (IPs) through the system. If all three equations for calculating IPs are used and all equal the same number, the logic of the system's structure is shown to be valid—meaning that the logic will work, but not that the logic does the right thing. The total number of paths through multiple valid linked systems is the sum of the individual IPs of the systems. This means that various subsystems can be analyzed separately, and their individual IPs can be summed to give the total number of IPs for the entire system.

The number of linearly independent paths through a system is usually the minimum number of tests required to exercise all paths in a structured system, one time. Looping and recursive scenarios will be controlled by the data input to the system. In Chapter 12, logic flow diagrams are applied to the sample application and used in the estimation process.

Path Analysis Samples for Further Exploration

Answer these questions for each of the following logic flow diagrams
You can check your answers in Appendix A.

1. Is this a valid logic flow diagram? Why or why not? Calculate the total independent paths, or TIPs, to help answer this question. If the diagram is not a valid logic flow diagram, construct a corrected version before proceeding to Question 2.

2. Find the total number of paths required to satisfy 100 percent coverage for branches, statements, total paths, and total independent paths.

Exercise 1

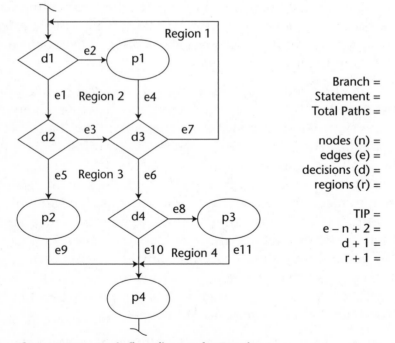

Branch =
Statement =
Total Paths =

nodes (n) =
edges (e) =
decisions (d) =
regions (r) =

TIP =
e − n + 2 =
d + 1 =
r + 1 =

Figure 11.11   Logic flow diagram for Exercise 1.

Exercise 2

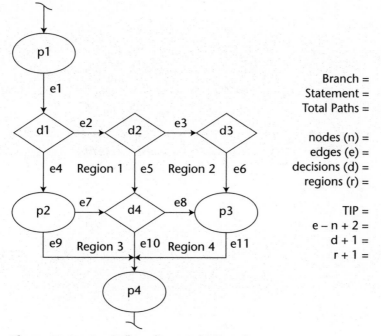

Branch =
Statement =
Total Paths =

nodes (n) =
edges (e) =
decisions (d) =
regions (r) =

TIP =
e − n + 2 =
d + 1 =
r + 1 =

Figure 11.12 Logic flow diagram for Exercise 2.

Exercise 3

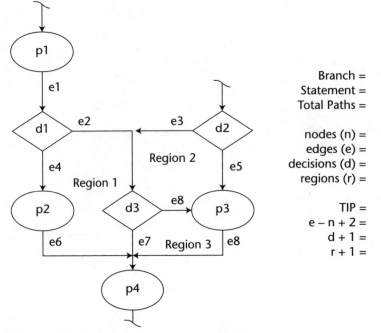

Branch =
Statement =
Total Paths =

nodes (n) =
edges (e) =
decisions (d) =
regions (r) =

TIP =
e − n + 2 =
d + 1 =
r + 1 =

Figure 11.13 Logic flow diagram for Exercise 3.

Exercise 4

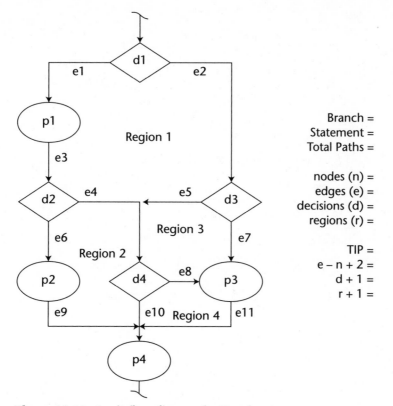

Branch =
Statement =
Total Paths =

nodes (n) =
edges (e) =
decisions (d) =
regions (r) =

TIP =
e − n + 2 =
d + 1 =
r + 1 =

Figure 11.14   Logic flow diagram for Exercise 4.

CHAPTER 12

Applied Path Analysis

S everal years ago when I first presented the material in this chapter at a software testing conference, it was very enthusiastically received, but the audience was very definitely divided into two distinct camps at the end of the presentation. Bill Silver, who is, among other things, a total quality management guru, was in the audience. Bill summed it like this: "When Marnie finished her talk, there were two types of people in the audience. The ones that understood exactly what Marnie was talking about, and the experts." The rest of this chapter is dedicated to trying to explain my approach to testing in terms everyone can understand.

Correcting Problems with Depth Perception: Or How This All Got Started

The project was a shopping application running on a large private network. The director in the project, a different one than the one I spoke of in the Introduction of this book, came to the presentation with only one foil. Everyone involved in the project was there—testers, developers, content producers, and network support. He began his presentation by putting up his foil. It had a picture similar to Figure 12.1 on it.

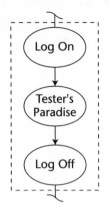

Figure 12.1 The director's foil.

"This is how it works," he said. "The users log on to the network. They jump to the application, they select products that they want to buy, fill in a shipping form, give a credit card number, and then log off. Two to 10 days later, their merchandise arrives at the address they provided. We know there are about 3,000 lines of new code here," he said, pointing to the first bubble, "45,000 lines of code here," pointing to the second bubble, "and 1,000 lines of code over there," pointing to the last bubble. "There is also some new code at the distribution centers. But it's not that complicated. We've sized the effort based on the new function, and we estimate that it shouldn't take more than 12 weeks to write and integrate the system. Based on the development effort, it should take about two weeks to test *it*. So, we should be ready for product rollout about 14 weeks after we start writing code." This is what is known in the industry as "the view from 50,000 feet." If this is the only view that management sees, those of us in the trenches are in trouble. This manager had no idea what was behind the bubbles on the diagram.

It's normal at this stage for the testers to have no more idea than the director what is behind those bubbles. Testers might even have agreed, given what they had just heard, that two weeks would be sufficient. In this particular case, the tester responsible for the project asked me to help out with the test estimation. Since all phases of that test effort were planned and executed using the MITs methods, it has become the example I prefer to use when teaching these methods.

The analysis of the application used the requirements, logical function paths, network paths, and data analysis to build the test inventory used for estimation. The starting point for the functional analysis was the GUI. Developers provided the network path details. Almost 400 end-to-end function test scenarios were required to provide adequate test coverage of that project. Even though the actual test effort was able to drastically reduce the time required to perform testing by using the methods presented in this book, along with automated test tools, it still took somewhat longer than two weeks to test the three-bubble application on the foil.

The Game Show Analogy

I searched for many years for an analogy that would explain the concepts and problems of dealing with user function paths though real systems in terms everyone could understand. My favorite way of explaining this is by the *Doom*[1] analogy. *Doom* is a hit video game that features an abundance of dark, confusing, monster-filled mazes, each tucked behind a color-keyed door. For those not familiar with video games, think of it like a television game show where contestants win whatever is behind the door they choose. Most people don't have too much trouble imagining a lot of stuff behind one of those doors.

A software system is like a maze full of doors. Each door is the entry-way to some other component or process in the system. At each door a decision will be made to open or not to open. Behind each one of those doors there are other mazes. It is possible to start at the user interface and descend through the layers of a system into the source code of program modules, and sometimes even into the processing instructions of the hardware. This type of testing is called *top-down testing*.

Imagine that each of those bubbles on the director's foil is such a door. This is a very good conceptual picture of the way internal logic paths of a software system look when viewed from the top down—that is, from the user's perspective. The tester must verify and validate or, if there is no map, *explore* what is behind those doors. Each component in the system has its own internal independent paths (IPs). The sum of all the IPs is the total for the system. Testing each component independently, *bottom-up testing*, will not verify that all the user functions will work properly.

---

[1] *Doom* is a trademark of id Software, Inc.

Getting a Map

Top-down testing can proceed very quickly if the tester has a map and knows from the beginning what he or she is up against—how big *it* is, where things are, and so on. In general, however, if there are to be any maps, it is the testers who will create them, usually as they go. Many test efforts are conducted without a map ever being created at all. It may just be a holdover from when I did my surveying school in the Canadian wilderness, but if I have to follow a path with more than two turns in it, I make a map.

True to this real-life scenario, the *Doom* game has a map function that shows the player a map of the corridors they have traversed up to their current point in the game. Such a map does not indicate how much of the maze remains unexplored. In testing, we call this a *dynamic analysis test tool*. In *Doom*, there are also master maps hidden in the maze that show the entire current maze, including hidden and secret corridors. This type of map is created by a *static analysis tool*.

In testing, commercial tools that perform static and dynamic analysis typically produce reports of different characteristics of the system, such as how many branches exist and the call tree structure. These tools will show the paths that have been traversed on the entire system map. This type of map combines both static and dynamic analysis and gives the viewer a graphical view of how much of the system has been traversed and how much remains. These maps are maps of the component-level paths. So while they are great aids for unit testing and module integration testing, they are generally too low level to be much help in a top-down system test. Also, these tools are platform- and language-specific and are generally expensive. If the system under test uses several hardware platforms, operating systems, and components written in several languages, this means a different tool for each. And there is no map of the paths between these disparate components in the system.

I have long lobbied for the inclusion of such mapping functions in applications and systems themselves as part of the code. But historically, diagnostic functions such as these are rarely included in the plan, and if they are, they are usually the first functions to be cut when deadlines approach. The result is that inexpensive and easily accessible user function maps have been rare until the advent of the Web.

While static analysis and mapping functions are not included in most traditional software applications, they are an integral part of a Web application. Most commercially available Web site creation tools offer site maps that show all the documents and links in a Web site. Figure 12.2 shows the hyperlink view of a page in the testersparadise.com Web site. Now standard in Web content creation packages, this type of tool creates graphical maps of the paths from a given page like the one shown here.

In addition, a series of reports are commonly available today in Web content creation and management tool sets that can be used to automatically certify that a Web site has no missing files, no extra files, and no broken links. While such tools can verify all the navigational links in a site, they cannot *validate* the links—that is, these tools cannot show that the links go to the logically *correct* location, only that they do navigate to a location that exists. Figure 12.3 shows the Web site Reports view from FrontPage 2002.

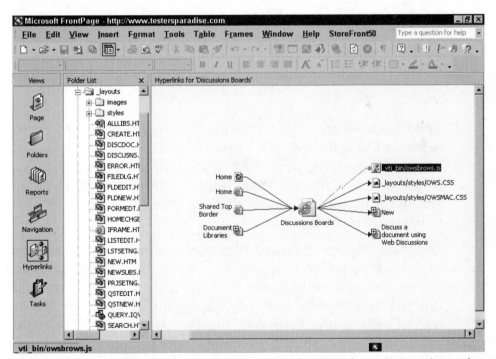

Figure 12.2 Automatic hyperlink analysis is a part of most Web content creation tools.

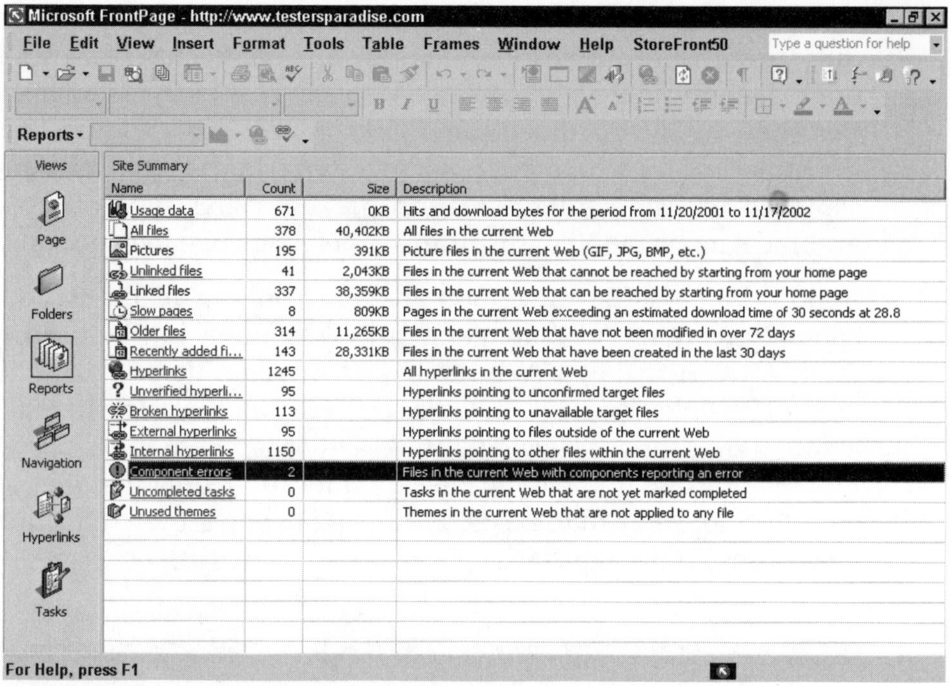

Figure 12.3 Automatic Web site Reports view in FrontPage 2002.

In addition to reporting statistics on hyperlinks, other reports show items such as unlinked files. These are effectively dead files that can't be accessed except by a direct link or via a search. The view in Figure 12.3 shows a Web technician most of the important points of failure in the site. In the figure, the line highlighted shows that two application components are reporting errors.

Because of their traceability, Web applications lend themselves to automated testing and monitoring. As a result, they are much more *testable* than traditional applications. Web test tools cost a fraction of their traditional counterparts, and they are readily available on the Web. The cost of testing and certifying the Web equivalent of a client/server application is only a fraction of the cost of testing a client/server application. But, unfortunately, as helpful as these Web analyzer maps are, they still do not take the place of a logic flow diagram, as we will see in a moment.

On the dynamic analysis side, the Web server keeps a log of every request made by a user and what the server did with the request, such as whether it sent the item, transferred the user to a different host, or returned an error message. Because of this feature, a wealth of information is available about how users find the site, what they do when they get there, what browsers they are using, and so on. The paths that users follow can be tracked and analyzed automatically; Figure 12.4 shows some of the most common usage reporting used in a Web site. There are specialized tools that can extract even more information than these 13 reports suggest. The graph in the background shows the number of visitors, page hits, and total hits to the site over a three-month period.

All of this information is valuable to both testers and administrators. Actual usage information is invaluable when predicting and monitoring the most important areas to test.

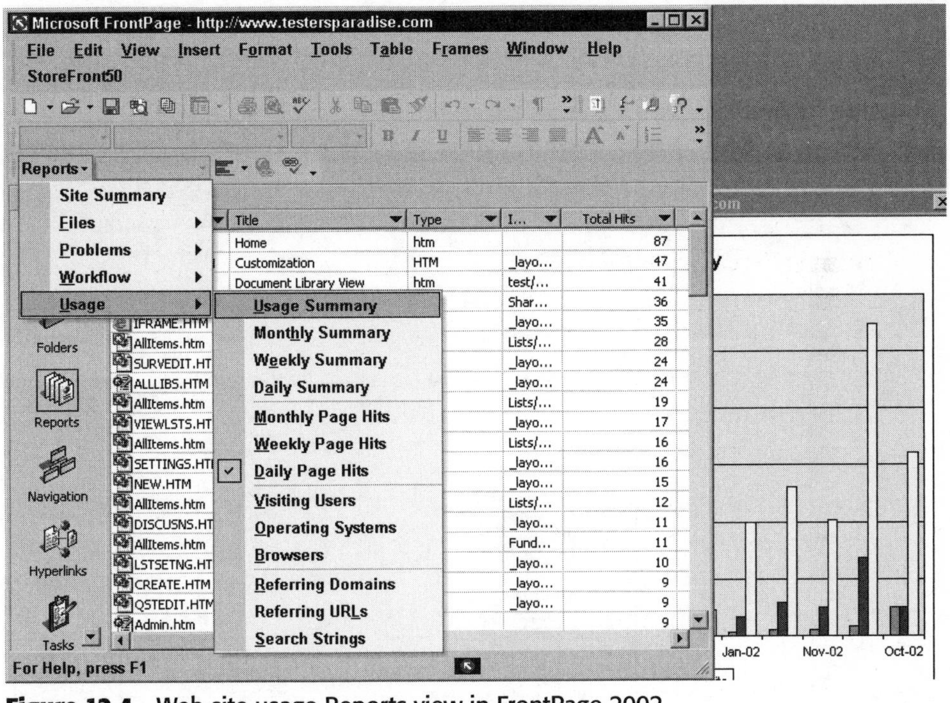

Figure 12.4 Web site usage Reports view in FrontPage 2002.

Divide and Conquer

Software systems typically involve connections between several code modules residing in various components that communicate with each other to accomplish user-selected functions. The following illustration, Figure 12.5, is a partial system map for a single menu option from the director's three-bullet foil. The code modules reside in various hardware components and communicate across networks, as shown in the illustration. When a user selects the menu option, the system interacts across network-based components in order to perform the function.

Testers routinely cross boundaries between different types of modules and system components to follow logical function paths of interest. These boundaries can be ignored or examined in detail. When there is an undesirable or unusual response from the system, testers routinely divide the test effort along these boundaries to verify input and output across these boundaries. When the flow between such boundaries is tested specifically and exhaustively, it is normally called *integration testing*.

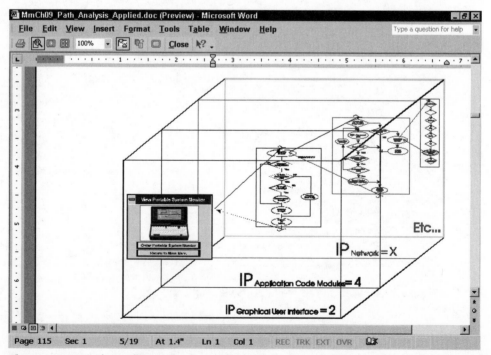

Figure 12.5 A three-dimensional representation of the internal paths in the director's three-bullet foil.

The strategy in integration testing is to send application requests between the components and then verify and validate the result. If the output of one component is not acceptable to the component receiving it, a deeper investigation is conducted to determine which component is not performing according to the specification. This approach to problem solving by decomposing the system into smaller and smaller components is called *divide and conquer*.

The total number of tests conducted is the sum of all the tests in all the components. The test planning process will identify tests in many components, as is indicated in Figure 12.5.

The Paths Not Counted

Testers will follow the component paths through the system to whatever level of detail is necessary to verify and validate the performance of the component. This means that some code modules will be trusted or assumed to be stable based on past performance, or point of origin, while other *untrusted* components will be examined in great detail.

Note: Any element given an IP of 1 is assumed to be stable.

The assumption that a component will behave correctly means that there is only one path through the component—that is, *the correct path*. Testers automatically publish this assumption about a trusted component when they give it an IP = 1. Examples of this simplifying assumption will be presented later in this chapter. The true count of all possible paths and therefore all possible tests is unbounded. The tests that are not counted and not performed as a result of simplifying assumptions like this one actually represent a lot of tests.

The Price We Pay for Using Divide and Conquer

Divide and conquer is an algorithm that human beings have used successfully to manage large problems for eons. The problem is, every time we divide the problem, we create a new interface that will need to be tested, tracked, and reintegrated at some point. When faced with a difficult problem, there is the temptation to keep dividing it into smaller and smaller pieces. This can result in a sorcerer's-apprentice-type scenario where we end up with a plethora of small problems that still defy our attempts at management simply because of their number. Care should be taken not to overuse the technique. In top-down testing the rule of thumb is "If it ain't broke, don't fix it."

Building Path Test Estimates Quickly

Let's take a look at what's behind door number 1 . . .

The screen shown in Figure 12.6 is from the second release of the shopping application called Tester's Paradise. The Tester's Paradise application began as a pseudo-application to allow safe use of statistics gathered in real three-bubble applications. It was such a good idea that it has since taken on a life of its own. The most current release is running on the World Wide Web.

If the user logs on to the network and navigates to Tester's Paradise Release 2, the menu shown in the figure is presented. It has five options; each one has a number of function paths behind it.

Application function paths are the logical paths through a function in an application or a *system,* as opposed to the paths through a block of source code, which is called a *function.* For example, following menu options through an application to perform some function, like "purchase a data flow checker," is exercising a function in the Tester's Paradise application. The actual number of paths through the source code of a program function is usually considerably larger than the number of system or program function paths. An application function path is most commonly accessed by the user via a menu option.

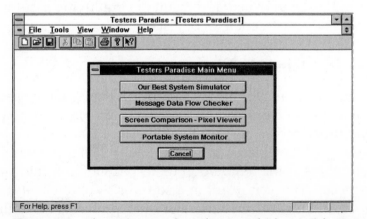

Figure 12.6 The main menu from the second release of the Tester's Paradise application.

The fastest way to get a quick estimate of how many functional tests need to be run is to count the navigation options on the system menus. These options are effectively the doors in the system maze. In a Web application, these navigation options are the hyperlinks. If the tester can't have a map of all the paths in the system up front, he or she can at least have a count of how many doors there are to be opened.

Step 1: Building a Menu Map of the System

Many types of maps can be built to help a tester understand and keep track of the system he or she is testing. The first map built for a system is usually the logic flow map for the highest level of functionality. In most cases, this is the map of the menu system or user interface. All the other maps for the system are maps of the details behind the menu options on this first high-level map.

Step 2: Counting All the Menu Options in the System

Counting all the menu options is the fastest way to determine the gross number of independent paths through the system. This is a big job, but it's not anywhere near as big a job as drawing all the exceptions.

Note: The number of independent paths from a menu is equal to the number of options on the menu.

Assumption #1. The user will never get *stuck* on a menu.

Figure 12.7 shows how the menu options can be modeled as a logic flow diagram. A menu is a case statement. In order to leave a menu, the user must select something. This means that the number of decisions on any menu is equal to the number of options minus one (the one that is selected). This method of counting ignores the trivial case where the user never leaves the menu—never gets out of the maze. If that case is considered, then the number of decisions is increased by 1. Each menu option then becomes a decision, and the number of paths on a menu is equal to the number of options plus 1.

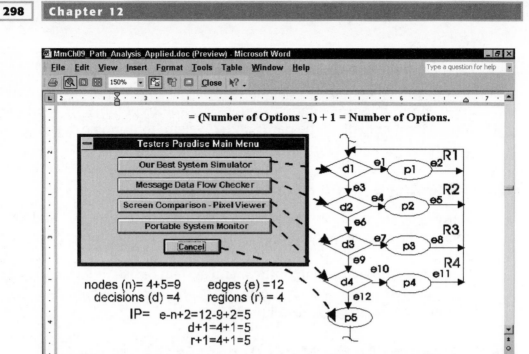

Figure 12.7 The Tester's Paradise main menu modeled as a logic flow diagram.

D = Number of options – 1

The IP = D + 1

    = (Number of options – 1) + 1 = Number of options

Assumption #2. The Cancel button is the same as the Close action from the window system menu. This means that it will not be counted as a separate option. It is assumed that the system menu will always work correctly.

Assumption #3. The Esc key will always back the user out of the current operation, and it will always work reliably.

It turns out that it is not a trivial case

I have recently encountered 3 different applications with "no-exit" pages—apparently there is a flaw in one of the new jsp designer tools that leaves out the navigation button(s) required to proceed to the next step, so users get stranded on the page. They can use the browser back button to go back, but they can't proceed forward. I guess if you live long enough you will see all your assumptions fail at some point.

These assumptions may be incorrect, but they are the reason that the Esc option and the system menu are neglected in all these menus. If any of these assumptions is proven to be incorrect, the condition that was neglected because of the assumption will have to be included and the number of paths on each menu will increase by one option. This will increase the total independent paths (TIPs) for each menu by 1 as well.

The illustration shows the first set of application screens presented by the designers. The arrows trace the new application function, View Portable System Monitor, from the main menu. There are eight menu options on the View Portable System Monitor function path. Each menu option has logic paths associated with it. The lower-level menus for Our Best System Simulator, Message Data Flow Checker, and the Screen Comparison-Pixel Viewer are not shown in this illustration. The IP total of the menus under each of these main options is shown next to each option.

Given the simplifying assumptions, there are 23 distinct menu options being considered in the Tester's Paradise Portable System Monitor menus. Their distribution is shown in Figure 12.8.

The menu option paths are not the only paths that must be tested, but menu options are important because they serve as key items in the test inventory. Other types of tests that are related to a menu option are typically grouped under the menu option title in the test inventory. Testing how many times the program is going to spin through a loop will be controlled by the data used in the function test. The test data is determined separately. The data tests for the entry fields on the form are discussed separately in Chapter 13, "Data Analysis Techniques."

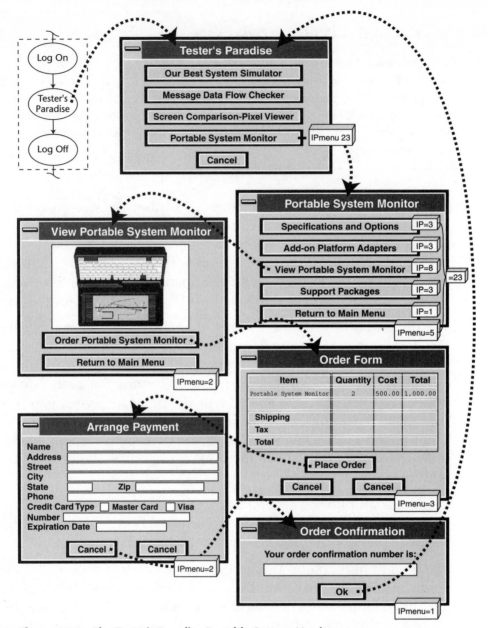

Figure 12.8   The Tester's Paradise Portable System Monitor menu.

Step 3: Counting the Exceptions for Each Menu Option

Each menu option has at least one exception condition associated with it. The most common case is the error window that opens if any menu selection is unavailable and when the menu option should *not* be available. One of the most frequently neglected test sets is the verification that menu options that should *not* be available during some function tests really are not available or are "grayed out."

One exception for each menu option is usually a reasonable estimate; however, this number should be tailored to suit the particular situation. Data entry fields that are required will have one or more error messages for each type of incorrect data response or *data exception.* Data-dependent error messages will be accounted for in the test inventory as part of the data analysis.

Calculate the IPs for the number of exceptions that will be tested. This number can be refined further if detailed analysis is conducted. This example will estimate based on one exception for each menu option.

Sample Test Inventory 2

The inventory created using the word processor is used as the base. New rows are added for the functions, and new columns are added for the path tests.

Tip for Microsoft Word

Fill any empty cells with "0" so that the Table Formula function can be used to automatically calculate the totals. The cells in the rightmost column, "TIPs," use the formula =SUM(LEFT). The totals in the bottom row, "Totals," use the formula =SUM(ABOVE).

For additional detailed information, select the Index function in Word's online Help (F1) and search for "formula." There is a topic that explains in detail how to perform calculations in a table.

Table 12.1   Tester's Paradise Test Inventory

Tester's Paradise (Release 2.0)	Total Path Tests			
	Menu Option Paths	Exception Paths	Program Paths	TIPs
Project Information:	0	0	0	0
Fix For Error #123	0	0	0	0
Fix for Error #124	0	0	0	0
Tester's Paradise Main Menu	5	5	0	10
Our Best System Simulator	0	0	0	0
Message Data Flow Checker	0	0	0	0
Screen Comparison — Pixel Viewer	0	0	0	0
Portable System Monitor (New Function)	5	5	0	10
Specifics and Options	3	3	0	6
Add-on Platform Adapters	3	3	0	6
View Portable System Monitor	2	2	0	4
Display Portable System Monitor	0	0	0	0
Order Form	3	3	0	6
Arrange Payment	2	2	0	4
Order Confirmation	1	1	0	2
Support Packages	3	3	0	6
Return to Main Menu	1	1	0	2
Cancel	1	1	0	2
Installation is automatic at logon	0	0	0	0
Totals	**29**	**29**	**0**	**58**

Step 4: Building the Logic Flow Maps for the System

Once all the menu options have been counted and cataloged, the next step is to find out what is going on behind all those menu option doors. It is time to build the logic flow maps of the system. Ideally, the processes behind the menu options will be described correctly in the project documentation. If the documentation is inadequate, or nonexistent, the information can be collected by interviewing the developers responsible for each part of the system. If the modules come from an outside party, it will be necessary to conduct interviews with developers within that organization to construct the logic flows. Interviews of some type may be the only way to verify the correctness of the documentation prior to actual tests of the system.

Some Procedural Notes on Interviews

I use a combination of techniques to conduct these interviews. The techniques that are used to conduct inspections and the techniques that are used to conduct audits supplemented by basic sales techniques used to identify compelling events work well.

People are individuals. Each person will require a unique approach. But these techniques are simple and fundamental. They work for almost every personality type or style. They can be used alone or in combination to formulate and execute an approach that will get good-quality results with virtually anyone.

Note: **Software testing is a contact sport.**

A successful tester has a lot of good contacts. I actively cultivate the developers on every project. I usually do this simply by being interested in what they are doing. I ask a lot of questions about "how things work." I not only want to know, I need to know. It is not usually hard to get the developer talking about her or his project. But like inspections, these interviews can be done well or poorly. Developers' time is in short supply and it must be utilized profitably.

1. Keep It Short and Sweet

The interview should be kept as short as possible. Keep the questions simple. "What happens first?" "What happens next?" "If this happens, then what?" It is possible to develop a detailed logic flow diagram after only a few minutes of interview time. Keep a log of how much time was spent in each session, who was there, general notes, and the logic flow diagram, or changes to a logic flow diagram, that came out during the session. Development managers will be quick to bar a tester from distracting a developer if they do not see a benefit from these discussions. By keeping these records and measurements, I have often been able to show that these techniques allow me to create project documents at a fraction of the normal cost.

2. Focus on the Facts

There will be many bits of murky, vague, or fuzzy logic during the design and implementation stages of a project. If a person cannot explain something succinctly, he or she either doesn't understand it or the person has a communications problem. In either case, a confrontational technique is rarely the most productive approach for getting an answer.

Instead, focus attention on something inanimate, like the logic flow diagram, a theoretical representation of the project. A drawing on the whiteboard or a picture on paper (that the tester can write on and take away) is less threatening than an across-the-table face-to-face discussion. If the answers aren't immediately forthcoming, write the questions down and come back to them later. At least the questions have been asked, and the next time there will probably be answers.

3. Draw the Logic Flow Maps

Draw the logic flow maps as soon as possible after the interview while the details are still fresh. Write down all your questions, and write down the answers you are given. Keep this question-and-answer log. I usually ask the same questions many times and of many people. I pay special attention to any questions that get different answers from different people or several different answers from the same person over time.

Never underestimate your powers of observation. If something doesn't *feel* right, there is probably a reason. If it seems like some topic is being avoided, it probably is. The normal reason for avoiding a topic is that it is not well understood. If the developers can't clarify a point for the testers, somebody does not understand the topic. I have found that if I have this problem, I am probably not asking the right question.

4. Conduct a Review of the Logic Flow Maps with the Developers

Take the logic flow maps of the system back to the developers for review. *Go over the maps with the developers*; don't just drop them off. This is the part of the process where I learn the most about what is really going on.

The review, like the interview, should not take long. I ask the developers to go over the diagrams with me. I ask if I have understood them correctly and if the maps are correct. The process of reviewing these maps almost always leads to disclosures of other related processes that were not mentioned previously for one reason or another.

Usually it takes one initial session and two to three review sessions to have an accurate map of the system, as it exists in reality or in concept at the current stage of development. As the logic flow changes during development, I encourage developers to make updates to the logic flow and forward them to me. The gain is that the logic flow maps are much quicker to create, update, and maintain than wordy documents. And they are mathematically verifiable.

In a perfect world, the designers would initialize the logic flow maps and the maps would be passed along with the system as it progresses through the development cycle. The diagrams would be updated by development as the system was developed and would always be available to other groups, such as the testers. The good news is that logic flow maps are such a flexible tool it doesn't matter who draws them or when.

Back to Work: Some Things to Remember

The additive property of linearly independent paths was introduced in the previous chapter. This property will be used to arrive at the total number of paths identified in the system after the analysis digs down into the internal processes of the application to identify them separately. The first interviews should focus on understanding how many of the menu processes will need to be analyzed in depth.

Note: The TIP is equal to the sum of the IPs in the system.

The highest level of logic flow maps generally comes directly from the GUI menus. Figure 12.9 is the logic flow map for the menu option View Portable System Monitor, shown earlier in Figure 12.8. It will be used as the starting point for the interviews and the analysis of the logic behind the menu options.

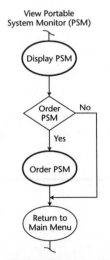

Figure 12.9 Logic flow map for the View Portable System Monitor menu option.

In this case, the user can either Order Portable System Monitor and Return to Main Menu, or the user can Return to Main Menu *without* ordering. There are two paths, *IP = 2*, through this logic flow diagram.

Note: Assigning any element a total independent path count of 1, TIP = 1, states implicitly that the element is assumed to be stable. Its internal paths are being ignored.

By assuming an element in a system is stable, we are conveniently ignoring the number of actual paths being executed inside it. If there is no apparent reason to examine the internal paths of an element, it is assigned a path count of 1. The assumption is that the element will only have one effective path, the correct path. If the assumption is found to be in error, the element can be analyzed and its internal path count added to the inventory. Tests can then be written to exercise the most important of those paths.

The First Logic Flow Maps

The logic flow maps in Figure 12.10 were the result of the first interview with developers and designers. This map shows the logic flow diagrams for Display Portable System Monitor and Order Portable System Monitor. Notice that the View Portable System Monitor logic flow diagram shows the number of IPs that have been counted inside the Display Portable System Monitor process node and the Order Portable System Monitor process node. This type of notation can be used on the menus to show how many paths are actually associated with each program menu option.

Once the user selects View Portable System Monitor, a sequence of events is triggered. The result is that a picture of the Portable System Monitor is delivered to the user, decompressed if necessary, and displayed. The function path that determines which type of picture to send and performs whatever processing is needed to display the picture is automatic as soon as the user selects View Portable System Monitor.

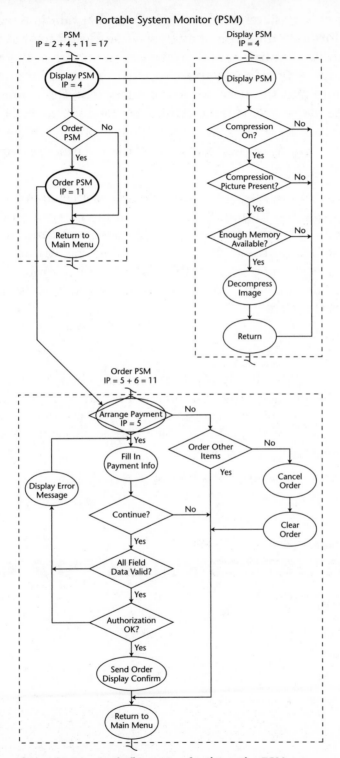

Figure 12.10 Logic flow maps for the entire PSM menu.

The Display Portable System Monitor logic flow diagram is a *process-level* diagram. Normally this type of analysis is sufficient to arrive at a good estimate of the number of tests that exist in a system. If a more detailed or rigorous approach is warranted, the number of internal IPs through the system and the network can be counted. The number of paths through the *source code* of the modules can be determined, if necessary, by automated tools that perform source code analysis like LDRA or Cantata. It is not usually cost-effective to conduct manual path analysis at the source code level.

The Arrange Payment process was given an IP = 5 as an estimate by the group as the time allotted for the interview ran out. Such estimates are normal and healthy. It is far better to record the best guess and publish the fact that there are untrustworthy paths behind the Arrange Payment door than to leave the process with an IP = 1, which implies that it is trustworthy. But they usually require additional analysis as the analysis process moves forward.

Step 5: Recording the Paths

Record the counts of the individual IPs on the main menu map and in the inventory and total the paths of interest on the lowest-level menu. Carry the internal path counts from the lower level menus up to the next-level menu and sum them. Repeat this step until all the internal paths in the system have been counted.

Table 12.2 shows the record from the Portable System Monitor.

Table 12.2 Record from Portable System Monitor

DISPLAY PSM PROGRAM PATHS	IP
Display PSM	4
Order Form	5
Arrange Payment	6
Return to Main Menu	2
Total IP	**17**

Order confirmation has been neglected for the moment.

The Menu Map

Notice that there is no distinction between different types of paths. The path triggered by selecting a menu option is counted in the same way and given the same importance initially as a path through source code or a path through the network. This approach to modeling a system is effective on both finite state and real-time event-driven systems. For event-driven systems, a set of assumptions are made about the system's state.

The other three options, Our Best System Simulator, Message Data Flow Checker, and the Screen Comparison-Pixel Viewer, were analyzed in Release 1. The only difference in these options is that the order process in Release 1 instructed users to dial an 800 number and place their orders through a sales representative. For the most part, the path counts shown in this inventory for those options are taken based on the actual tests used in the Release 1 test effort.

Table 12.3 Sample Test Inventory 3

Tester's Paradise (Release 2.0)	Total Path Tests			
	Menu Option Paths	Exception Paths	Program Paths	TIPs
Project Information:	0	0	0	0
Fix For Error #123	0	0	3	3
Fix for Error #124	0	0	0	0
Tester's Paradise Main Menu	5	5	0	0
Our Best System Simulator	0	0	65	65
Message Data Flow Checker	0	0	61	61
Screen Comparison – Pixel Viewer	0	0	76	76
Portable System Monitor (New Function)	5	5	0	10
Specifics and Options	3	3	0	6
Add-on Platform Adapters	3	3	0	6
View Portable System Monitor	2	2	0	4
Display Portable System Monitor	0	0	4	4
Order Form	3	3	6	12
Arrange Payment	2	2	5	9
Order Confirmation	1	1	0	2
Support Packages	3	3	0	6
Return to Main Menu	1	1	0	2
Cancel	1	1	0	2
Installation is automatic at logon	0	0	0	0
Totals	**29**	**29**	**220**	**268**

Path and Data Dependencies

The Display Portable System Monitor module is executed unconditionally every time the View a Portable System Monitor menu option is selected. The logic flow paths associated with Display Portable System Monitor are controlled by internal conditions in the system, rather than data (see Figure 12.11). These internal conditions are configuration- and environment-related items, such as whether the picture must be decompressed before it can be displayed, how much memory is available, and so on. For any particular system, these conditions will be fairly static once they have been established. This means that on a given system the same paths will be traversed through this element each time the Portable System Monitor is displayed. The functional complexity of the Display Portable System Monitor is said to be *path dependent*.

Another way to look at this type of function, from the perspective of the World Wide Web or a client/server environment, is that this is a downstream-only function. The server sends the requested data out, and no further action is required by the user or client.

The paths through Order a Portable System Monitor are controlled by user input, including the type and quantity of items ordered, what method of payment will be selected, and so on. This data will be very dynamic, and so the number of paths through Order a Portable System Monitor will be dynamic. The function paths of the Order a Portable System Monitor section are said to be *data dependent*.

The total number of paths that will be exercised by the test set through the system function is a function of the number of linearly independent paths plus the number of data set tests.

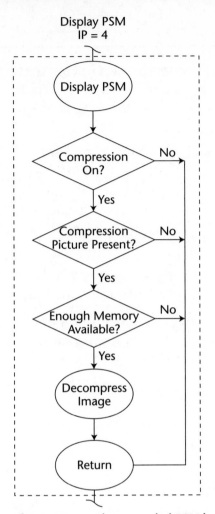

Figure 12.11   The expanded PSM logic flow map.

Summary

Much of the success of a test effort is dependent on having a good estimate of the size of the test effort in the beginning. It is very common for test projects to be underestimated because too little is understood about their depth.

A good estimate starts with a good analysis. A map of the menu options alone is a quick way to begin to understand the depth of the project. A logic flow map is an invaluable tool for understanding the size of the undertaking and for tracking what has and has not been accomplished.

The map-building process is incremental. It does not matter who builds the map; any work that is done will help improve the test sizing estimate. The map constructed so far shows the function paths through the application. The paths controlled by data are analyzed next.

There is considerable pressure to do the minimal amount of testing. As a result, top-down approaches are popular. A top-down divide-and-conquer approach can yield a highly effective test effort.

CHAPTER 13

Data Analysis Techniques

I once had a job interview that involved a three-week contract to test a new mouse driver. During the interview, I was asked how many tests I thought would be needed to test a new mouse driver on a 640 x 480 display. I did a quick calculation and responded that I would need to perform 307,200 tests for a rigorous test effort, but that most of the bugs would probably be identified in the first 153,600 tests.

This answer took only a few seconds, but the explanation of how I got it took considerably longer and ended up involving most of the test department. That answer is presented in this chapter. In the end, I did not get a job to test the mouse driver; the test department wasn't comfortable working with someone who wanted to run a minimum of 153,600 tests in three weeks. I did get a contract to write an automated test tool to run the tests that were eventually selected.

In this chapter, I show you my favorite methods for analyzing the data requirements of the application, along with the techniques I use to cut the number of data sets down to a manageable size. I am not going to try to do justice to this vast topic here. For a complete set of techniques to use in determining answers to this type of question, see Boris Beizer's book, *Black-Box Testing* (Wiley, 1995), which is the best source I have ever found.

Testing Data Input by Users (the GUI)

Most of the data testing we do these days is user input, and that is what we concentrate on in this book. I have included one example about testing raw data in quantity—the real-world shipping example mentioned repeatedly throughout the book. That was the one test project I had in 10 years in which I tested raw data in quantity. One part of the integration effort was to test the integration of the acquired company's car movement data stream with the parent company's car movement data stream.

The team accomplished this testing in a completely manual mode even though millions of messages had to be analyzed and verified. The testers were all SMEs and senior staff members. The complexity of their analysis could not be automated, or even taught to professional testers. Every verification and validation required the experiences of a lifetime and the expertise of the very best.

The effort was an enormous undertaking and cost four times more than the estimates. I believe that budget money was appropriated from every other department at the parent company to pay for it. Nevertheless, it was mission-critical that those data streams maintained 100 percent integrity, and consequently, no price was too high for the test effort that ensured the success of this integration effort.

Data-Dependent Paths

Some paths will be more data-dependent than others. In these cases, the number of tests performed is a function of the number of data sets that will be tested. The same path, or at least parts of the same path, will be exercised repeatedly. The data will control the branches taken and not taken.

If you approach data analysis without considering the independent paths, you will certainly miss some important paths. In my experience, this is how many hard-to-reproduce bugs get into production. Someone tests all the main, easily identified data sets without considering all the possible exception paths. This is why I recommend performing the path analysis and then populating the paths with the data sets that are required to exercise the most important paths, rather than the other way around.

Having said that, I must add that users do some unexpected things with data, and so an examination of paths alone will not suffice to cover all the exceptions that will be exercised by the user.

Some Thoughts about Error Messages

Error messages for data exceptions are an important consideration in a good test effort. In my study of production problems at Prodigy, it became clear that virtually all of the most tenacious, expensive, and longest-lived production problems involved one or more missing or erroneous error messages. These problems had the most profound impact on customer service as well.

Data-dependent error messages need to be accounted for in the test inventory as part of your data analysis. I haven't seen a complete list of error messages for an application since 1995. In today's object-oriented architectures, they tend to be decentralized, so accounting for them usually requires exploration. I generally estimate how many I should find when I do my path analysis. There should be at least one error message for each exception path and at least one data error message for each data entry field. This area of testing may be a minor concern to you or it may be a major issue. Here are a couple of examples of what I mean.

There was a startup company with a B2B Web application that I tested during the dot-com boom. There was only one error message in the entire Web application. The text of the error message was just one word: "Wrong." This developer's error message "placeholder" appeared whenever the application encountered a data error. The testers complained about the message, and they were told that it would be replaced by the appropriate text messages in due course. Of course, it was never fully eradicated from the system, and it would pop up at the most inconvenient times. Fortunately, this company went into the sea with the other lemmings when the dot-coms crashed.

On the other end of the spectrum, I had the pleasure to write some white papers for a Danish firm that developed and marketed the finest enterprise resource planning (ERP) products I have ever seen. Reviewing (testing) their products was the most wonderful breath of fresh air in testing I have had since Prodigy. Their products were marketed throughout Europe and America, and simultaneously supported many languages.

To ensure high-quality, appropriate, and helpful error messages in many languages, they incorporated the creation and maintenance of the error message text for any required language into their development platform. The development platform kept a to-do list for all unfinished items, and developers could not check in their code as complete until the error messages were also marked complete. The company hired linguists to create and maintain all their text messages, but it was the responsibility of the developer to make sure the correct messages were attached to the exception processors in their code.

This system worked wonderfully in all its languages. The helpful text messages contributed to both high customer satisfaction and fewer calls to customer service.

Boundary Value Analysis

Years ago I read a headline somewhere that said something to the effect that "boundary value analysis is the most important test technique there is." My reaction was, "Of course it is; every animal on my farm can tell you that." Boundary value analysis (BVA) is one of the most fundamental survival techniques there is. The trick is recognizing the boundaries as boundaries and then cataloging their properties correctly.

Boundary value analysis is a test data selection technique in which values are chosen to lie along data extremes. Boundary values include maximum, minimum, just inside and outside boundaries, typical values, and error values. The hope is that if a system works correctly for these special values, then it will work correctly for all values in between. These values are the most important test cases.

Boundary Value Analysis Example

I will continue to use the method of payment test items from Chapter 12. Figure 13.1 shows the payment details page from the Tester's Paradise Web application. Let's consider the matter of credit card authentication.

There are two types of tests that need to be conducted on this page. First, we need to verify that the individual data fields are being validated correctly, and second, we need to verify that the data set produced by validated field values from this page is being validated correctly.

A Survivalist View of Boundary Analysis

There is a path on my farm that leads from the barnyard down to the pond and then around the pond to the pasture. My ducks follow this each day as they make their way from breakfast in the barnyard to the water for their day's activities and then back again in the evening for dinner and sleep. One morning there was a branch from an old oak tree about 18 inches in diameter lying across the path. It had fallen during the night.

The ducks approached it cautiously. Each duck inspected the log carefully from the barnyard side, paying special attention to the area where the log met the path. There were gaps between the log and the path, but none big enough for a duck to squeeze through. Once the ducks were satisfied of this, they began to inspect the top of the log, and stretching as far as their necks could reach on tip toe, they examined the other side.

The log was just big enough that they couldn't quite see the ground on the other side, so they would not risk leaping over onto uncertain ground. A couple of the ducks returned to the barnyard. A couple of the ducks decided to explore to the ends of the branch to see if they could find a way around it. And the largest and bravest duck found a way to climb up to the top of the log, and she continued her inspection of the far side from there. Eventually, she found a gentle, branching way to get down to the path on the pond side.

One of the ducks who tried to go around the log through the brush succeeded in getting through and also made it to the pond. The last duck met a big black snake in the brush and would have probably been bitten except for the intervention of the dog.

A few minutes later, I came to the log while walking my horse out to the pasture. He stopped and gave it a similar inspection. First checking, by eye and by smell, the side closest to him, then the log itself, and finally using his height, he thoroughly inspected the far side. He was not interested in stepping over the log until he was quite satisfied with the ground on both sides and the log itself. After the duck's adventure with the snake, I was not inclined to rush him. The interesting thing was that coming back that evening, he again refused to step over the log until he had completed the same inspection from the pond side.

Horses are prey animals, and consequently they do not rationalize obstacles. That means that just because it was safe to go across the log in one direction didn't mean it was safe to go across in the other direction. They treat every side of a boundary as a unique challenge and potential threat. This is a fundamental survival instinct.

I first told this story to a group of testers in a corporation that manufactures huge boom-ables. The consensus was that the ducks were very good testers. But the horse must have been a tester in a safety-critical industry in some past life.

Field validation can happen in the browser or on the server. It is normal to try and do simple field validation in the browser, because it saves the round trip to the server and offloads this minor processing to the client, freeing the server's resources for more important tasks.

A credit authorization requires a valid credit card number of the type of credit card selected—Visa or MasterCard in this case—and a valid expiration date. The expiration date must have a valid month and a valid year and must be the correct expiration date for that particular card number. Further, the user must also provide the correct four-digit security code, called a card verification number, found on the back of the card.

Drop-Down Selection Boxes Only Keep Out Honest People

If you are looking at the drop-down selection box in Figure 13.1 and thinking, *What is she talking about? You can't test a "-1" or a "13" in the month field since it's a drop-down*, then you should think again. Drop down boxes like this one have done a lot to help keep incorrectly typed data from getting to our applications, but they are not a panacea.

Recently, a Web store owner I know called to ask f I could help figure out what was going wrong in his electronic store. It seemed that something locked it up on a regular basis, but the server logs showed nothing. The Visual Basic (.asp)-scripted store would simply stop creating pages about every three days. It required a full server restart to get the store functioning again. The hosting company was not happy to interrupt service on all the Web sites in the server every three days so the store could go on.

I agreed to take a look. Sure enough, I managed to dig up an obscure application log that seemed to have lots of funky-looking command strings in it. After a bit of thinking, I realized I was looking at a series of artificially generated bogus command strings. The store had logged them because it had not been able to process them.

It turns out that it was an easy matter to send edited command strings to the store and lock it up. So, some hacker was creating these command strings in a text editor and sending them to the store. The store's response to these bad command strings was to lock up. Locking up was the only exception processing in the software; there seemed to be no data validation taking place in the application logic. The store's ASP developers were depending entirely on the HTML/ASP user interface to validate the user input.

Hackers have a field day with such weak applications, and someone obviously was onto this one.

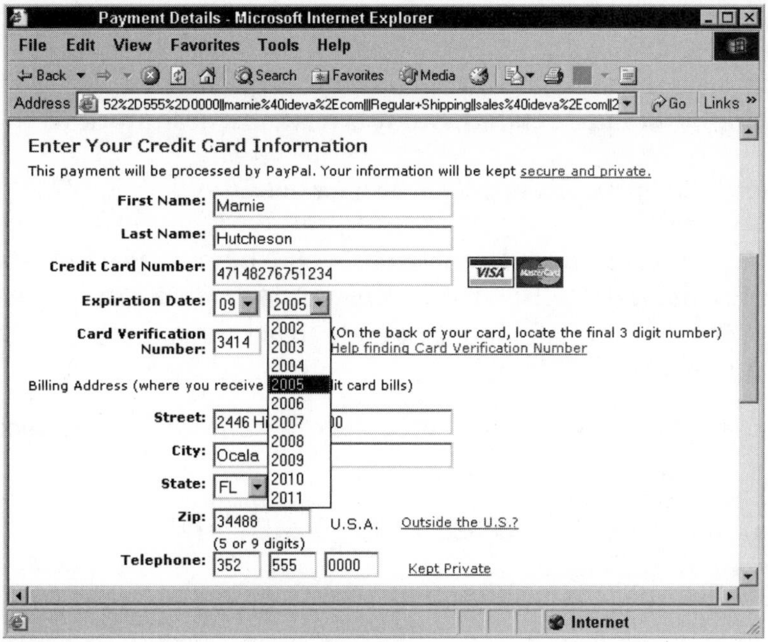

Figure 13.1   The Payment Details page.

Field Validation Tests

As the first example, I will use BVA and a data-reducing assumption to determine the minimum number of tests I have to run to make sure that the application is only accepting valid month and year data from the form.

Translating the acceptable values for boundary value analysis, the expiration month data set becomes:

$1 \leq$ month ≤ 12

BVA-based data set = {0,1,2,11,12,13} (6 data points)

The values that would normally be selected for BVA are 0, 1, 2, and 11, 12, 13.

Using simple data reduction techniques, we will further reduce this number of data points by the following assumptions.

Assumption 1.   One of the values, 2 or 11, is probably redundant; therefore, only one midpoint, 6, will be tested.

Month data set = {0,1,6,12,13} (5 data points)

This next assumption may be arbitrary, especially in the face of the hacker story that I just related, but it is a typical assumption.

Assumption 2.   Negative values will not be a consideration.

Figure 13.2 shows how I like to visualize the boundaries for this range. Every value that falls within the hatched area, including my test data, 1, 6, and 12, is valid, and all values outside these areas, for example, 0 and 13, should fail.

Likewise, the valid field data set for the expiration year becomes

$2002 \le year \le 2011$

BVA year data set = {2001,2002,2003,2010,2011,2012}

Again, I will apply a simplifying assumption.

Assumption 3.   One of the values, 2003 or 2010, is probably redundant; therefore, only the midpoint, 2006, will be tested.

BVA year data set = {2001,2002,2006,2011,2012}

These two fields, a valid month and a valid year, are combined to become a data set in the credit authorization process. These are the data values that will be used to build that test set. But before I continue with this example, I need to mention one more data reduction technique that is very commonly used but not often formalized.

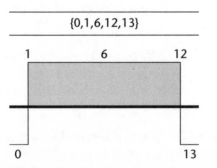

Figure 13.2 The boundary value range for a valid month.

Matrix Data Reduction Techniques

We all use data reduction techniques whether we realize it or not. The technique used here simply removes redundant data, or data that is likely to be redundant, from the test data sets. It is important to document data reductions so that others can understand the basis of the reduction. When data is eliminated arbitrarily, the result is usually large holes in the test coverage. Because data reduction techniques are routinely applied to data before test design starts, reducing the number of test data sets by ranking them as we did with the paths may not be necessary.

Note: **Generally use matrix data reductions rather than data ranking.**

The following section illustrates some good defensible data reduction techniques. But there are a couple of rules:

1. Do not apply this data reduction technique to individual data items—only to data sets.
2. Use your assumptions and the test inventory to document your data reductions.

The matrix data reduction is accomplished by building the matrix of possible combinations of the individual data and removing redundant sets. Again, be sure to write down the assumptions you use to remove data sets from your test set. In the previous section, I made the assumption that any point between the two boundaries would be OK as a test point—that I didn't need to test a number immediately adjacent to the boundary. In this case, I will be making a similar type of assumption, but the results can have a profound impact on the total number of tests that are left after reduction.

This is a very typical assumption that testers make all the time, but they rarely write it down. Typically, we make a guess about boundaries. In my testing over the last year, I have found that the single biggest source of error is in boundaries in the data entry field.

For the data reduction matrix, I will combine the two individual data sets that were just created in order to make a set of month, year combinations. Once I have done this, I will have to test to validate the month and year. If I have a good month but a bad year, the test is going to fail, or vice versa. Now I will show you how to build a data set matrix that allows you to consider further data reduction of your test sets.

Data Set Tests

A valid expiration date field must have both a valid month and a valid year using the two data sets selected previously:

{0,1,6,12,13} and {2001,2002,2006,2011,2012}

This gives us, {month, year} → 5 × 5 data combinations = 25 possible combinations. Figure 13.3 shows the possible combinations of these data and their truth table outcome.

Note: **If I had used all 6 BVA data items, there would be 6 × 6 = 36 data sets to test. So the data reduction assumption saved 11 data set tests. Looking at it another way, applying this data reduction technique reduced the BVA tests by 31 percent.**

Notice the True (T) and False (F) value notation. The shaded areas in the matrix, all the values around the edges, should fail because they contain at least one false value, so the month, year set should fail. There are 16 data sets that should fail. The nine data sets in the middle of the matrix are all true, so they should pass. Notice that there are almost twice as many exceptions as there are passing sets.

This matrix provides a systematic way of visualizing how the data sets behave. I can use this pattern to my advantage if I need to reduce the number of data tests. If I select sets from this matrix, I can make sure I get a representative set, because I can see the pattern, rather than some ad hoc random sampling. I can test the extremes, the mixed sets, and the all-true sets—without testing every single value.

I can make a good guess at the proportions of TT, TF, FT, and FF sets I need to test because I can see how many of each there are. I also know that I have almost twice as many sets that should fail as sets that should pass. Let's say that I want to cut the number of tests in half. I can probably pick a representative test set by choosing

$$16/2 = 8 \text{ failing sets}$$

I would select all four FF sets, 2 TF sets, and 2 FT sets.

And for

$$9/2 = 4.5 \text{ (round up to 5) passing sets}$$

I would select each of the corner TT sets, {1,2002}, {12,2002}, {1,2011}, {12,2002}, and the one in the center of the matrix, {6,2006}.

0,2001 FF	1,2001 TF	6,2001 TF	12,2001 TF	13,2001 FF
0,2002 FT	1,2002 TT	6,2002 TT	12,2002 TT	13,2002 FT
0,2006 FT	1,2006 TT	6,2006 TT	12,2006 TT	13,2006 FT
0,2011 FT	1,2011 TT	6,2011 TT	12,2011 TT	13,2011 FT
0,2012 FF	1,2012 TF	6,2012 TF	12,2012 TF	13,2012 FF

Figure 13.3 The data set for a valid date field expanded.

Note: **This would reduce the number of test sets I plan to test down to 13, or 36 percent test coverage of the original BVA estimate of 36 test sets.**

This is a small and simple example, but it clearly demonstrates the principle of using the matrix data reduction technique. This method is systematic and reproducible—as long as you document your assumptions. In a completely new environment where no components are trustworthy, it would be far better to test all the data sets, but I don't usually have time.

Building the data sets this way is a bottom-up process. I may test from top down, but I build my data sets from the bottom up whenever I can. With that in mind, let's go on to look at another technique for building test data set requirements from the bottom up as we go on to the next step, determining the data sets required to test credit authorization.

Data Set Truth Table

At first glance, Table 13.1 might seem trivial. Obviously, all these values need to be valid or we will never get a credit card authorization to pass. But consider it a different way. Let's say we put in a valid date and a valid credit card number, but we pick the wrong type of credit card. All the field values are valid, but the data set should fail. To build the data sets that I need, I must first understand the rules. This table tells me how many true data values I need for each one card to get a credit authorization.

Note: **My goal is to build the fewest number of test sets possible. If I can, I will build the data sets to verify credit authorization using data that will verify the field processors at the same time. So, I can run one test series and verify both the fields and the function.**

Table 13.1 The Credit Authorization Truth Table

Data Set 1-The set of all Valid Data, all in the data set	Is a valid value for the field	Is a valid member of this Data Set	Minimum Number of Data to test	Minimum Number of Data Sets to test
Cardholder Name				1
1. First Name	True	True	1	
2. Last Name	True	True	1	
Billing Address				1
2. Street Address	True	True	1	
3. City	True	True	1	
4. State	True	True	1	
5. Zip	True	True	1	
Credit Card Information				1
6. Card Type	True	True	1	
7. Card Number	True	True	1	
8. Expiration Month	True	True	1	
9. Expiration Year	True	True	1	
10. Card Verification Number	True	True	1	
OUTCOME:	**True**	**True**	**10**	**1**

Published Assumptions

Assumption: Once the field processors have been verified for one credit card, they will be assumed to be stable for all credit cards.

We're going to assume once the field processors have been verified for one card, they are going to work for both credit cards. In one test effort our team did assume this initially, and it was a bad assumption, but happily it didn't bite us because we published it in the test plan.

One of the programmers came forward and told us that the field processor for the credit card number in the client was checking to make sure that only numeric data was placed in the field; however, there was another process to validate that it was a valid credit card of the type selected, for example, Visa or MasterCard. This second validation took place after the information was submitted to the online application. The application was using a specific algorithm for each type of card selected by the user.

This is a common problem when testers can't know for sure "where" validation is occurring. We would only have been testing one of the algorithms; we wouldn't have validated both of them. Because we stated this assumption in the test plan, the developers picked up on it and let us know.

The card verification number is another field that might be processed by a different logic routine depending on the type of card. This is another example of one of those hidden boundaries that testers don't know about. If I only define tests to test what I know about, I will probably just run two tests for each card, one valid and one invalid. That's four data set tests in all:

10 valid data + 10 invalid data = 20 field tests for each card

These two test sets should yield two test sets for one card; one will pass authentication and one will fail. This will test each of the field validation processors once.

We have to perform all these tests for both credit cards:

$$20 \times 2 = 40 \text{ field tests for 2 credit cards}$$

But as I have just explained, this is too small a test set to detect any hidden boundaries, unless I get very lucky. So, I will want to add some data values to help me probe the code just a bit. Before I add any tests, there is another assumption that I want to consider.

Assumption: Whether field data will pass or fail is independent of validity of the data set.

The field tests don't verify any data sets; they just verify that field tells us that data. Mixing valid data from different sets will cause the data set to be invalid, even though all the field processors have been satisfied. Could be a good credit card number and a good date, but they may not work together. So the field test set is only going to tell us about the field problems. This assumption also addresses the logic flow of the field data validation processing. Whether field data pass or fail is independent of the data combination. I am assuming that once the field processor tells us whether or not it's good data, it will always be able to tell us if it's good data, regardless of whether or not some other field is valid.

So when we count up the minimum number of field tests on the data in all those fields, at minimum there are 10 valid data to make one set, and

10 invalid data. One good case and one bad case. At the very minimum, we have to come up with 20 field data items for one card. Then we have a total for two credit cards, so we multiply by 2 for a total of 40 field tests.

As I said, I don't think that this is enough coverage to provide an adequate test effort. If you are wondering if extra coverage is necessary, see the discussion on Web services in the *Caveats* section coming up. I don't want to just beat on the application in a random fashion. I would like to identify potential hidden boundaries and test them. I need a tool to help me decompose this large data set into its components so that I can visualize where such hidden boundaries might be found. Table 13.2 shows one approach to accomplish this.

Table 13.2   Data Set Validation Table

Data Set Credit Card #1	Field Test Outcome	Data ∈ Set	Data Set Test Outcome
1. (All Valid & ∈ set)	Valid	Valid	Valid
2. (All invalid data)	Invalid	Invalid	Invalid
3. Card Type ∉ Set	Valid	Invalid	Invalid
4. Card # ∉ Set	Valid	Invalid	Invalid
5. Exp. date ∉ Set	Valid	Invalid	Invalid
6. Card Verification # ∉ set	Invalid	Invalid	Invalid

∈ means "is a member of"

∉ means "is NOT a member of"

Each of the six items in Table 13.2 has two distinct possible outcomes for the field and data set validations. Each of these six items is a data set. According to this table, I need six data sets to test the card validation process. This gives me the opportunity to try multiple values for each data item. I will use this number of tests in my actual test count.

The Process for Building Sufficient Data Sets from the Bottom Up

The following is the process I recommend for building sufficient data sets from the bottom up—and which I use for all my work:

1. I start with two good sets of data, one for each card. This will ensure that I have tested the most important all-true paths.

2. Next, I prepare a list of all the invalid data values that I want to test to verify the field validation routines. For example, if I need to check for negative numbers, or nonnumeric characters in numeric fields and so on, then I will quickly build up several tests for the numeric fields—and that means more than two complete test sets. If this happens, I will create more data sets to accommodate these field tests.

3. Most important, I will try to get a look at the logic paths that do the credit authorization. I want to know how the application is verifying the data set for the credit authorization. If I can identify any data boundaries in the application validation logic, I will add test data to create test sets to test those boundaries.

Stated as it is here, this may seem like a trivial example, but it is no accident that most credit card authorization is handled by specialized companies as secured Web services. Anytime there is an opportunity to commit fraud, there are hackers ready to try.

In all, I will prepare at least five sets of invalid data for each credit card. This gives me the opportunity to test at least five exceptions for each data field.

(1 valid set of data + 5 invalid sets) × 2 credit cards = 12 data sets

The next example on the test inventory is the new Purchase Option: Not available in some states (data). This is an adjunct process that must consider each product and compare the buyer's state rules against the rules of the selling state. This is actually an international issue rather than a U.S. interstate issue. Some products can't be sold in some countries. The processing that verifies and says yes or no to a particular sale is quite complex and beyond this discussion.

I have approximated it here by stating that each state will require a test, so the number of tests is 50.

Finally, Minimum Order must be $30.00 (data). I assumed a simple BVA for this test, for example, $29.99, $30.00, and $31.00. Interestingly enough, I recently broke an application trying to make a purchase that was for too large an amount. Having completed this much data analysis, Table 13.3 shows the most recent version of our sample test inventory. The total data set tests, 77, will be carried to the MITs Totals page in the spreadsheet. I will show you the results of the analysis we conduct in Chapters 12 and 13 in the next chapter, "What Our Analysis Tells Us and What's in Store in the Near Future."

Table 13.3 Sample Test Inventory 3

Tester's Paradise (Release 2.0)	Data Sets	Existing Data Tests	System Data Tests
Project Information:			
Fix For Error #123	0	7	0
Fix for Error #124	0	4	0
Tester's Paradise Main Menu			
Our Best System Simulator			
Message Data Flow Checker			
Screen Comparison — Pixel Viewer			
Portable System Monitor (New Function)			
Specifics and Options			
Add-on Platform Adapters			
View Portable System Monitor			
Display Portable System Monitor			
Order Form			
Arrange Payment			
Method of Payment (Path)			
Method of Payment limited to 2 credit cards (Data Sets)	12		
Purchase Option: Not Available in some states (data)	50		
Minimum Order must be $30.00 (data)	3		
Order Confirmation			
Support Packages			
Return to Main Menu			
Cancel			
Installation is automatic at logon			1
Totals	65	11	1

Total Data Tests	77

Caveats

BVA isn't always enough. There can be problems and times when you reduce the data set too far, as I have just pointed out. Here are some of the things to keep in mind as you plan your data testing.

Hidden Boundaries

Boundary value analysis provides us with an invaluable data reduction technique for test data selection. The risk of missing a significant error in some other part of a number line is very small when you use good boundary analysis techniques—unless there is another boundary in your test range that you don't know about. For example, when we tested the logon application at Prodigy, we used boundary value analysis to determine the test set. The testing went well, and the application was sent to production. But soon after it went live, we started experiencing user profile corruption problems.

The Prodigy Services ID was made up of four alpha characters, two digits, and one alpha character—for example, HFDC15A. Non-alpha and nonnumeric characters were not allowed, for example, spaces and punctuation characters.

The testers tested all the forbidden characters in the first four slots, and they tested several permutations of punctuation and alpha characters in the numeric slots 5 and 6, and so on. The one thing they did not think to test was a space in the fifth slot. Of course, almost immediately a clever user did perform this test when he or she was trying to log on the first time.

First-time logons were very special events back in the days when we were using data tape, DASD, to store our information. It turned out that a failed first attempt ruined the entire user profile. So the user would need to call customer service and receive a new ID before he or she could join the service.

This was a very hard bug to isolate and reproduce, because users who encountered it could not remember exactly what they had done. And as far as they were concerned, they hadn't done anything wrong.

We finally found the bug by building a complete test suite that systematically tried every character on the keyboard in each slot. When the space was typed into the fifth slot and the logon was submitted, an error was generated and the user profile was corrupted. With this evidence in hand, we were able to find the problem.

What Was Really Going On

Bug no. 1.   Unknown to us, there was a boundary at the fifth character—a different subroutine. A numeric validation routine evaluated slots 5 and 6, and it did not have the logic to check for a space character. A simple omission.

Bug no. 2.   When the space character was sent to the logon application in the mainframe that verified the user profile, which did not have logic to protect it from an illegal character (that was supposed to be handled at the client), the mainframe process overwrote the profile with the bad information and corrupted the record.

Bug no. 3.   The error message sent to the user told them that they had committed a security breach. This, of course, was not quite correct.

Boundary value analysis automatically picks the most important data points. Ranking is not usually necessary. This really cuts down the number of tests that you have to run while still minimizing the risk of missing some point of failure.

Web Services

Back in the late 1980s, users typing data into fields on a GUI was the unknown territory. All the validation code, the processing code, and the messages were brand-new and not to be trusted. The network protocols and interfaces were nowhere near as stable as what we have today. Server technology was in its infancy. However, we could at least be sure where our application logic was coming from. We could make bold statements like, "The application had been tested and was ready to go to production." I fear this will not be the case in the coming years.

Software as a service has been threatening to become a part of the application landscape for over 20 years. It was inevitable that some day it would become acceptable and profitable. Slowly but surely, Web-based software subscription services are becoming a reality in the Internet landscape. For example, look at eBay and PayPal. Taken together, these are a first-generation retailer Web service, robust and thriving. Anyone can become a shopkeeper. Next, consider the now-ubiquitous virus checkers and operating systems that automatically go "home" to check for updates in the background, and you don't need to know about it. There is Quicken Online, TurboTax—the list is getting longer every day.

Most of us have come to appreciate at least a few of these services even if we don't entirely trust the direction they are taking us. The caveat I see has more to do with the current "next generation" of Web services. These XML-based programs can live on any Web server and advertise their services in globally available search engines in the Universal Description Discovery and Integration (UDDI) servers. Programs can automatically locate and identify these Web services through their UDDI listings, which define the entire contract for the Web service, including what they provide and how you have to compose your requests to get these offerings.

Developers envision this to be the next opportunity for the independent development entrepreneur. Since these Web services are not high pro- file like eBay, they are background processes for the most part, and they will be hard to track. These contracts are all made programmatically behind the scenes. No humans need to be involved. The users have no idea where the actual processing is being done. It may be, for example, that your travel company contracts with a reservation Web service to get flight information, a Tester's Paradise Web service to find hotels, and so on.

How can we be sure that the Tester's Paradise Web service is legitimate? How can we be sure where they are sending our data?

How can we enforce a service-level contract when we can't be sure we are still using the Tester's Paradise Web service?

I don't have simple answers for any of these questions. I have already had a couple of bad experiences trying to debug problems when a third- party Web service was involved. I don't look forward to testing this next generation of Web services. If they really catch on, we testers will probably have to go back to an IP traffic monitor to even be sure who or what the application is talking to.

I mention this here because it has a profound impact on the verity of the applications and the very boundaries we take for granted, that we think are static and dependable. If you don't know where your data is coming from, or what module is performing the business logic calculations in your application, if these processes can be replaced without warning or sign, we cannot assume the things will work the same tomorrow as they did today.

Summary

Users can do unexpected things when entering data, and hackers will definitely test the limits. But in my experience, the most important data comes into most systems through the user interface.

Boundary value analysis is a powerful technique for picking the most probable failure points in the data. You can reduce the amount of testing by two-thirds or three-quarters based on your assumptions. Just beware of hidden boundaries, because with such a reduced test set, there are huge holes in your test coverage.

When testing the data-handling capabilities of an application, I like to build my data sets from the ground up and then perform data reduction on the resulting sets, to cut down the number of tests based on probable redundancy. I continue this process until I have a test set that is both concise and doable in the time allowed.

We instinctively use boundary analysis constantly. Be sure to document it when you do it, so that others have the chance to correct your faulty assumptions. Data reduction is another powerful technique for further reducing the number of tests that you may have to run. This is another technique that we use instinctively. Again, be careful to document your assumptions.

Watch out for the things that you didn't expect or plan for. I try to throw in a few extra off-the-wall tests just to see what happens. Every once in a while, something unexpected does happen, and the truth is always stranger and more interesting than fiction.

For those of you wondering about the mouse driver data estimate in the beginning of the chapter, the number came from the following matrix:

640×480 pixels = 307,200 possible locations for the mouse to click on

When you expand the problem, it produces a matrix much like Figure 13.3, only bigger. By boundary value analysis, most of the bugs would occur in a well-selected 50 percent test coverage scenario, or the first 153,600 tests. Based on what I showed you in this chapter, by using the matrix, we could probably identify most of the bugs in 92,160 tests, or 30 percent of the matrix—although screen quadrants are not quite the same as valid month/year combinations. The technique certainly worked well in this case.

CHAPTER 14

What Our Analysis Tells Us and What's in Store in the Near Future

"So, what did your analysis tell you?" my manager asked.

"That we need to do more testing than we thought," the tester said.

"I expected as much," my manager said, smiling.

Table 14.1 shows the total MITs that were established through path and data analysis covered in Chapters 12 and 13. The actual number is larger than the estimate, as I predicted, but not only for the reason that I would have expected.

The MITs path and data analysis yielded 38 more tests than we originally estimated. The real surprise was that it turned out there were more existing tests than we thought. And after the past performance of the first version, no one was sure which tests we could drop, safely.

Table 14.1 The Total Tests Identified for the Effort through MITs Analysis

Tester's Paradise (Release 2.0)	Total Path Tests				Data Tests			MINs	
	Menu Option Paths	Exception Paths	Program Paths	MIPs	Data Sets	System	MIDs		Existing Tests
Project Information:	0	0	0	0					
Fix For Error #123	0	0	3	3					7
Fix for Error #124	0	0	0	0					5
Tester's Paradise Main Menu	5	5	0	10					
Our Best System Simulator	0	0	0	0					65
Message Data Flow Checker	0	0	0	0					61
Screen Comparison— Pixel Viewer	0	0	0	0					76
Portable System Monitor (New Function)	5	5	0	10				3	
Specifics and Options	3	3	0	6					
Add-on Platform Adapters	3	3	0	6					
View Portable System Monitor	2	2	0	4					
Display Portable System Monitor	0	0	4	4				3	
Order Form	3	3	6	12				3	
Method of Payment limited to 2 credit cards (Data Sets)				0	12				
Purchase Option: Not Available in some states (data)				0	50				
Minimum Order must be $30.00 (data)				0	3				
Arrange Payment	2	2	5	9					
Order Confirmation	1	1	0	2					
Support Packages	3	3	0	6					
Return to Main Menu	1	1	0	2					
Cancel	1	1	0	2					
Installation is automatic at logon	0	0	0	0		1			
Totals	29	29	18	**76**	65	1	66	9	
				76			66	9	214

Total all tests MIPs + MIDs + MINs =	**151**
Existing Tests	**214**
Total Tests	**365**

So how good was the estimate? Actually, it was pretty good. Table 14.2 shows the raw worksheet with the MITs tests added in. Initially, the new numbers in the MITs column make it look like the test effort doubled, but we were able to contain the effort to the original estimated time line. Take a look at Table 14.2, and I will explain.

Table 14.2   The Testers Paradise Release 2.0 Sizing Worksheet with MITs

Tester's Paradise (Release 2.0)	Estimates	MITs
Total Tests for 100% coverage (T) from MITs Totals row on Test Calc. Sheet	**315**	
MITs Recommended number of scripts	**232.00**	365.00
MITs Minimum number of scripts from MITs Totals Sheet	208.00	
MITs estimate for recommended coverage – all code	**74%**	
MITs estimate for minimum required coverage – all code	66%	
Number of existing tests from Version 1	131.00	214.00
Total New Tests identified	113	151
Number of tests to be created	**101.00**	151
Average number of keystrokes in a test script	50	40
Est. script create time (manual script entry) 20 min. each -> (total new tests × 20/60) = person-hours total	32.58	50.33
Est. Automated replay time total MITs (including validation) 4/60 hrs./script = replay hr./cycle total (For each test environment)	**15.47**	24.33
Est. manual replay time for MITs tests (including validation) × (20/60) = hours/cycle (For each test environment)	**77.33**	**121.67**
LOC Approx. 10,000 C language, 2,000 ASM	12,000 lines	
Est. Number of errors (3 errors/100 LOC) = 400	400 errors	
Number of code turnovers expected	4	
Number of complete test cycles est.	5	
Number of test environments	6	
Total Number of tests that will be run (against each environment) 4 complete automated cycles = Total MITs × 4	**928**	**1,460**
Total Tests – all environments in 5 cycles × Total MITs × 6 environments	**6,960**	**10,950**
Pre-Turnover: Analysis planning and design	80 hrs.	
Post-Turnover:		
Script creation & 1st test cycle (manual build + rerun old suites) = Hours	41.31	64.60
4 Automated Test cycles (time per cycle × 4) × Running concurrently on 6 environments (in Hours)	**61.87**	**97.33**
Total: Script run time with automation Running concurrently on 6 environments (1 manual + 4 automated) = weeks to run all tests through 5 cycles on 6 environments	**7.22**	**11.35**
Total: **Script run time all Manual** (5 manual cycles) = weeks for 6 environments – Best Recommendation for automating testing!	**58**	**91.25**
Error logs, Status etc. (est. 1 day in 5 for each environment) weeks	1.73	2.72
Total: Unadjusted effort Total Run Time + Bug Reporting (in Weeks)	8.95	14.07
Factor of Safety adjustment = 50% Total adjusted effort (Total effort in Weeks)	13.43	21.11

We added six test machines so we could run the test suites in half the time. Then we also decided to only run the tests for Release 1 two times: once at code complete and once after any bug fixes were integrated, just before shipping the code to production. The strategy worked very well, and we were able to implement the extra 38 tests for the new code and still fit the test effort into the original 14-week estimate.

The bugs we found in this application were not in the field processors of the user interface. They were embedded in the interactions of the system, and that leads me to my next topic: what testers will need to test in the next generation of software.

You are not going to be testing trivial field processors, and no, you won't be able to rerun every test from the last release. Most development shops are trying to be Agile in order to compete while they keep just enough of the trappings of the traditional effort so that they can claim their products are commercially hardened, reliable, viable, and whatever other "ables" marketing requires. If the test effort can't demonstrate its value, then it is likely to be cut.

Software development is still being treated as a commodity, driven by entrepreneurial forces in the market. Until we raise our expectations about safety and reliability, we will continue to build software that is not prepared to survive the events that will probably happen to it.

Testing: The Next Generation

The Internet lowered the cost of communications to virtually nothing and gave us a cheap, globally accessible distribution system for software, e-commerce, and e-business. However, that was just the beginning. As more and more services move onto the Net, our expectations are that "everything" should be doable on the net, and we "need" to be connected more and more of the time. And this is where testers are going to be needed the most.

Collaboration

New Internet-based collaboration technologies enable projects to spread around the globe. Typically, e-business initiatives focus on the transaction systems, but the reality is that they are fundamentally based on people working together. Capabilities such as instant messaging, team rooms, and application sharing are being integrated within software such that they naturally become a part of the work environment. When considered in light of the sharp rise in telecommuting to more than 30 million U.S. workers in 2001, this all points to an impending demand for integrated collaboration tools that are accessible from both land-based and mobile devices. This demand will undoubtedly drive business adoption of new expanded wireless application services.

These services will include proactive and interactive features. Proactive features like notification are called push technology because applications and other users on the network can push messages and data to the mobile device. Data *pull* functions allow the user to access private corporate applications and data, as well as public Web services, and "pull" data from the application or service into their mobile device, where they can manipulate it.

The dedicated interface and the client/server application will probably be around for a while, but they will not be the major players. Embedded systems will still be around, but more and more of them will be network-connected over IP.

Mobile Computing

As I write this, many of you are in the process of moving your first application software to the mobile Internet. By the time this book is published, most of us in the testing community will be working on some form of mobile Internet application. A survey of development managers in Fortune 1000 companies conducted in early 2002 shows that, on average, 76 percent of the development budgets had been allocated to mobile Internet application development projects.

Your first mobile application might be as simple as a Web application that looks up contact phone numbers and sends the pages to a browser in a mobile phone, or it may be a full-blown mobile client for an ERP application running in a Pocket PC using an 802.11 Ethernet card or a cell modem for connectivity. The point is, we are about to enter a new age of computing.

At this time, it is not possible to say whether the Smartphone or the Pocket PC will win the impending mobile computing race. It doesn't matter if it is one or the other, or both—cost factors and mobility will drive the masses to the handheld computing device.

There are many examples that involve mobile personnel in industries where field workers need access to support services on the company intranet. Many of these workers have never used PCs in their jobs, but the Internet-connected mobile device will give them access to the same applications that have traditionally been accessible from a PC on the corporate LAN. These industries are expecting to experience large improvements in speed and efficiency in their service provisioning and customer care.

Back in my Prodigy days, we were limited by slow data transmission rates, small displays, limited memory, and slow processors. We had limited diagnostics tools and strict performance requirements. Applications had to become granular, rather than monolithic. They had to be broken into functional bits so that only the function that was required would be called—not an entire block of logic. The user interface had to be structured into small bits as well, so it could be downloaded quickly and then reassembled to run on computers using the small DOS operating system. This didn't seem to fit with the bigger, faster, smarter, get-DSL-in-your-own-home-and-watch-movies-over-the-Internet way things have been going recently.

MITs Methods and the Next Generation

Grace Hopper, the inventor of the software compiler, is the person who first popularized the notion of a computer bug.[1] She is also credited with saying something to the effect that each new tool we create to improve the way we write code removes whole classes of bugs from existence; simultaneously, it introduces new and different ones to take their place.

As I have said, most of the biggest quality improvements in software over the past 10 years have been due to standardization and improved development methods rather than improved quality assurance or testing. But having said that, when I take stock of where we are today, I have to agree with Grace's quote. There are new bugs coming at us all the time. So even though we don't need to spend too much time verifying and validating data field processors today (unless we are concerned that hackers might attack a weak application that relies on the user interface to prequalify data, rather than validating its own data), we do

---

[1] For the full story, see www.jamesshuggins.com/h/tek1/first_computer_bug.htm.

need to test. However, the things we are testing are changing from simple computing logic to complex multisystem integration issues.

The bugs I am seeking today may have very confusing symptoms; they are usually virtually impossible to reproduce, and they often have far-reaching effects. They can be very hard to diagnose, yet on any given day, this type of bug can affect thousands of users.

My role as a tester has changed a lot over the past 10 years. But I still use the MITs methods. Ten years ago I was shocked and appalled when management suggested that I simply fix the bugs that I was finding and send a report back to development. But today, I routinely fix systems issues and send the report to the responsible party. I draw the line at changing compiled code; I still won't do that. However, I am often expected to redesign the user interface based on test results.

> **Note:**   I still use the same MITs methods even though my testing job has changed a lot.

Today, my role as an integration tester is like the role of a doctor. I am a technician who diagnoses systemic ailments by observing symptoms and performing tests. Once I have made a diagnosis, I prescribe a medication or a cure. I may refer the matter to another technician who may be a specialist in that field. And, the client may choose to ignore my advice.

The Challenges

Now we stand on the threshold of a new era of Internet development: The mobile Internet is upon us even now. By the end of 2002, there will be 1.5 times more Web-enabled cell phones in the hands of the public than PCs. People who have never used PCs will begin using mobile Internet applications on their cell phones, in both their business and personal lives.

In most places, they will be limited by slow data transmission rates over existing cell networks and 320-pixel-wide displays, as well as limited memory and storage. Applications will be broken into small bits so that they can be called as needed—in other words, Web services. And new delivery mechanisms will evolve to ensure that data is delivered to users who will be sometimes connected and sometimes disconnected from the network.

This new (or resurgent old) architecture requires new (or resurgent old) testing techniques. The methods, techniques, and tools in this book were developed in just such an environment, and they are an excellent fit for the needs of testers facing the challenge of testing distributed applications running on handheld Internet-capable mobile devices.

Testing is going to be challenged again, as it was when PCs were introduced. The new connectivity and interoperation of these complex systems, where old technology meets new technology, will be a challenging and stimulating environment for the journeyman tester.

Even if some developers are screaming that no testing is required, there will be those more cautious and mature among the sheep who will be willing to risk a bit on an evaluation, saying, "We really need testers on the Internet; people have been writing code and sticking it out there for years without testing anything." (That quote came from the lead developer in my last eXtreme development project.)

If you can apply MITs methods like the inventory, filled with measurements, you have a good chance of adding value to your client's product, and your testing will be considered worthwhile.

Note: I use MITs no matter what the maturity of the software development is.

It is important that the maturity level of the test effort meet or exceed the maturity level of the software development. Otherwise, the test effort will be perceived as deficient. There are several such maturity models for software testing. For organizations using the Software Capability Maturity Model (SW-CMM) program, there is also a Software Testing Maturity Model (SW-TMM) program that maps testing activities to development activities.

The methods and metrics that I have discussed in this book fulfill all of the major requirements for a maturity level 5 testing process. I use them successfully to test development projects that are functioning on any CMM level. I simply use the best MITs tools, methods, metrics, and techniques for the job at hand.

I differ with most of the test maturity models in two areas. First, there some organizational issues that I believe need to remain flexible for each organization—for example, how to control and monitor the testing process. Second, I differ with most mainstream thinkers in the area of quality assurance. You can find my views on this topic in Chapter 2, "Maintaining Quality Assurance in Today's Software Testing Environment."

Overall, I believe that existing maturity models don't demand enough from the testers to make the test effort worthwhile. I have tried throughout this book to give you insights into how to show management (and yourself) the value that you add to the product. I do hope that you are able to take advantage of some of these techniques.

Until next time, Happy Testing.

Answers to Exercises

Chapter 7: How to Build a Test Inventory

Answers to all exercises in Chapter 7 are explained in detail at www.testersparadise.com.

Chapter 11: Path Analysis

Exercise 1

Remember:

Do not count the edges entering or leaving the system.

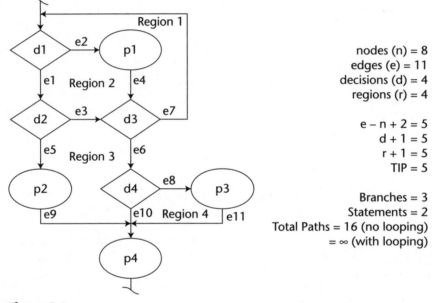

nodes (n) = 8
edges (e) = 11
decisions (d) = 4
regions (r) = 4

$e - n + 2 = 5$
$d + 1 = 5$
$r + 1 = 5$
TIP = 5

Branches = 3
Statements = 2
Total Paths = 16 (no looping)
$= \infty$ (with looping)

Figure A.1

Is this a valid logic circuit? Yes, this is a valid logic flow diagram, because all three equations total the same number of paths and no rules are broken.

Exercise 2

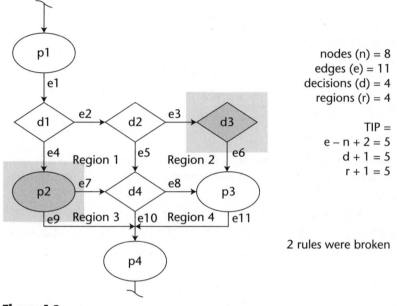

nodes (n) = 8
edges (e) = 11
decisions (d) = 4
regions (r) = 4

TIP =
e − n + 2 = 5
d + 1 = 5
r + 1 = 5

2 rules were broken

Figure A.2

Is this a valid logic circuit? All three equations do add up to the same number, but this is *not* a valid logic flow circuit. Two rules were broken here, and the net effect is that mathematically they cancel each other out of the calculations. This is a common occurrence in actual testing. The person doing the logic flow misses the exception clause when he or she is figuring out or explaining how the system works. A superficial inspection will not find these bugs. Care should be taken when the system is reviewed to look at each individual node and be sure it complies with the rules.

✔ **Rule: You can only have one edge leaving a process.**

The p2 process was actually a decision. When this change is made, the equations no longer total to the same number.

$$IP = Edges - Nodes + 2$$
$$\rightarrow 11 - 8 + 2$$
$$= 5$$
$$IP = Regions + 1$$
$$\rightarrow 4 + 1$$
$$= 5$$
$$IP = Decisions + 1$$
$$\rightarrow 5 + 1$$
$$= 6$$

✔ **Rule: A decision can have more than one edge coming into it, but it is better to use a process node to collect the edges and feed a single edge into the decision.**

Adding a collector or process node and one edge does not add to the total number of paths through the system. From the equation we can see that these additions cancel each other out.

$$IP = Edges - Nodes + 2$$
$$\rightarrow 12 - 9 + 2$$
$$= 5$$

Adding one edge and one process node makes the model clearer. If the collector node is necessary for conceptual clarity, it is probably necessary for programmatic clarity as well. This is one of the first things we identify in a reengineering effort. Take out the multiple entry points, and funnel all entries through a collector node. Not only does such a procedure node help structure a system, it is the perfect place to install a diagnostics trace to aid in testing the system.

Adding a collector node and diagnostics can have other benefits as well. It is not uncommon to discover that several of the edges that were thought to enter the new collector node are defunct or erroneous. One of the most productive uses of measurement is to verify actual usage. In one project, when a collector node and usage counts were added at the entrance to a report writer on a large system, it was discovered that only about 15 percent of the system reports were ever requested. This information was used to accurately reapportion the maintenance budget. The result was a better-balanced workload for support personnel and huge cost savings.

✔ **Rule: A decision must have two edges leaving it.**

The d2 decision has only one edge leaving it. We will assume that it was really a process. When this change is made, the totals of all three equations agree:

$$IP = Edges - Nodes + 2$$
$$\rightarrow 8 - 11 + 2$$
$$= 5$$
$$IP = Regions + 1$$
$$\rightarrow 4 + 1$$
$$= 5$$
$$IP = Decisions + 1$$
$$\rightarrow 4 + 1$$
$$= 5$$

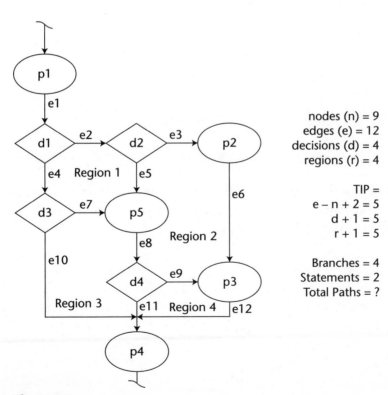

nodes (n) = 9
edges (e) = 12
decisions (d) = 4
regions (r) = 4

TIP =
e – n + 2 = 5
d + 1 = 5
r + 1 = 5

Branches = 4
Statements = 2
Total Paths = ?

Figure A.3

Exercise 3

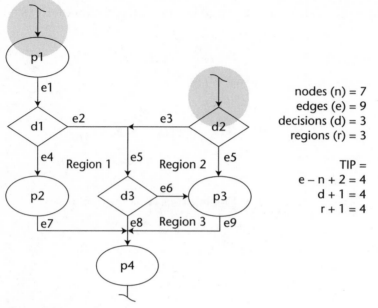

nodes (n) = 7
edges (e) = 9
decisions (d) = 3
regions (r) = 3

TIP =
e − n + 2 = 4
d + 1 = 4
r + 1 = 4

Figure A.4

Is this a valid logic flow circuit? No. Why not? It has two entrances.

✔ **Rule:** **You can only have one entry point and one exit point in a structured system.**

The system is not a valid logic circuit, because it's not a structured system. It requires five linearly independent paths to cover this system. The calculated value is erroneous.

Exercise 4

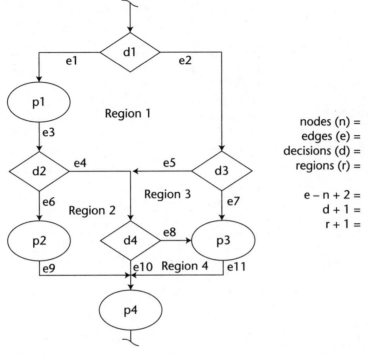

nodes (n) =
edges (e) =
decisions (d) =
regions (r) =

$e - n + 2 =$
$d + 1 =$
$r + 1 =$

Figure A.5

Is this a valid logic flow circuit? Yes.

There are five linearly independent paths possible through this system.

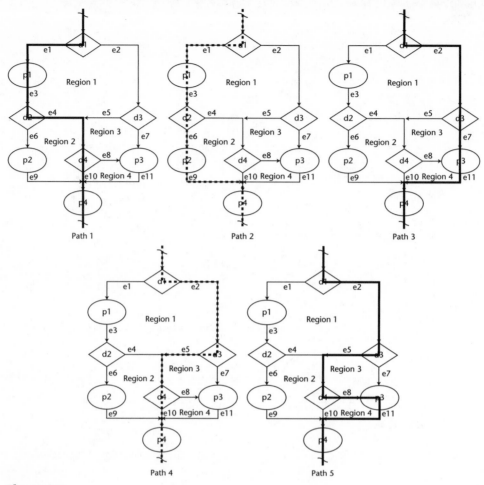

Figure A.6

However, these five paths can be covered in four traversals. If the order in which the nodes are covered is not important, then Path 4 is not necessary. All the path segments that it covers are covered in the other four traversals. There are a total of six different ways to traverse the five linearly independent paths that exist in this system.

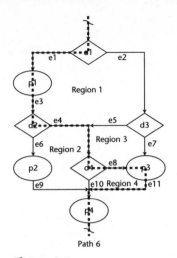

Figure A.7

> **Note:** Calculating the number of IPs does not tell where the paths are in the system, only how many exist.

The number of linearly independent paths is not *always* the minimum number of traversals required to cover all path segments one time. However, it requires detailed analysis to determine whether or not a system can be covered in fewer than the calculated number of linearly independent paths. For the purpose of estimating the number of path traversals that will be traversed as a minimum, the number of linearly independent paths is still an excellent metric.

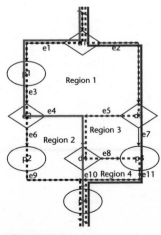

Figure A.8

Software Testing Questionnaire, Survey, and Results

I f you are going to measure how far you have come, you must first note the position where you started. In land surveying this is called the *benchmark*. A surveyor picks a good solid spot, paints an "X" on and says, "This is the benchmark; its elevation equals 100 feet." It doesn't matter where the benchmark is as long as it stays put for the duration of the survey. The "100 feet" elevation is arbitrary. It doesn't matter what its actual elevation is, such as its height above sea level, because everything is being measured relative to that point.

As the landscape becomes more civilized, durable monuments will be erected to be used as permanent benchmarks. Their arbitrary elevations and displacements will have been replaced by ones that have been normalized to fixed standards. In land surveying the standards are sea level, latitude, and longitude. Once the normalized elevation, latitude, and longitude of a benchmark have been established, the data is used to produce maps. In this way virtually all of the United States has been measured.

Making Your Benchmark

The following survey is nine years old. It had been completed by more than 1,350 people before they were exposed to these methods and metrics. To create your own benchmark, to measure your knowledge relative to the survey groups, and to measure your progress, complete this questionnaire before you read the results, and see where you fit.

The Test Questionnaire

Area in which you work:

Mainframe Computer: ☐   Both: ☐

Personal Computer: ☐   Other: ☐ _____

How long have you worked in this area?

_____

Are you:

Management: ☐   Not Management: ☐

Do you work primarily on:

Mainframe Computer: ☐   Both: ☐

Personal Computer: ☐   Other: ☐ _____

Have you participated in any organized software testing classes or workshops?

_____

If so, how long ago?

_____

Please indicate the types of testing you perform or are involved with:

1 = Never, 2 = Rarely, 3 = Infrequently, 4 = Frequently, 5 = Most Frequently

	1 2 3 4 5		1 2 3 4 5
Unit Testing	☐☐☐☐☐	Integration Testing	☐☐☐☐☐
Function Testing	☐☐☐☐☐	System Testing	☐☐☐☐☐
User Acceptance Testing	☐☐☐☐☐	Other:_____	☐☐☐☐☐

How many days per week (on average) do you spend involved in testing?

1 2 3 4 5
☐☐☐☐☐

If less than 1 day per week, please indicate how many hours per week:

_____hours.

Please indicate the software metrics that you use in your work:

1 = Never, 2 = Rarely, 3 = Infrequently, 4 = Frequently, 5 = Most Frequently

	1 2 3 4 5		1 2 3 4 5
Lines Of Code (LOC)	☐☐☐☐☐	Cyclomatic Complexity	☐☐☐☐☐
Halsteads Constant	☐☐☐☐☐	Function Points	☐☐☐☐☐
% Function Coverage	☐☐☐☐☐	Other:_____	☐☐☐☐☐

Are you currently using any automation tools in your testing?

Yes ☐   No ☐

If you are, please name the tools:

_____

_____

Do you have plans to automate your testing in the next six months?

Yes ☐   No ☐

If you do, please indicate what testing you intend to automate:

	1	2	3	4	5		1	2	3	4	5
Unit Testing	☐	☐	☐	☐	☐	Integration Testing	☐	☐	☐	☐	☐
Function Testing	☐	☐	☐	☐	☐	System Testing	☐	☐	☐	☐	☐
User Acceptance Testing	☐	☐	☐	☐	☐	Other:_____	☐	☐	☐	☐	☐

Please indicate the types of test tools you are interested in and your level of interest:

1 = None, 2 = Some, 3 = Medium, 4 = High, 5 = Highest

	1	2	3	4	5		1	2	3	4	5
System Simulators	☐	☐	☐	☐	☐	Network Simulators	☐	☐	☐	☐	☐
Capture/Replay (DOS)	☐	☐	☐	☐	☐	Capture/Replay (OS/2)	☐	☐	☐	☐	☐
Capture/Replay (Host)	☐	☐	☐	☐	☐	Source Analyzer	☐	☐	☐	☐	☐
Testers Workbench	☐	☐	☐	☐	☐	Document Generator	☐	☐	☐	☐	☐
Results Tracking	☐	☐	☐	☐	☐	Test Script Generator	☐	☐	☐	☐	☐
Test Script Repository	☐	☐	☐	☐	☐	Coverage Analysis	☐	☐	☐	☐	☐
System Analyzer	☐	☐	☐	☐	☐	Other:_____	☐	☐	☐	☐	☐

Please supply definitions for the following terms: (If you are not familiar with a term, please say so.)

Test: _____

_____

_____

Unit Test: _____

_____

_____

Statement Testing: _____

_____

_____

Branch Testing: _____

_____

_____

System Test: _____

_____

_____

Integration Test: _____

_____

_____

Black Box Testing: _____

_____

_____

White Box Testing: _____

_____

_____

Function Testing: _____

_____

_____

Structural Testing: _____

_____

_____

End-to-end Test: _____

_____

_____

User Acceptance Testing (UAT): _____

_____

_____

Ad Hoc Testing: _____

_____

_____

The State of Knowledge in Commercial Software Testing

The core material in this book is called *The Most Important Tests—MITs—Test Management Method. MITs* has been offered as a seminar since 1991. Beginning in 1992, students were asked to fill out the written test survey before the class. A voice survey was added in 1993 when the seminar was offered for the first time in Europe.

The Written Survey

The written survey sought to establish the following:

- The respondent's role as practitioner or manager, and the type of group in which the respondent worked, such as development, test, or operations.

- The respondent's level of knowledge of software testing basics and ability to define the test activities he or she performs regularly.

- The type of testing being conducted.

- The types of metrics, if any, that are in use.

- The level of interest in test automation and the automation tools being used.

- The level of competency respondents have in the tasks identified as those they are expected to perform in their job. (Respondents were asked to identify the types of testing they perform in their job and then provide definitions of those tasks. Definitions provided by respondents are good indicators of competency in the tasks identified.)

The Voice Survey

- Supplemented the written survey and collected information that students might not want to write on a survey form.

- Determined how long respondents had been involved in testing.

- Requested educational background of the respondents.
- Determined commonly used metrics for bug tracking and measuring the effectiveness of the test effort, analysis methods, and attitudes about these metrics.

Results of the Seminar Evaluations

The methods taught in the seminars that have been identified over the years as most useful are listed according to the respondent's perceptions of their ease of implementation.

Easiest to Implement

- Bug Tracking and Bug-Tracking Metrics
- The Test Inventory and Test Coverage Metrics
- Planning, Path Analysis, and Data Analysis
- MITs Ranking and Ranking Criteria
- The Test Estimation Worksheet
- Test Performance Metrics

More Difficult to Implement

- S-Curves
- Test Rerun Automation
- Automated Test Plan Generation

Results of the Written Test Survey

The results presented here were taken from a sample of 657 written test surveys. In some cases, the results of surveys administered in the United Kingdom are presented separately from the results of the U.S.-administered surveys.

Composition of the Respondents

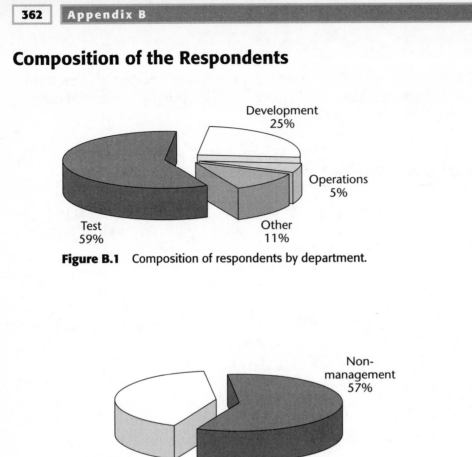

Figure B.1   Composition of respondents by department.

Figure B.2   Composition of respondents, management or nonmanagement.

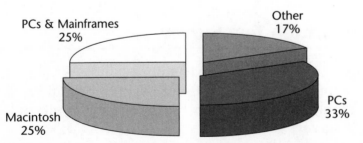

Figure B.3   Composition of platforms tested by respondents.

"Other systems," noted as 17 percent of the total, includes specialized computer systems and subsystems such as those found in car braking systems, telephone switching equipment, pagers, and medical diagnostic equipment.

Education

Of all respondents, 47 percent had some previous training in software testing. For respondents from the United Kingdom, 60 percent had previous test training—on average, 22 months before the current seminar. For the respondents from the United States, only 40 percent had received training, generally within the previous 12 months.

Test Activities

The bar chart in Figure B.4 shows the most and least common test activities as reported by the respondents. System testing was reported to be the primary focus of most of the respondents, with function and integration the next most common types of testing performed by the respondents. User acceptance and unit testing were the focus of the fewest testers responding to the survey.

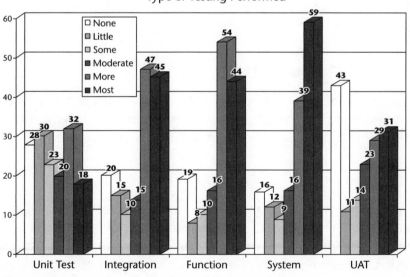

Figure B.4 Type of testing performed by respondents.

Types of Metrics Used

Very few respondents reported using any metrics at all. Lines of code and percent function coverage were the two most used metrics cited by survey respondents. Function points, cyclomatic complexity, and Halstead's metrics were used only rarely (see Figure B.5).

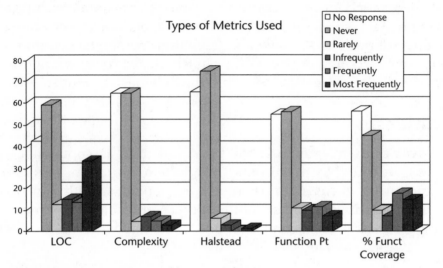

Figure B.5 Test metrics used by respondents.

Types of Formal Methods Used

Few respondents reported using formal methods such as inspection or structured analysis. In fact, the most commonly cited reason for attending the seminar was to learn formal software testing methods.

Test Automation

Test automation elicited great interest in 1994 and 1995. Of particular interest to 69 percent of all respondents were automated script replay and test tracking. The majority of respondents (76 percent) had some experience with automated test tools. Most of the tools listed by respondents were used by only one respondent. The largest group (29 users) used proprietary tools. Of the most frequently named commercial offerings, nine reported using Autotester; eight used SQA Test

Tools, QA Automator, or Mercury Interactive's XRunner, and four reported using Microsoft Test.

Knowledge of Common Test Terms

The respondents from the United Kingdom and Europe scored consistently higher than respondents from the United States in defining the 13 test terms. The average score for the respondents from the United States ranged from 30 percent to 60 percent correct. The average score for the respondents from the United Kingdom and Europe ranged from 40 percent to 80 percent correct. The average scores for the definitions of the most commonly performed types of testing—system test, integration test, and function test—were markedly lower among respondents who claim to perform these tasks frequently or most frequently than among respondents who do not claim to perform these tasks. This trend was consistent across all groups from the United Kingdom, Europe, and the United States. This runs contrary to the expectation that the people doing the work would also be the most knowledgeable about the work.

Recognized Survey Deficiencies

The written survey did not ask how long the respondent had been testing or if test coverage, test effectiveness, and test performance metrics were in use. Nor did it ask specific questions about the type of bug-tracking metrics being used, such as the bug-find and bug-fix rates. These questions were added to the seminars in 1994 by way of a voice survey. They were added to the written survey in 1995.

Results of the Voice Survey

The voice survey was conducted during the workshop, with students responding with a show of hands. These results are general and approximate.

Question: How long have you been testing?

   Answer: United States—The vast majority were new to testing or had been testing for fewer than two years.

   United Kingdom—More than half of the respondents had been testing for two to four years.

Question: How many have a Bachelor of Science degree or a Computer Science degree?

Answer: United States—Only one or two persons in 50 had a science or engineering degree.

United Kingdom—Typically 50 percent to 70 percent of all students had science degrees.

Question: Does your organization track the bugs you find?

Answer: Everyone counted bugs.

Question: Do you rank the bugs by severity?

Answer: Ranking schemes were commonly used to identify the severity of each bug. They varied from two categories such as "Must fix" and "Would like to fix," to five or six categories ranging from "critical" to "design issue."

Question: How do you track these bugs?

Answer: Some organizations tracked bugs manually, on paper. Most respondents reported using some sort of database. Most were looking for a better tool.

Question: Do you measure bug-find rate and bug-fix rate of the test effort?

Answer: Between 25 percent and 30 percent said "yes." Many students expressed concern that such analysis would be used negatively by management.

Question: Do you analyze fault or defect density or error distribution? If so, do you look at the bug densities by module or by development group to find out where the bugs are?

Answer: Between 25 percent and 30 percent said "yes" to the fault analysis question. When questioned, it became clear that this analysis is generally accomplished by gut feel, not by counting the number of bugs or faults discovered. Many students expressed concern that such analysis would be used negatively by management.

Question: Do you measure the effectiveness, efficiency, or performance of the test effort?

Answer: Only about 1 person in 100 answered "yes" to this question. Of those, *efficiency*, or cost per unit of work, was generally cited as the metric used.

Conclusions Drawn from the Surveys

- The respondents who were not actively testing provided the most accurate definitions of the testing terms. The people performing the testing supplied the poorest definitions of the testing tasks that they were performing most frequently.

- Respondents from the United Kingdom scored much higher than the U.S. respondents in the definition of testing tasks. They had more science and engineering education than respondents from the United States. They used more automation tools, but they did not use significantly more metrics than their counterparts in the United States.

- Few respondents reported using formal methods such as inspection or *structured analysis*, meaning some documented structured or systematic method of analyzing the test needs of a system The most commonly cited reason for attending the seminar was to learn some software testing methods.

- The only type of metrics used regularly had to do with counting bugs and ranking them by severity. Only a small percentage of respondents measured the bug-find rate or the bug-fix rate. No other metrics were widely used in development or test, even among the best educated and seemingly most competent testers. It could also be inferred from these results that the companies for which these testers worked did not have a tradition of measuring their software development or test processes.

- Survey respondents rated the methods and metrics in this book as valuable and doable.

Test Collateral Samples and Templates

The following documents are offered as an aid, and a guide, feel free to copy and paste whatever bits you can use into your own effort. You can find these and other materials online at www.testersparadise.com in electronic form.

Sample Memo to Describe the Interview Process

RE: Project [Project Name Here]

System Test Design Project and SME Interview Process

This system test effort differs from integration test and IT-conducted system tests in that it seeks to verify that critical business functions are operating properly across the entire system. The system test effort includes function, performance, and load testing. Rather than focusing on the new data flows through the system, it focuses on day-to-day business functions both before and after the system is subjected to the new data flows. In theory, very little function will change, but loads on various systems will be increased.

The test inventory is the tool used in this system test effort to identify the scope of the test effort and prioritize it based on each inventory item's risk potential. The inventory is intended to be an enumeration of the software system's testable items that have been identified in the project. The initial test inventory was prepared from the available project documentation and is included in the master test plan. Initial priority ratings were applied to each item in the inventory based on the available project documentation. The inventory also contains the reference to the systems touched by a given item. This initial test inventory serves as a starting place for the SME interview process.

The interview process is the most efficient method for reviewing, correcting, and enriching the test inventory and building the system-level process flows. The information gathered during the interviews is used to correct and refine the test inventory, and to identify data dependencies, as well as interproject/intersystem dependencies. Currently, two levels of interviews are planned for the system test planning effort. They are high-level interviews (duration 15 to 30 minutes) and mid-level interviews (duration 30 to 60 minutes). Interviewees are solicited from each of the project areas: IT, support, and system groups.

The product of the interview process is a mature prioritized test inventory that encompasses the entire system and includes the expert input of all the participants. The test inventory and its prioritized test items are used to build cost, sizing, and scheduling estimates during the planning phases. During the test effort, the test inventory becomes the test repository and test metrics database.

High-Level Interviews (Duration 15 to 30 minutes)

See the sample questionnaire at the end of this Appendix.

Goals

1. Identify (for this expert's area):

- The project deliverables
- Owners of deliverables (mid-level interviewees)
- Project dependencies and run requirements
    - Interproject
    - Cross-domain

- Database and shared files
- Business partners' projects
- The location of, and access to, the most recent documentation

2. Get the expert's opinion on the following:

- Ranking priorities (at the project level)
- Schedules:
  - Delivery
  - Testing

3. Go through the day-in-the-life scenarios to understand and document:

- Where do the new projects fit? (If they don't fit, identify the missing scenarios.)
- How do the systems fit together? How does the logic flow?
- Which steps/systems have not changed and what dependencies exist?

Mid-Level Interviews (Duration 30 to 60 minutes)

Goals

1. Build and/or review:

- The logic flows for the projects and systems
- The test inventory
  - Enumerate and rank additional test items and test steps in the test inventory
  - Data requirements and dependencies
  - All systems touched by the project

2. Get answers to the following questions (as they apply):

- What will you or have you tested?
- How long did it take?
- How many testers did you need?
- What do you think we need to test?

3. **Identify additional test sequences.**

4. **Identify requirements for test tools.**

Sample Project Inventory and Test Questionnaire for the Interviews

Preliminary Test Inventory

REQUIREMENT	TS	DESCRIPTION	SIZE	P	CONTACT	DATABASE	DEPENDENCIES
MGT0033		Fixed Assets & Project Accounting	5				
MGT0218		Convert XRR to XSXT ORACLE Purch and Mat					
MGT0219		Convert XRR to XSXT Accounts Payable Sys	5				
MGT0145		Budgets—XRR Acquisition	5				
MGT0034		Interface XRR to XSXT Oracle General Ledger					
MGT0203		XRR to XSXT Car Repair Billing	3				
MGT0030		Convert XRR to XSXT Expenditure Billing Sys	1				
MGT0026		XRR to XSXT Property Management	3				
MGT0139		Property Tax	4				

TS = Test Sequence; Size, default: KLOC; P = Priority, 1 = Most critical, 5 = Least critical

Test Questionnaire

What test domains will be most important?

Function___   Performance___   Load___   Stress___   Other_____

Who will perform unit testing?_____

Who will perform module or function testing prior to integration? _____

_____

What functions do we need to test?	Verification	Dependencies (test with . . . or integrate with . . .)

What else?_____

_____

_____

How long will it take you to test it? _____

_____

_____

How many testers will you use? _____

_____

_____

What else do I need to know? _____

_____

_____

References

AgileAlliance. "Abile Software Development Manifesto." February 13, 2001. Published online at www.agilemanifesto.org.

Amler, Scott. *Agile Modeling*. New York: Wiley, 2002.

Beck, Kent and Martin Fowler. *Planning eXtreme Programming*. Reading, Mass.: Addison-Wesley, 2001.

Beiman, James M., and Janet L. Schultz. "Estimating the Number of Test Cases Required to Satisfy the All-du-paths Testing Criteria." Proceedings of the COMPASS 90 conference. 1989 ACM 089791-342-6/89/0012/0179.

Beizer, Boris. Software Testing Techniques. New York: Van Nostrand Reinhold, 1983.

Beizer, Boris. *Software System Testing and Quality Assurance*. New York: Van Nostrand Reinhold, 1984.

Beizer, Boris. *Black-Box Testing: Techniques for Functional Testing of Software and Systems*. New York: Wiley, 1995.

Berge, C. *Graphs and Hypergraphs*, Amsterdam, The Netherlands: North-Holland, 1973.

Bergman, Mark. "The Evolution of Software Testing Automation." Proceedings of the 8th International Conference on Testing Computer Software, June 19, 1991.

Boehm, B. W., and R. W. Wolverton. *Practical Strategies for Developing Large Software Systems*. Reading, Mass.: Addison-Wesley, 1975.

Boehm, Barry, and D. Port. "Balancing Discipline and Flexibility with the Spiral Model and MBSDE." *STSC CrossTalk*, December 2001, pp. 23-30. Published online at www.stsc.hill.af.mil/crosstalk/2001/dec/boehm.pdf.

Boehm, Barry. "Get Ready for Agile Methods, with Care." *IEEE Computer*, January 2002.

Boehm, Barry W. "A Spiral Model of Software Development and Enhancement," Proceedings of IEEE Second Software Process Workshop, ACM Software Engineering Notes, March 1986 and May 1988.

Brown, J. R., and M. Lipow. *The Quantitative Measurement of Software Safety and Reliability.* TRW Report SDP 1176, 1973.

Cockburn, Alistair. *Agile Software Development,* Reading, Mass.: Addison-Wesley, 2001.

Crosby, Philip B. *Quality Is Free,* Mentor, 1980.

DSDM Consortium. Dynamic Systems Development Method. Version 3. United Kingdom. Published online at www.dsdm.org.

Farr, W. H. "A Survey of Software Reliability Modeling and Estimation." Naval Surface Warfare Center Technical Report, NSWC TR 82-171, June 1983.

Gilb, Tom. *Principles of Software Engineering Management.* Reading, Mass.: Addison-Wesley, 1988.

Gilb, Tom, and Dorothy Graham. *Software Inspection.* Reading, Mass.: Addison-Wesley, 1993.

Goodenough, J. B. *Research Directions in Software Technology.* Cambridge, Mass.: MIT Press, 1979.

Gordon, Geoffrey. *System Simulation.* Upper Saddle River, N.J.: Prentice Hall, 1978.

Halstead, Maurice H. "Software Science Measures." Published in *Elements of Software Science*, 1977.

Halstead, Maurice H. *Elements of Software Science, Operating, and Programming Systems Series.* Volume 7. New York, NY: Elsevier, 1977.

Highsmith, Jim. *Agile Software Development Ecosystems.* Reading, Mass.: Addison-Wesley, 2002.

Howden, William E. "Validation Programs without Specifications." Proceedings of COMPASS 90, 1989 ACM 089791-342-6-89/0002.

Humphrey, Watts. *A Discipline for Software Engineering,* Reading, Mass.: Addison-Wesley, 1997.

Hutcheson, Marnie. "Production Problems in an Application Running on the Prodigy Service." Proceedings of the Fifth Annual Compass Conference on Computer Assurance, 1990, IEEE, Washington, DC, Section 3.

Hutcheson, Marnie. "Using S-Curves to Measure Test Progress." Proceedings of the ASM Metrics Conference, La Jolla, California, November 1994.

Hutcheson, Marnie. "Testing of a Shrink-Wrapped (RAD) Product." Proceedings of Eurostar '94, 1994 1.3.

Hutcheson, Marnie. "The Most Important Tests (MITs) Test Management Method." Prodigy Services Co. Internal Publication, 1992 Proceeding of UNICOM Seminars. Fall 1993.

The Institute of Electrical and Electronics Engineers. *IEEE Standard Dictionary of Measures to Produce Reliable Software.* The Institute of Electrical and Electronics Engineers. April 30, 1989.

Johnson, David E., John L. Hilburn, and Johnny R. Johnson. *Basic Electric Circuit Analysis.* 2d Edition. Upper Saddle River, N.J.: Prentice Hall, 1984.

Jones, Capers. *Applied Software Measurement: Assuring Productivity and Quality.* New York: McGraw-Hill, 1991.

Jones, Capers. *Software Quality for 1995: What Works and What Doesn't?* Software Productivity Research, Inc., 1994.

Jones, Capers. *Function Point Metrics and Civilian Best Practices.* Software Productivity Research, Inc., 1995.

Kaner, Cem, Jack Falk, and Hung Quoc Nguyen. *Testing Computer Software,* 2d Edition. New York: Van Nostrand Reinhold, 1993.

Kitchenham, Barbara. *Experimentation in Software Engineering.* Systems/Software, Inc., 1990.

Lauterback, L., and W. Randall. *Experimental Evaluation of Six Test Techniques,* Research Triangle Institute, P.O. Box 12194, Research Triangle Park, NC 27709, 1991.

McCabe, Thomas J., and Charles W. Butler. "Design Complexity Measurement and Testing." *Communications of the ACM.* December 1989, Volume 32, Number 12.

McCabe, Thomas, J. "Structured Testing: A Software Testing Methodology Using the Cyclomatic Complexity Metric." *Computer Science and Technology,* NBS Special Publication 500-99, U.S. Department of Commerce, December 1992.

Microsoft Corporation. *Microsoft Excel Developer's Kit.* 2d Edition. Redmond, Wash.: Microsoft Press.

Microsoft Corporation. *The Windows Interface: An Application Design Guide.* Redmond, Wash.: Microsoft Press, 1992.

Microsoft Corporation , *Microsoft Word Developer's Kit.* 3d Edition. Redmond, Wash.: Microsoft Press, 1995.

Myers, Glenford. *The Art of Software Testing.* New York: Wiley, 1978.

Ostrand, Thomas J., and Marc J. Balcer. "The Category-Partition Method for Specifying and Generating Functional Tests," *Communications of the ACM.* June 1988, Volume 31, Number 6.

Paulk, Mark C., Charles V. Weber, Bill Curtis, and Mary Beth Chrissis. *The Capability Maturity Model: Guidelines for Improving the Software Process.* Reading, Mass.: Addison-Wesley, 1995.

Rowland, John H., and Yu Zuyuan. "Experimental Comparison of Three System Test Strategies" Preliminary Report. 1989, ACM 089791- 342-6/89/0012/0141.

Shortley, George, and Dudley Williams. *Elements of Physics,* 5th Edition. Upper Saddle River, N.J.: Prentice Hall, Inc., 1971.

Silver, Bill. "Application of Software Test Measurement." *Software Quality World.* June 18, 1991.

Treinish, L. A. "Visualization Techniques for Correlative Data Analysis in the Earth and Space Sciences." *Animation and Scientific Visualization: Tools and Applications.* San Diego: Academic Press/Harcourt Brace & Company, 1993, pp. 193-204.

Webster's New World Dictionary of the American Language, Second College Edition. Upper Saddle River, N.J.: Prentice Hall, 1984.

Weyuker, Elaine J. "The Evaluation of Program-Based Software Test Data Adequacy Criteria." *Communications of the ACM.* June 1988, Volume 31, Number 6.

Yamada, S. M. Ohba, and S. Osaki. "S-Shaped Reliability Growth Modeling for Software Error Detection." *IEEE Transactions on Reliability.* BOL. R-32, No. 5, December 1983, pp. 475-478.

Yourdon, Edward, *Decline and Fall of the American Programmer.* Upper Saddle River, N.J.: Prentice Hall, 1993.

Glossary

ad hoc.   For this specific purpose; for a special case only, without general application [an *ad hoc* committee].

adjunct processor.   A secondary CPU that is in communication with a primary CPU. This secondary CPU or processor handles a specific task or function. Typically, the primary CPU sends traffic to the adjunct processor to be processed. Also called an *attached processor*.

Agile development methods.   See AgileAlliance. "Agile Software Development Manifesto." February 13, 2001. www.agilemanifesto .org

art.   1. The human ability to make things; creativity of human beings as distinguished from the world of nature. 2. Skill; craftsmanship. 3. Any specific skill or its application (the art of making friends). 4. Any craft, trade, or profession or its principles. 5. Making or doing of things that display form, beauty, and unusual perception; art includes painting, sculpture, architecture, music, literature, drama, the dance, etc. 6. Artful or cunning. 7. Sly or cunning trick; wile. (*Webster's New World Dictionary of the American Language, Second College Edition,* Prentice Hall, 1984)

assumption. 1. The act of assuming, a taking upon oneself, taking over, or taking for granted. 2. Anything taken for granted; supposition. 3. Presumption. (*Webster's New World Dictionary of the American Language, Second College Edition*, Prentice Hall, 1984)

basis suite. A highly optimized test suite used to establish the baseline behavior of a system. See also *diagnostic suite.*

behavioral testing. Tests that verify the output is correct for a given input, without verifying the process that produced the output; data testing.

benchmark. 1. A surveyor's mark made on a permanent landmark of known position and altitude; it is used as a reference point in determining other altitudes. 2. A standard or point of reference in measuring or judging quality, value, and so on. (*Webster's New World Dictionary of the American Language, Second College Edition*, Prentice Hall, 1984)

bias. Error we introduce by having knowledge and therefore expectations of a system.

black box testing. See *behavioral testing.*

bottom-up testing. Each module or component is first tested alone (see *unit test*), and then the modules are combined a few at a time and tested with simulators used in place of components that are necessary but missing.

brainstorming. Using group synergy to think up ideas.

branch. In program logic, a branch refers to a decision in the code, usually a conditional branch such as an if statement, but it could also be an unconditional branch like a goto statement.

branch coverage. The count of the minimum number of paths required to exercise both branches of each decision node in the system. Best known in unit testing as the number of logic branches in the source code (such as the number of if statements multiplied by 2).

branch test. A test that exercises a logic branch in a program. Traditionally part of unit testing.

calculate. To determine by using mathematics, to compute.

Capability Maturity Model (CMM). Scheme for measuring the levels of process maturity in a company. Developed at Carnegie Mellon University.

client/server. A name given to the architecture that gives the user or client access to specific data through a server.

code generator. A software application that generates program source code.

code inspections. A formal process where the source code is inspected for defects.

coding. The act of writing a software program. Program language statements are called *code*. This is an old term from precompiler days when programmers translated programming instructions directly into machine language.

CPU. Central processing unit.

cyclomatic complexity. A term used interchangeably with the *cyclomatic number*.

cyclomatic number. The minimum number of linearly independent paths through a structured system.

data. Things known or assumed; facts or figures from which conclusions can be inferred; information.

data analysis. The process of analyzing data.

data dependent. Something that is dependent on the value of a given piece of information. For example, which branch of an if statement will be selected is usually dependent on the information being processed at that specific time.

database. A large collection of data in a computer, organized so that it can be expanded, updated, and retrieved rapidly for various uses.

debug. Given a program that has a bug, to track the problem down in the source code.

decisions. A branching node with multiple edges entering and one edge leaving; decisions can contain processes; in this text, for the purposes of clarity, decisions will be modeled with only one edge entering.

deformation. The changing of form or shape induced by stress.

design. 1. To make preliminary sketches of; sketch a pattern or outline for; plan. 2. To plan and carry out, especially by artistic arrangement or in a skillful way. 3. To form (plans, etc.) in the mind; contrive. 4. To plan to do; purpose; intend. (*Webster's New World Dictionary of the American Language, Second College Edition*, Prentice Hall, 1984)

diagnose. To ascertain why a system responds to a set of stimuli the way it does.

diagnostic suite. A highly optimized test suite used to establish the current behavior of a system, used to isolate the site (or source) of a failure.

document inspection. A formal process where the project documentation is inspected for defects.

edges. In logic flow diagrams, these are lines that connect nodes on the logic flow map.

effectiveness. 1. Having an effect; producing a result. 2. Producing a definite or desired result; efficient. 3. In effect; operative; active. 4. Actual, not merely potential or theoretical. 5. Making a striking impression; impressive. 6. Equipped and ready for combat. (*Webster's New World Dictionary of the American Language, Second College Edition*, Prentice Hall, 1984)

efficiency. 1.Ability to produce a desired effect, product, and so on with a minimum of effort, expense, or waste; quality or fact of being efficient. 2. The ratio of effective work to the energy expended in producing it, as of a machine; output divided by input. (*Webster's New World Dictionary of the American Language, Second College Edition*, Prentice Hall, 1984)

empirically. Determined by trial or experiment.

end-to-end testing. Type of testing where the entire system is tested—that is, from end-to-end.

engineering. 1. (*a*) The science concerned with putting scientific knowledge to practical uses. (*b*) The planning, designing, construction, or management of machinery, roads, bridges, buildings, and so on. 2. The act of maneuvering or managing. (*Webster's New World Dictionary of the American Language, Second College Edition*, Prentice Hall, 1984)

environment catalog. A catalog or list of the elements of a given environment, usually includes description and specifications.

excellence. The fact or condition of excelling; of superiority; surpassing goodness or merit, and so on.

expected response. A standard against which a test is compared.

experimentation. The act of conducting experiments.

expert testers. Testers who are experts in their areas.

feature richness. A measure of the abundance and quality of the features offered by a product.

formal. Following a set of prescribed or fixed procedures.

fourth-generation languages (4GL). 4GLs are characterized by natural language-like commands and/or application generators. 4GLs are typically easier to use than traditional procedural languages. They can be employed by end users to develop applications quickly.

function paths. The logic paths that are taken when a program function is executed.

function points. A synthetic software metric that is composed of the weighted totals of inputs, outputs, inquiries, logical files or user data groups, and interfaces belonging to an application.

function test. A test of program functions normally conducted from the user interface.

fundamental metric. A measurement of a physical quantity, where what is measured is the name of the metric, for example, errors per 100 lines of code.

graphical user interface (GUI). Computer user interface where the user can manipulate objects to accomplish tasks.

IEEE. Institute of Electrical and Electronics Engineering.

incremental delivery. A strategy for delivering a system to the users in increments. Each increment delivered adds function to the previous product. Such systems are generally delivered using incremental development or modular development techniques.

incremental development. Modules that implement function to be delivered are developed and unit tested; then they are assembled, integrated into the existing system, and tested as they become available. The system is stabilized after each addition. Theoretically, this means that there is always a stable version ready to be shipped.

independent function paths. The discrete logical paths that can be executed through a function in an application or a system where each one is independent from the others.

innovate. Renew, alter, introduce new methods, devices, and so on; to bring in as an innovation.

inspection. The process of examining something carefully and in detail.

integration test.   This is the process where systems are built. Units that make up a system are combined, and the interfaces and data flow within the system are tested. Units are usually added one at a time, and the system's stability is reestablished before the next unit is added.

integrator.   One who integrates.

integrity.   The quality or state of being complete; unbroken condition; wholeness.

invent.   1. To come upon, meet, or discover. 2. To think up; devise or fabricate in the mind [to invent excuses]. 3. To think out or produce [a new device process, etc.]; originate, as by experiment; devise for the first time. (*Webster's New World Dictionary of the American Language, Second College Edition,* Prentice Hall, 1984)

inventory.   A detailed list.

keytrap tool.   A software test tool that captures and saves the keystrokes typed by the user. Also called *capture/replay* and *capture/playback*.

linear independence.   A line that is independent of other lines. For system traversals, this means that each linearly independent path through the system must traverse some unique path segment that is not traversed by any other traversal through the system.

lines of code.   The count of the lines of program code in a software module or system.

load testing.   Testing the load-bearing ability of a system. For example, verifying that the system can process the required number of transactions per time period.

logic flow map.   Graphic depiction of the logic paths through a system, or some function that is modeled as a system.

logic schematics.   A logic scheme, plan, or diagram.

magnitude of a physical quantity.   Specified by a number and a unit, such as bugs per thousand lines of code or per minutes of test.

management.   The act, art, or manner of managing, or handling, controlling, directing, and so on.

measure.   "The act or process of determining extent, dimensions, and so on; especially as determined by a standard," (according to *Websters New World Dictionary*). The IEEE definition is "A quantitative assessment of the degree to which a software product or process possesses a given attribute." [IEEE043098]

menu. A program element that offers the user a number of choices; menus do not involve data entry.

metric. A measure.

metric system. A set or system of measures.

Most Important Tests (MITS). The tests most likely to be of interest on the basis of probable importance and risk of failure.

node. From the Latin *nodus*, meaning knot. A dilemma or complication; a point of concentration. In logic flow mapping, both processes and decisions are nodes.

object-oriented languages. A programming system where program functions and utilities are precompiled into *objects* that have distinct properties and behaviors.

paper documentation. Documentation printed on paper.

path. A track or way worn by footsteps; also a line of movement or course taken; any traversal through a system.

path analysis. Examining and enumerating the paths through a program or system.

path-dependent function. A program traversal that follows a particular path regardless of the current data.

percent function coverage. The percent of all functions that are being tested.

performance. 1. The act of performing; execution, accomplishment, fulfillment, and so on. 2. Operation or functioning, usually with regard to effectiveness, as of a machine. 3. Something done or performed; deed or feat. 4. (*a*) A formal exhibition or presentation before an audience, as a play, musical program, show, and so on. (*b*) One's part in this. (*Webster's New World Dictionary of the American Language, Second College Edition*, Prentice Hall, 1984)

performance testing. See *load testing*.

physical quantity. The description of the operational procedure for measuring the quantity.

plan-driven. Term coined by Barry Boehm in his article, "Get Ready for Agile Methods, with Care" to describe traditional waterfall-style development methods. See the "References."

process. A continuing development involving many changes.

processes. In logic flow mapping, a process is a collector node with multiple edges entering and one edge leaving; a process node can represent one program statement or an entire software system, as long as the contents are consistent throughout the logic flow diagram.

production system monitoring. The act of watching a production system; the object is to detect anomalies or failures as they occur.

programmatic paths. The logic flow through the code statements in a program.

proprietary. Privately owned and operated. Held under patent, trademark, or copyright by a private person or company.

quality. The degree of excellence that a thing possesses. The degree of conformance to a standard.

quality assurance. According to the British Standard 4778, this standard cites all those planned and systematic actions necessary to provide adequate confidence that a product or service will satisfy given requirements for quality.

quality control. According to the British Standard 4778, the operational techniques and activities that are used to fulfill requirements for quality.

random. Without specific order.

rank. An orderly arrangement; a relative position, usually in a scale classifying persons or things.

rapid application development (RAD). A development process that evolves a product through multiple trial-and-error cycles.

regions. Any area that is completely surrounded by edges and processes.

regression test. Retesting something that has been tested previously. Usually conducted after some part of the system has been changed. Regressing; going back, returning.

review. To look at or go over again.

science. 1. Systematized knowledge derived from observation, study, and experimentation carried on in order to determine the nature and principles of what is being studied. 2. A branch of knowledge or study, especially one concerned with establishing and systematizing facts, principles, and methods, as by experiments and hypotheses. 3. (*a*) The systematized knowledge of nature and the physical world.

(*b*) Any branch of this. 4. Skill or technique based upon systematized training. (*Webster's New World Dictionary of the American Language, Second College Edition,* Prentice Hall, 1984)

scientific method.   The systematic attempt to construct theories that correlate wide groups of observed facts and are capable of predicting the results of future observations. Such theories are tested by controlled experimentation and are accepted only so long as they are consistent with all observed facts.

severity.   The quality or condition of being severe; strictness; harshness.

software application.   A computer program that performs some set of functions.

Software Capability Maturity Model (SW-CMM).   A scheme for measuring the levels of process maturity in a company. Developed at Carnegie Mellon University, Software Engineering Institute. The Capability Maturity Model uses a conceptual framework based on industry best practices to assess the process maturity, capability, and performance of a software development organization.

source code.   In programming, the actual statements of programming language in a program.

spaghetti code.   Referring to poorly constructed, disorganized, and unstructured source code.

statement.   The thing stated; account; declaration. In programming, a single line of program code, a single program action.

statement coverage.   A method of path counting that counts the minimum number of paths required to walk through each statement in the source code.

statement test.   Testing statements in a software program at the source code level.

static code analyzer.   A software tool that analyzes the program source code, in an uncompiled state. As opposed to dynamic code analyzers, which analyze the activity of code while it is being run.

structural test.   A test that verifies the structural integrity of a set or system of program elements.

structured system.   A system or subsystem that has only one entry point and one exit point.

system. A set or arrangement of things so related or connected so as to form a unity or organic whole. A set of decisions and processes that as a group have one entry point and one exit point. A group of units that can interact, as well as act independently.

system test. This term is often used interchangeably with *integration test*, but it really refers to testing a system that is built. The functions of the complete system are verified.

technique. The method or procedure (with reference to practical or formal details), or way of using basic skills, in rendering an artistic work or carrying out a scientific or mechanical operation.

test. Ascertain the response of a system to stimuli and compare that response to a standard. Evaluate the quality of the response with respect to the standard. Given some software and a list of the functions it is supposed to perform, find out if it performs these functions as they are described. Additionally, find out if it does other things that are not described. (Validate and verify.)

test. (IEEE) A set of one or more test cases.

test case. A condition to be tested that includes its own identification and the expected response. Sometimes used interchangeably with *test script*.

test coverage. The percentage of everything that could be tested that was actually tested.

test effort. Process by which testers produce their product, involving developing and evaluating a software system by conducting tests and getting bugs removed.

test inspection. A formal process where the tests are inspected for defects.

test inventory. The complete enumeration of all known tests; path, data, module, design, system, and so on.

test script. A collection of tests or activities that are performed in sequence. Used interchangeably with *test case*.

test set. Term used to describe a group of tests. See also *test suite* or *test inventory*.

test suite. A group of tests run sequentially.

testing. (IEEE) The process of analyzing a software item to detect the differences between existing and required conditions (that is, bugs) and to evaluate the features of the software item.

theoretical. Limited to or based on theory.

theory. 1. A mental viewing; contemplation. 2. A speculative idea or plan as to how something might be done. 3. A systematic statement of principles involved. 4. A formulation of apparent relationships or underlying principles of certain observed phenomena that has been verified to some degree. 5. That branch of an art or science consisting in a knowledge of its principles and methods rather than in its practice; pure, as opposed to applied, science, and so on. 6. Popularly, a mere conjecture, or guess. (*Webster's New World Dictionary of the American Language, Second College Edition,* Prentice Hall, 1984)

top-down testing. A testing process that first assembles a system and then tests the entire system at once from the user's perspective.

total independent paths (TIP). Total number of linearly independent paths being considered.

Underwriters Laboratory (UL). An establishment in the United States licensed to certify that electronic products meet established safety standards.

uniformity. State, quality, or instance of being uniform.

unit. A discrete, logical set of function(s). This can be a single small program.

unit test. To test a program unit, a separately compiled module, an object, or a group of closely related modules.

universal description discovery and integration (UDDI). A cross-industry effort driven by major platform and software providers, as well as marketplace operators and e-business leaders within the OASIS standards consortium. UDDI creates a standard interoperable platform that enables companies and applications to quickly, easily, and dynamically find and use Web services over the Internet. http://www.uddi.org/

unreproducible bug. A bug that cannot be reproduced by following the same steps that produced it originally.

user acceptance test (UAT). Tests performed by the user to determine if the system is acceptable.

validate. To confirm the validity of.

validation. The act of confirming; to declare valid.

validity. The state, quality, or fact of being valid (strong, powerful, properly executed) in law or in argument, proof, authority, and so on.

verification. Verifying or being verified; establishment or confirmation of the truth or accuracy of a fact, theory, and so on.

verify. 1. To prove to be true by demonstration, evidence, or testimony; confirm or substantiate. 2. To test or check the accuracy or correctness of, as by investigation, comparison with a standard, or reference to the facts.

versioning. A process used by the first version.

white box testing. Testing that examines and verifies the process by which program functions are carried out; path testing.

working hypothesis. To provide a basis for further investigation, argument, and so on of an unproved theory.

WYSIWYG. What you see is what you get.

M arnie Hutcheson creates technical courseware for Microsoft Corporation and travels around the world training the trainers who teach these technologies to the world. She is an internationally published author and speaker in the areas of software development, testing and quality assurance, and systems administration.

She began her career in engineering at Prodigy Services Company in 1987 as the Lead Systems Integrator for Shopping, and later Banking and Financial Services. Over the years, she has become a leader in the development of the Web and has helped corporations like GTE and Microsoft develop and launch several major Internet technologies.

Prior to that, she was a student of the performing arts for over 25 years. She performed on stage, in classical ballet, musical theater, folk singing, and opera for 10 years in Denver, Montreal, Boston, and New York.

She also taught dance in institutions and colleges during those years. In the late 1970s, she was the dance instructor and assistant choreographer to U.S. Olympic skating coach, Don Laws, and Olympic choreographer Riki Harris. She worked with U.S. Olympians, elite skaters, and gymnasts in the United States and Canada.

I live in a software development world where product development is not an orderly consistent march toward a tangible goal. "The Project Plan" usually consists of a laundry list of functions dropped off by somebody from marketing. Management embellishes "The Plan" with start and end dates that are of highly questionable origins and totally unreachable. The design and implementation of the product are clandestinely guarded by developers. The product routinely arrives in test virtually unannounced and several weeks late. The tester has not finished the test plan because no one is quite sure what the thing does. The only sure thing is the product must ship on time, next week.

That is software development—chaotic and harried. This book is dedicated to the proposition that this development system is primitive and enormously wasteful. This book presents several methods that provide better ways to perform the business of understanding, controlling, and delivering the right product to the market on time. These methods, taken singly or in groups, provide large cost savings and better-quality products for software developers.

I am a practitioner. I work where the rubber meets the road. I am often present when the user puts their hands on the product for the first time. I deal with real solutions to real problems. I also deal with the frustration of both the customers (who are losing money because the product is failing in some way) and the front-line support people. Front-line support is typically caught in the middle between development groups, who have other priorities, and the customer, who needs the system fixed "right now."

I work with the developer, whose job is to write good code. Developers do not have time to fill out all those forms quality assurance wants, or to compose an operations document that the test and support groups need. I work with the testers, who really don't know what's going on back there in the system. They keep breaking it, but they can't reproduce the problems for development. And I work with the document writers, who can't understand why the entire user interface changed just two weeks before the end of the test cycle.

My role is to prevent failures and enhance productivity through automation and process optimization. I work primarily on applications running in large networks. These systems are huge and contain a variety of components that need to be tested. Typically, there are object-oriented modules and graphical user interfaces (GUIs), and browser-based interfaces. These applications typically interact with databases, communications networks, specialized servers, and embedded code, driving specialized hardware—and all of them need to be tested. The methods in this book are distilled from experiences, both failures and successes, with projects that have touched all of these areas.

This is also a work about "how to solve problems," so it is rich with commentary on human factors. Systems are designed, written, integrated, tested, deployed, and supported by human beings, for human beings. We cannot ignore the fact that human factors play a major role in virtually all system failures.

What This Book Is About

This book is a software tester's guide to managing the software test effort. This is not a formula book of test techniques, though some powerful test techniques are presented. This book is about defensible test methods. It offers methods and metrics that improve the test effort, whether or not formal test techniques are used. It is about how to use metrics in the test effort. There is no incentive to take measurements if you don't know how to use the results to help your case, or if those results might be turned against you. This book shows how to use measurement to discover, to communicate those discoveries to others, and to make improvements.

Some time back I was presenting an overview of these methods at a conference. Part of the presentation was a case study. After these methods were applied, a test inventory was built, and the risk analysis was performed for the system, it was determined within this case study that the optimal test coverage given the time and resources allowed was 67 percent coverage of the entire test inventory.

During the question-and-answer session that followed my presentation, a very distinguished and tall fellow practitioner (he stands well over six feet) said, "Excuse me for mentioning this, but it strikes me that you are a very small person. I was wondering where you find the courage to tell your managing director that you only plan to test 67 percent of the system?"

My answer: "It is true that I am only 5'6", but I am big on the truth. If management wants to give me enough time and resources to test every item on the inventory, I will be happy to do so. But if they want me to do with less than that, I am not going to soft sell the fact that they will get less than 100 percent test coverage. If there isn't time and resources to test everything, then I want to be sure that the tests conducted are the *most important tests*."

I am also going to tell management how good that selection of tests was, how many bugs the test effort found, how serious they were and how much it cost to find them, and if possible, how much was saved because we found and removed them. I will measure the performance of the test effort and be able to show at any time whether we are on schedule or not, if the error densities are too high, or if the bug-fix rate is too low. If we cannot stay on schedule, I can give management the high-quality information it needs to do what it does best, specifically, manage the situation.

Industry and Technology Trends: Why I Think It's Time to Publish This Book

I began developing these methods in the late 1980s when I worked at Prodigy. They evolved to suit the needs of a fast-paced development environment feeding a large, complex real-time system. They were called the Most Important Tests method, or MITs. MITs quickly became the standard for testing methods at Prodigy, and I began writing and publishing case studies of MITs projects in 1990. I took MITs with me when I left Prodigy in 1993, and it continued to evolve as I tackled more and more testing projects in other industries. I spent most of the last 10 years helping businesses embrace and profit from integrating large systems and the Internet.

The (PowerPoint-based) syllabus that I developed to teach MITs since 1993 is based on the first seven chapters that I wrote for the original book, *Software Testing Methods and Metrics*. The emphasis then was on client/server testing, not the Internet, and that is reflected in the original chapters.

First offered in 1993, the course has been taught several times each year ever since. I put the original first four chapters on my Web site in 1997. The number of people reading these four chapters has increased steadily over the years. This year some 17,000 visitors have downloaded these chapters. The most popular is Chapter 2, "Fundamental Methods." Because of its popularity and the many e-mail discussions it has sparked, it has been expanded here into Chapter 3: "Approaches to Managing Software Testing," and Chapter 4: "The Most Important Tests (MITs) Method."

Changing Times

I spent most of 2001 working on Microsoft's .NET developer training materials, and in the process, I became very familiar with most of the facets of .NET. Bottom line is, the new .NET architecture, with its unified libraries, its "all languages are equal" attitude about development languages, and its enablement of copy-and-run applications and Web services brings us back to the way we did things in the early 1990s—those heady days I spent at Prodigy. The big and exciting difference is that Prodigy was small and proprietary; .NET will be global and public (as well as private).

It will be two years before we really begin to see the global effects of this latest shortening of the software development cycle. Literally, anyone can deploy and sell software as a Web service on global scale, without ever burning a CD, or writing a manual, or paying for an ad in a magazine. And at some point, that software will be tested.

The picture becomes even more interesting when you consider that we are now just beginning the next wave of Internet evolution; the mobile Internet. Just as the PC revolutionized the way we do business today, the smart phones and pocket PCs will allow more people than ever before to access dynamic applications on small screens, with tenuous data links. The methods in this book evolved in just such an environment, and were successful.

Software testing must show that it adds value, and that it is necessary for product success. Otherwise, market forces will encourage competitive shops to forego testing and give the product to the users as fast as they can write it and copy it to the server.

This book is about fundamentals, and fortunately, "fundamental" concepts, while sometimes out of style, evolve very slowly. The examples in the original Prodigy work were out of style in the client/server days; they are very much back in style in the .NET world. In many ways, revising this work to be current today is actually taking it back to its original state.

Scope of This Book and Who Will Find It Useful

This book is a field guide aimed squarely at testers and management involved with developing software systems and applications. It contains practical solutions, not theory. Theory and background are presented only to support the practical solutions.

This is a tester's survival guide because it helps testers supply answers that management understands and respects. Testers need to answer the question, "Why can't you have it tested by next week?" This work is also a manager's survival guide because managers have to explain why things are the way they are, how much it's going to cost, and why.

The methods presented here were developed in large networks. Often these networks are running a combination of Web-based and client/server-based applications, some on the public Internet and some running privately behind the firewall. These systems are generally written at least in part using object-oriented languages, and all are accessed using graphical user interfaces, be they dedicated clients or Web pages running in a browser. These test methods have been used to test a rich variety of other software systems as well, including telecommunications, business applications, embedded firmware, and game software.

The process described in this book is a *top-down approach* to testing. These methods can be used to test at the unit level, but they are more useful in integration, system, and end-to-end test efforts. These test methods are often used later in the project life cycle, in load testing, performance testing, and production system monitoring. Opportunities for automation or test reuse are noted as appropriate.

Last, this is not an all-or-none test guide. A process improvement can result from implementing parts of these methods, like adding a metric to test tracking, or prioritizing tests and keeping track of how long each one takes to run.

How This Book Is Organized

The chapters have been organized to parallel the process flow in most software development and test efforts. Successive chapters tend to build on what came in the chapters before; so jumping right into the middle of the book may not be a good idea. It is best to proceed sequentially.

Case studies, notes on automation, test techniques, usability issues, and human factors appear throughout the text. It is broken into three main blocks:

Chapters 1 to 5 concentrate on background and concepts.

Chapters 6 to 8 focus on the inventory and how to make it.

Chapters 9 to 14 cover tools and analysis techniques for test estimation, sizing, and planning.

The Standard for Definitions in This Book

The standard for all definitions given in this book is *Webster's New World Dictionary of the American Language* (College Edition, Prentice Hall). However, any good dictionary should be acceptable. When I refer to a definition from some other work, I will cite the work. I have tried to limit such references to works that are readily available to everyone today.

One of the major stumbling blocks I have encountered in educating people involved in developing and testing software is the lack of consensus on the meaning of basic terms. This is richly illustrated in the test survey discussed in Chapter 1 and presented in Appendix B of this book.

The biggest reason for this lack of consensus is that while there are plenty of standards published in this industry, they are not readily available or easy to understand. The second reason for the lack of consensus is simple disagreement. I have often heard the argument, "That's fine, but it doesn't apply here." It's usually true. Using the dictionary as the standard solves both of these problems. It is a starting point to which most people have access and can acknowledge. It is also necessary to go back to basics. In my research I am continually confronted with the fact that most people do not know the true meaning of words we use constantly, such as *test, verify, validate, quality, performance, effectiveness, efficiency, science, art,* and *engineering.*

To those who feel I am taking a step backward with this approach, it is a requirement of human development that we must learn to creep before we can crawl, to crawl before we can walk, and to walk before we can run. The level of mastery that can be achieved in any phase of development is directly dependent on the level of mastery achieved in the previous phase. I will make as few assumptions as possible about my readers' level of knowledge.

We software developers and testers came to this industry from many directions, many disciplines, and many points of view. Because of this, consensus is difficult. Nevertheless, I believe that our diversity gives us great strength. The interplay of so many ideas constantly sparks invention and innovation. The computer industry is probably home to the largest cooperative inventive undertaking in human history. It simply needs to be managed.

Vincent Kunkemueller, and all the others who were so patient and supportive as they added their talents to the making of this work. And finally, many thanks to my research assistants, and my artistic staff, Velvalee Boyd and Dane Boyd.

When a subject is well understood, it can be explained in a few words, but the road to that understanding can be a long one, indeed. Every human being since the beginning of time has understood the effects of gravity—you trip, you fall down. Yet Sir Isaac Newton explained this phenomenon briefly and accurately only recently on the human time scale.

I have been working on developing the material in this book and circulating it back to testers and their management for many years. Most of the methods and techniques presented here are simple, but good answers don't have to be difficult. Many of these methods are about as old and patentable as oatmeal; others are new. Many of these methods have been discussed and debated for months and even years with colleagues.

The first four chapters of the original version of this book have been available online for four years. In that time the number of readers has risen steadily; presently about 350 visitors read these chapters each week. More than 2,500 software testers and managers in various industries reviewed this work and provided feedback on it. To all those who took part in those discussions, asked questions, picked nits, or came back and reported which steps they tried to implement and how it worked, I want to say again, "Thank you. And don't stop the feedback; that's how we improve our knowledge."

Thanks to Minna Beissinger, Joseph Mueller, Eric Mink, Beate Kim, Joan Rothman, L. Gary Nakashian, Joy Nemitz, Adrian Craig Wheeler, Lawrence Holland, John Chernievsky, Boris Beizer, Dorothy Graham, Roger Sherman, Greg Daich, and Tom Gilb.

I want to express my special thanks to my technical reviewer, researcher, and product developer, David Mayberry. This work would probably not exist except for his patience and continuing efforts. I also want to thank my editors at Wiley; Ben Ryan and Scott Amerman,